Youth Offending and Youth Justice

RESEARCH HIGHLIGHTS 52

Research highlights in social work

This topical series examines areas of particular interest to those in social and community work and related fields. Each book draws together different aspects of the subject, highlighting relevant research and drawing out implications for policy and practice. The project is under the editorial direction of Professor Joyce Lishman, Head of the School of Applied Social Studies at the Robert Gordon University in Aberdeen, Scotland.

Other books in the series

Public Services Inspection in the UK
Edited by Howard Davis and Steve Martin
ISBN 978 1 84310 527 5
Research Highlights in Social Work series 50

Co-Production and Personalisation in Social Care
Changing Relationships in the Provision of Social Care
Edited by Susan Hunter and Pete Ritchie
ISBN 978 1 84310 558 9
Research Highlights in Social Work series 49

Developments in Social Work with Offenders
Edited by Gill McIvor and Peter Raynor
ISBN 978 1 84310 538 1
Research Highlights in Social Work series 48

Residential Child Care
Prospects and Challenges
Edited by Andrew Kendrick
ISBN 978 1 84310 526 8
Research Highlights in Social Work series 47

Managing Sex Offender Risk
Edited by Hazel Kemshall and Gill McIvor
ISBN 978 1 84310 197 0
Research Highlights in Social Work series 46

Social Work and Evidence-Based Practice
Edited by David Smith
ISBN 978 1 84310 156 7
Research Highlights in Social Work series 45

Women Who Offend
Edited by Gill McIvor
ISBN 978 1 84310 154 3
Research Highlights in Social Work series 44

Youth Offending and Youth Justice

Edited by Monica Barry
and Fergus McNeill

RESEARCH HIGHLIGHTS 52

Jessica Kingsley Publishers
London and Philadelphia

First published in 2009
by Jessica Kingsley Publishers
116 Pentonville Road
London N1 9JB, UK
and
400 Market Street, Suite 400
Philadelphia, PA 19106, USA

www.jkp.com

Library of Congress Cataloging in Publication Data
Youth offending and youth justice / edited by Monica Barry and Fergus McNeill.
    p. cm. -- (Research highlights ; 52)
  Includes bibliographical references and index.
    ISBN 978-1-84310-689-0 (pb : alk. paper) 1. Juvenile delinquency--Great Britain. 2. Juvenile delinquents--Great Britain. 3. Juvenile justice, Administration of--Great Britain. I. Barry, Monica. II. McNeill, Fergus.

  HV9145.A5Y67 2009
  364.360941--dc22

                    2009009627

British Library Cataloguing in Publication Data
A CIP catalogue record for this book is available from the British Library

ISBN 978 1 84310 689 0

Printed and bound in Great Britain by
Athenaeum Press, Gateshead, Tyne and Wear

Contents

Part Two Youth Offending and Youth Justice in Practice

Figures and Tables

PART ONE

Youth Offending and Youth Justice in Context

CHAPTER 1

Introduction

Monica Barry and Fergus McNeill

Introduction

This may seem like an odd way to begin a book, but when the Research Highlights Editorial Board first approached us about editing this collection, Fergus had serious doubts. So many good collections, most notably the excellent twin volumes edited by Goldson and Muncie (2006) and Muncie and Goldson (2006), had been produced in recent years, that it was not immediately obvious exactly what yet another volume on youth justice might hope to achieve. Against this hesitation stood a loyalty towards the Research Highlights series that had its origins in the many contributions that the series had made to Fergus's own professional and academic development. Obviously the latter impulse won the day but, more to the point, it influenced the way in which we jointly sought to shape and structure this volume.

When we approached the contributors we made clear that this collection aimed to provide social work, youth justice and youth work practitioners, managers, policymakers, students and academics with an accessible but scholarly account of contemporary youth justice research in the UK. By gathering contributions from leading researchers we hoped to provide insightful and critical analyses of at least some of the key issues and developments in the field. We also wanted the collection to engage constructively with contemporary policy and practice debates, and to that end we have encouraged the authors of each chapter at least to conclude with some thoughtful consideration of the policy and practice implications of the research that it reviews. We hope that the book offers not just an important and new contribution to existing scholarship but also an important and new contribution to public policy and professional practice in an area of great contemporary interest.

In introducing a collection on youth offending and youth justice it might make some sense to seek to define our key terms. However, we chose not to seek to impose a definition of 'youth' or 'youth justice' on the contributors, not least because this is problematic even across the UK jurisdictions and far more so internationally, where both ages of criminal responsibility and the age-related scope of youth justice systems vary. Similarly, we did not seek to define precisely the timescales which chapters should address, but suggested that authors might want to look back at least over the last decade and, where appropriate to their argument, over the last two or three decades.

The Editorial Board for the Research Highlights series suggested that each chapter should seek to include reference to all four UK countries, though a principal focus on one jurisdiction would be acceptable. As editors we gave contributors considerable latitude in this regard, preferring to allow them to write to their strengths, but seeking to ensure an appropriate jurisdictional reach across the collection as a whole. With hindsight, it is highly regrettable – and perhaps an unpardonable failing in editors all too used to neglecting smaller jurisdictions – that youth justice in Northern Ireland does not feature more prominently in this collection than it does; not least because Northern Ireland has gone much further than most jurisdictions in mainstreaming restorative youth justice. A chapter on that experience would doubtless have strengthened this collection.

The Editorial Board also asked us as editors to consider how we would handle issues around gender, ageism, ethnicity and diversity; care and control; interfaces between childcare, youth justice and criminal justice systems and issues of poverty and discrimination. Though we considered seeking chapters on these important issues and many others, on balance we settled for asking our contributors to pay some attention to these issues within their chapters, as appropriate to their topic. We leave it to readers to judge to what extent they have received adequate coverage, although we are confident that many of these issues emerge very clearly and receive very thoughtful attention.

We reminded the contributors that the Research Highlights series has played a significant role in developing the interfaces between research and practice in social work. Having now seen the project come to fruition and reviewed the excellent chapters that our contributors have provided we rest assured in our original hope that this collection can usefully further that tradition in an area of practice about which all of us are concerned and to which all of us are committed.

Youth offending and youth justice

The rate of youth crime has not risen in recent years, contrary to popular belief fuelled by a sensation-seeking media. And yet the political and legislative machinery is in overdrive, anxious to be seen to be doing something about young people's seeming disaffection with the rule of law. However, the context which ferments such 'disaffection' itself is largely ignored, and young people themselves are scapegoated because of their age, their (non-)status, their disregard for 'adult' norms and their seeming inability to conform. But perhaps that is just one side – the adult side – of the story.

Young people see themselves as largely conformist. They may be disaffected, but that is more to do with their inability to infiltrate the perceived 'closed shop' of adult society because of their status as 'young people'. Such status in transition renders them deficient in terms of citizenship rights and meaningful responsibilities. Such status results in marginalisation, stigmatisation and discrimination by those (adults) in authority over them. Arguably, for some of them offending is a means of denying that status and relieving the pressure of non-integration.

Whilst youth offending is not increasing, and may in fact have decreased in the last decade or two, there is no doubt that it *is* an issue in our society. However, this book counters the concern about the problem of youth offending with the argument that youth justice systems, at least as they currently operate in many jurisdictions, are not necessarily the appropriate solution to that problem. Youth offending is not just a question of rational choice by young people, it is also the result of a lack of structural opportunities for young people, in terms of education, employment, housing, adequate income and constructive leisure opportunities. However, this duality between agency and structure in youth crime is rarely seriously considered by politicians and policymakers. The emphasis is very much on blaming young people alone for their propensity to offend and making them responsible for their offending behaviour and the consequences of such behaviour, often through increasingly punitive means. Some argue that youth justice systems in many jurisdictions have lost their 'social justice' ethos. Although they purport to offer multi-disciplinary and welfare-oriented services, their emphasis is increasingly on containment, surveillance and blame within a criminal, rather than a youth justice, ideology.

If the world economy from late 2008 has been described as a 'system on life support' (Mason 2008), then many youth justice systems over the last decade or more could arguably be described in similar terms, not only in respect of their funding and philosophy but also in respect of their impact on young offenders. The book is therefore timely in re-focusing attention on what really matters for young offenders, victims of youth crime and wider publics in terms of making youth justice a social and moral, as well as a political and legal, issue.

Layout of the book

This book is in two parts. The first part puts youth offending and youth justice in their social, theoretical and political contexts. In Chapter 2 Brown suggests that youth and crime are social constructs dependent more on negotiating life course events than on chronological age per se. Nevertheless, she argues that criminality has been defined downwards by policy to an unprecedented younger age and to a broader range of behaviours. Brown describes the recent 'legislative binge' in England and Wales which criminalises not only children but also their parents and is fuelled by a hungry media more interested in demonising children than accurately stating the facts. Children and young people are not considered to be 'citizens' or to have rights in such a climate which increasingly marginalises and penalises them at an ever-younger age.

McVie, in Chapter 3, focuses on the research evidence underpinning developmental and life course criminology. Government policy is heavily influenced by developmental theories of offending, and particularly their efforts to predict later offending from early childhood experiences. But she asks to what extent crime is determined by and predictable from childhood, not least when most children who offend do not continue such behaviour into adulthood. McVie explores the literature on the age-crime curve and on criminal careers and identifies a range of dimensions which show promise in increasing our understanding about the developmental processes which lead to prolonged offending. However, she concludes that youth justice policies based on risk identification, prediction and prevention run the risk of inadvertently stigmatising and criminalising young people.

The criminalisation of young people, according to Morgan (Chapter 4), is a complex issue resulting from increased and earlier involvement of the youth and criminal justice systems in the lives of children and young people. Summary justice developments now mean out-of-court justice, which results in more young people being drawn into the system, greater police powers, less legal accountability, stricter interventions, greater likelihood of breach and consequent labelling of young people as 'criminals'. Whilst youth crime rates are stable or falling, the criminalisation and incarceration of young people is increasing. Whilst Morgan acknowledges that the Youth Justice Board has made some considerable improvements in the way the youth justice system operates in England and Wales, the fact remains that the system is still failing young people who offend.

Barry (Chapter 5) explores theories of desistance from crime at both the agency and structural level. She argues that current youth justice policy in the UK is somewhat at odds with much of this theoretical underpinning, with individual 'deficits' in young people forming the basis of much youth justice policy at the expense of wider structural constraints. In particular, Barry focuses on the Youth Crime Action Plan for England and Wales which promotes enforcement and punishment, non-negotiable support and earlier intervention as the basis for work with young offenders. Drawing on two studies of looked after young people's perceptions and experiences of offending and desistance, she offsets the policy rhetoric against the views of young offenders themselves to illustrate how current policy is more likely to undermine rather than encourage desistance amongst this age group.

Finally in Part One, Maruna and King (Chapter 6) question from where the increased punitiveness towards young people has emerged in contemporary society. Conventional wisdom oscillates between agreeing that young people will 'grow out of crime' and fearing that 'once a criminal, always a criminal'. The authors explore the extant literature on public attitudes to crime before outlining some of the findings of their own study of householders' views about crime and criminals, including 'generational anxiety' about young people. Maruna and King conclude that if the public are pessimistic about the 'redeemability' of young people, they are more likely to be punitive. However, if the public have a greater awareness of the external influences on offending, they will be less likely to fear, condemn and give up on young people.

Part Two of the book focuses on more practical or specific issues relating to work with young offenders, not only issues for professionals but also for young people themselves. Phoenix opens this section, in Chapter 7, with an exploration of the way youth justice practitioners in England and Wales make sense of the process and techniques of risk assessment to highlight the dichotomy for workers between welfare and punishment and between subjective and objective decision making. She points to a move from rehabilitation to assessment and management of risk so as to fulfil the Government's aim of reducing reoffending. Drawing on a wider study in England of youth justice practitioners' decision making relating to risk and need, Phoenix explores the possibility that risk assessment tools such as ASSET 'dematerialise' youthful offending by 'individualising' risk. How practitioners negotiate this individualisation in their recommendations to the court is hampered in a climate of structural constraints. Phoenix concludes that the welfare principles that practitioners nonetheless retain in their risk assessments may inadvertently result in more rather than less punitive interventions, not least when such interventions are only available within the confines of the youth justice system.

In Chapter 8 McNeill reviews a wide range of evidence about the effectiveness of community supervision and about 'what works?' in interventions with young people, arguing that an interrogation of the evidence about 'what works?' necessarily leads us towards moral questions about 'what's right?'. McNeill argues that current correctionalist policy and practice is liable not only to limit the effectiveness of supervision but also to undermine the desistance process. He concludes that supervision needs to give greater precedence to relationships between young people, professionals and others, not least when such relationships are crucial to reducing offending, and that if youth justice is to be legitimate (and thus effective) it cannot but attend to the injustices that many young offenders have suffered.

Halsey and Armitage (Chapter 9) focus on juvenile detention centres in Australia and the effects of custody on non-Indigenous and Indigenous young offenders as well as on professionals working with them. Some 650 10–17-year-olds are held in secure units across Australia, with the majority being males aged 15–17. Whilst Indigenous young people constitute less than 5 per cent of the overall youth population, over half of all incarcerated young people in 2006 were identified as Indigenous. The authors explore some of the cultural issues for such young people, as well as power relations, care versus control, education and contact with family and friends. They also explore the issues for caregivers, such as emotional detachment and their experience of the care versus control dichotomy. Halsey and Armitage conclude that more needs to be done to address the needs of young people within and beyond secure care, particularly the needs of Indigenous persons. They argue that young offenders and youth justice professionals alike require a greater say in how policy and practice in such establishments should develop.

In the penultimate chapter Souhami gives an overview of the rationale and practicalities of working beyond professional boundaries within a multi-agency context. In England and Wales, on which Chapter 10 focuses, youth justice professionals work in multi-agency Youth Offending Teams overseen by the Youth Justice Board. Souhami argues that although multi-agency work can produce creative, coherent and innovative practice, it also brings into focus complex and unsettling questions about professional identity, culture and conflict which can constrain and disrupt collaborative working.

The book concludes with an exploration by the editors of the key themes to emerge from the preceding chapters. This task has been made easier by the perhaps surprising – and certainly unanticipated – unanimity amongst the contributors about the essential factors affecting youth offending and youth justice in recent years. These include the increasing criminalisation and stigmatisation of young people; the relentless drive to punish and blame young people entirely for their own predicament; the emphasis on responsibilising young people and their parents and the fact that many youth justice policies are more likely to exacerbate rather than alleviate the problem of youth crime.

References

Goldson, B. and Muncie, J. (2006) *Youth Crime and Justice*. London: Sage.

Mason, P. (2008) 'A Last Chance' *New Statesman*. 6 November London: New Statesman.

Muncie, J. and Goldson, B. (2006) *Comparative Youth Justice: Critical Issues*. London: Pine Forge Press.

CHAPTER 2

The Changing Landscape of Youth and Youth Crime

Sheila Brown

Introduction

This chapter attempts to map the defining contours of the landscape of youth and youth crime over recent decades and to identify how these have changed to produce particular problems for young people, and challenges for those working with young people and for policymakers who shape young people's lives. The discussion is not intended as an analysis of developments in youth justice per se, which are considered elsewhere in this volume. It does, however, take the view that childhood, youth, and crime are socially constructed categories, rather than facts (James and Prout 1990; James, Jenks and Prout 1998). It is the socially negotiated life course, not chronological age, that most shapes young people's experiences of youth and crime (Hockey and James 1993). As such, legislative, policy and political discourses, as well as media representation, are an inherent part of the symbolic landscape through which the cultural meanings of childhood and youth, as well as what counts as 'crime', are produced. In that sense, the redefining of youth and youth crime, and the redefining downwards of youth crime to child crime, is significant. The discussion follows four broad dimensions:

1. The extended criminalisation of young people's behaviour through defining criminality downwards in the life course by

the State (for example by removing *doli incapax* in England and Wales, extending punitive and in particular custodial sentencing downwards in age and, of recent importance, the rejuvenated policy discourse of the proto-criminal child, reframed with a preventative gloss and a punitive edge).

2. The dualism of disempowering young people of agency, economically and socially, and abrogating their human rights under international conventions, whilst increasingly redefining children as viable authors of evil.

3. The broadening out of young people's 'criminality' by increasingly criminalising their everyday cultures, from music to social interaction, and by pre-criminalising increasingly 'low level' behaviours as 'anti-social' or otherwise demanding of State intervention that carries criminalising entailments.

4. A change in the profile of the youth and youth crime landscape, specifically arising from trans-border flows (embracing cultural, economic and politico-legal dimensions) in the context of global and (g)local dynamics.

This chapter is therefore concerned with certain interlocking processes: the symbolic *construction* of youth and youth crime through the languages of the media and the increasingly intertwining discourses of policy and politics – the process, in essence, of viewing young people through a prism of crime and disorder, and turning them by default into proto-criminals *sui generis*; the lived *experiences* of young people themselves in terms of culture, agency and structure and some of the major effects of global *flows* upon our purview of youth and youth crime. It focuses principally on the English jurisdiction, where these changes have been most starkly effected, but makes reference to Wales, Scotland and Northern Ireland, particularly in the sense that the cultural climate in these countries has produced various degrees of rejection and resistance to what might be termed the 'punitive disease' of the English.

Symbolic landscapes and the shaping of youth and crime

Hard times: redefining problem youth through policy

Detailed accounts of the many twists and turns of youth justice legislation in the UK over recent decades are widely available (see for example Bottoms and Dignan 2004; Brown 2005; Muncie 2004; Muncie, Hughes and McLaughlin 2002; Pitts 1988, 2001) and I do not propose to rehearse these here. From the original retreat from 'welfarism' in England and Wales during the recession of the 1970s under Labour, through the Conservatives' political crisis of legitimacy in the late 1970s and early 1980s during a maelstrom of economic and industrial disasters (Brake and Hale 1992; Hall *et al.* 1978; King 1991; Marr 2008) a tsunami of legal measures began to build, which were to progressively criminalise young people (King 1991). This occurred in tandem with the rolling back of the welfare state, and it was legislation in the fields of welfare, training, housing and education in the 1980s that consolidated the victim-blaming process of defining youth (in a time of burgeoning structural unemployment) as ill-disciplined, workshy and criminogenic (Carlen 1996). When unemployment soared at the turn of the 1970s it became politically and fiscally expedient to coercively 'warehouse' unemployed young people into low-paid work through 'training schemes' to massage unemployment statistics downwards (Coles 1995, pp.35–40). The meaning of youth had changed from one of fluid transition from school to work to consumer to adult, to an extended period of economic marginality and state and/or parental dependency. Young people on housing estates in areas of high unemployment were deemed to constitute a major part of a disintegrating, disassociated, frequently criminal, 'underclass' (Murray 1990).

Evil children, urban decay and getting tough: the 'ever younger, ever worse' decade

Following this redrawing of the meanings of youth and 'youth crime' came an even more disturbing phenomenon in the redefining of *childhood*. In the wake of the murder of two-year-old James Bulger (Brown 2003, 2005; Carlen 1996; Jewkes 2004; Young 1996) by two ten-year-old boys, childhood was almost overnight declared to have ended – in England at least.

This tragic event opened the floodgates by sensitising tabloid antennae to a small number of spectacular acts of delinquency by younger children: boys as young as six and seven were reported joyriding (taking cars for fun); an 11-year-old Hartlepool boy featured on the tabloid front pages after a joyriding spree, 'swaggering' from court wearing an SAS mask after receiving a community disposal (Brown 2005). (The boy was to later die choking on heroin he was trying to hide from the police in 2002, aged 18.) Meanwhile, even the *Hobart Mercury* captured the exploits of 13-year-old 'rat boy': 'UK police capture estate's "rat boy"… BRITISH police said yesterday they had captured a teenager known as the "rat boy" who had been living in the air ducts and tunnels of a Newcastle housing estate and terrorising residents' (1 March 1993). No oxygen of publicity was given to the extreme circumstances of these boys. 'Rat boy' for example, had run away from care 30 times and been completely rejected by his birth family. Instead, such cases were homogenised by the media and politicians into the 'evil child' category. Thus in the 1990s official 'war' was declared on child offenders. In introducing Secure Training Orders for 12–14-year-olds, the 1994 Criminal Justice and Public Order Act made it clear that young people in conflict with the law were culpable young *criminals* – not child offenders with multiple social needs. Alongside this, dramatic outbreaks of pyrotechnics in shows of urban unrest involving young males, police, cars and arson across deprived housing estates in the early 1990s (Campbell 1993) gave the media one long party on alleged child rioters (BBC 2006; Brown 2005). More in-depth reports on these events revealed the poor conditions on the estates in question, with high levels of long-term unemployment, child poverty and lack of local resources that made them unviable as living environments in any proper sense of the term. Locally, this prompted regeneration enterprise; for Party politics, it was grist to the political mill and fed into the now historical slogan: 'tough on crime, tough on the causes of crime', holding up a Labour Party Manifesto in which the rendering of children criminal was cynically used to help create a landslide electoral victory for the Party in 1997.

The subsequent 1998 Crime and Disorder Act saw younger children and young teenagers become a fully fledged category of social demon. Alongside its explicitly preventative mission, the Act produced the abolition of *doli incapax*; the introduction of curfews, parenting orders, action plan orders and child safety orders; the replacement of multiple cautioning by a dramatically pared-down reprimand and final warning system; and the expansion of criminal justice legislation into the realm of 'incivilities' via the Anti-Social Behaviour Order – in addition to the Crime (Sentences) Act 1997 that already allowed for public 'naming and shaming' of juveniles. The legislature expanded both the breadth of, and the intensity of, symbolic constitution of childhood and youth as a social threat. We were all to be urged to 'Shop a Yob' (Brown 2005, p.70).

Into the millennium, New Labour surpassed itself in its *iterative* reframing of children and young people as overwhelmingly negative forces through specific legislative and policy discourses. Those commentators who favour the phraseologies of 'new' youth justice and 'new' punitiveness (Goldson 2000, 2004, Newburn 2002; Pitts 2001) are not without reason, for the seemingly endless parade of punitive youth crime legislation produced by New Labour is without historical precedent.

Binge legislating and the languages of risk and blame: the creation of pre-crime

Perhaps the most insidious aspect of this legislative binge is the extent to which legal and policy discourses around youth crime since 1998 have been deployed under the rubric of 'prevention' just by the device of Section 37(1) of the Crime and Disorder Act, with an accompanying trumpeting of 'restorative' justice. In ten years a discursive avalanche in English and Welsh legislation has buried children, young people and their hapless parents under 'Child Protection Orders', 'Parenting Orders', 'Acceptable Behaviour Contracts', 'Common Assessment Frameworks' and of course the infamous 'Anti-Social Behaviour Orders', originally aimed at adults but now associated principally with children and young people. The 2003 White Paper *Respect and Responsibility: Taking a Stand against Anti-Social Behaviour* (Home Office 2003) firmly redefined that most youthful of all youthful activities, 'hanging around', as proto-criminal. Young people in public spaces were placed on a par with street rubbish.

Young children and their families are now to be screened for 'risk factors' allegedly predictive of future prolific offending from 'temperament' to 'mother has low IQ' to 'low economic status' (Home Office 2008a). Such risk factors will trigger 'Parenting Early Intervention Projects' in families of

8–13-year-olds (Youth Crime Action Plan 2008, p.29). One commentator has argued that the cutting edge of criminology is in fact now a 'pre-criminology' of actuarialism, risk management and surveillance (Zedner 2007, p.10).

Moreover, these alarming languages of pre-criminal construction find inspiration (or justification) in academic research. The latest Youth Action Plan (Home Office 2008a) imports Farrington's longitudinal predictive work (Farrington 2002). In Farrington's research 'prevention requires change within individuals' (Farrington 2002, p.661; for a critical review see Brown 2005, pp.101–103) and his predictive factors of low IQ, family breakdown, single parenthood, low family income and so on are introduced explicitly in current government policy discourse in that sense. Social justice is not an issue. The combination of a positivist research language and neo-Liberal politics literally suck disadvantaged families into the purview of the criminal justice system by inexorably pre-criminalising them.

Repressive blaming systems are, anthropologically speaking, the product of weak constitutions (Douglas 1994). Contemporary blaming systems also rely on legitimating public representation, and in that sense the production of 'youth' and 'youth crime' and of the risky child 'pre-criminal', depend upon their acquiring substance via mass mediated representation, otherwise they remain but chimera of distrusted politicians. The trajectories detailed above have little bearing upon a humanitarian concern with the welfare – in the everyday sense of the word, not the policy construction – of children and young people. They represent a history of what Redhead defines as 'panic law': 'to denote the frenzied-but-simulated state of law and justice at the end of the century, as in Jean Baudrillard's use of "panic crash" to describe global economic stock-exchange breakdowns' (Redhead 1995, p.112). The *excess* of law, almost a frenzy of law, becomes a supra-mediated and representational field framing childhood and youth, but children and young people are not the true objects of these representations: the representational field is directed at holding on to legitimated power at any cost. The result, as Jewkes (2004, p.68) notes, is that 'it appears that the political process in Westminster and media discourses are…mutually constitutive'.

Mediatisation and panic law: young people and meltdown-talk

Following from the foregoing, none of the constructions of youth and crime produced by legal and policy discourse can be understood without reference to their embeddedness in a mediatised culture (Brown 2003). I have discussed elsewhere the emergence of a 'total panic' surrounding children and young people, which emerged in the 1990s and is distinctively different to the discrete 'moral panics' of former decades (Brown 2005, pp.58–65). The total panic, perhaps now even beyond 'panic', is part of a media orchestrated twenty-first-century meltdown language that links all domains from banking systems to military strategies, and heralds a 'permanent state of exceptionality' (Shearing and Wood 2007) that justifies almost any political response. This way of framing the world requires a continual supply of 'the Other' (Brown 2003; Young 1996) and is incapable of embracing diversity without hostility (Hudson 2008).

The latest 'knife crime epidemic' (2008) is a case in point. The third in a series of meltdown discourses around young people and knives since 2002, the latest barrage was prompted by the stabbing of the brother of a soap actress. Interviewed on BBC Radio 4, a range of newspaper editors acknowledged that the saturation coverage given to the 'knife crime epidemic' of 2008 stemmed from having a cachet of celebrity attached to it: the attractive young female 'Brookside' actress was soon drawn into the *Sun* newspaper 'campaign' against knife crime (Soodin 2008). Not least, the 'knife crime panic' has been used to quickly lever in less accountable street policing, which will inevitably impact most upon young (black, male) people by withdrawing the requirement for police to use recording forms (Home Office Press release on Hallam Centre for Community Justice Portal, 2008b www.cjp.org.uk/news/archive). The press release continues: 'Home Secretary Jacqui Smith said…"Giving police the means to dramatically reduce form-filling bureaucracy in these ten priority areas will free up valuable officer time to further clamp down on knife crime".' Reading the notes at the end of the press release one sees that under 'Operation Blunt 2', 'in London, 77,000 stop and searches [and] 3,300 arrests have occurred', and '2,200 knives were recovered'. That is, 2.8 per cent of those stopped were carrying knives. The Offending Crime and Justice Survey (Home Office 2008c, p.16, 21–22) found that 3 per cent of 10–25-year-olds admitted carrying a knife in the preceding 12 months, and *of this 3 per cent of* respondents, 4 per cent had used the knife to threaten someone and 1 per cent to occasion injury. Forty-six per cent of knives carried were penknives. The general seriousness of these constructive processes is simply illustrated by the following: *The Times* reported in July 2008: "'Knife crime has overtaken terrorism as the No 1 priority for the Metropolitan Police", one of Britain's most senior officers said yesterday' (5 July 2008).

Resistances and localisms: the un-English stemming of the penal tide

Is panic law a specifically English phenomenon? Turning to Scotland, the major difference in the symbolic production of child criminals compared to England and Wales has historically occurred through the operation of the Children's Hearing system, in that despite the low age of criminal responsibility (at age eight in Scotland), the major focus for under 16-year-olds has been for four decades on the social and welfare needs of the child. Under a Labour administration numerous policy and legislative changes attempted to bring the Scottish policy framework much closer to its punitive English counterpart from 2002 (Audit Scotland 2007). In sections of the Scottish media, however, this English infiltration did not go unchallenged:

> Last week, the deputy justice minister, Richard Simpson, did what a senior politician should never do: he spoke the truth, namely, that juvenile courts are a disaster in England. It is a proposition with which few would argue, and legal reformers in England have long sought to introduce the children's hearing system because – shock, horror – it actually works. In Scotland, youth crime is down, though you would hardly believe it from the rhetoric of this administration. (MacWhirter 2002)

Resistance to changes in Scottish cultures of welfarism has been substantial, causing wrath in the English tabloids, which combine anti-Scottish sentiment with anti-youth sentiment to achieve sublime heights of jingoism. The *Daily Mail* fumed on 10 September 2008, 'A nation at the mercy of feral youths: 8,000 child criminals terrorize Scotland'. Continuing the crusade later in the month, the *Daily Mail* protested that 'Powers to target parents of feral children have never been used…not one Parenting Order in three years since legislation was introduced' (22 September 2008). Local councils, it seems, have preferred not to use the Orders, with the regional preference still being for Children's Hearings. ASBOs for young people have been left almost unused and the rolling out of the youth court pilots has been postponed. The Scottish National Party (SNP) administration it seems, under Justice Minister Kenny MacAskill, was not prepared to join in the uneasy 'second order consensus' described by Downes and Morgan (2002, p.317), and was not minded to challenge localised resistance from councils, sheriffs and social workers. Complex historical cultures, including cultures of professional practice and ambivalent broader social attitudes towards childhood and youth, can operate to resist punitive turns where there is political will to support this.

Northern Ireland is also resisting the 'penal tide'. The situation here is particular for a number of reasons; not least that devolution only occurred in 2007. Northern Ireland's policy interpretation of responding to children and young people in conflict with the law as legislatively framed by the Justice (Northern Ireland) Act 2002, which, as in England, defines the aim of the youth justice system as 'to protect the public by preventing offending', is different to England. The Northern Ireland Government has constructed the aim of prevention as prioritising of youth restorative practices, through the establishment of the 'Youth Conference Service' for 10–18-year-olds. Together with community supervision, youth conferencing orders accounted for the majority of sentences in 2006 (Youth Justice Agency Northern Ireland website: www.youthjusticeagencyni.gov.uk) and youth conferencing is also used as a diversionary measure. In this emergent and rapidly changing landscape, still definitively characterised by sectarian history and issues surrounding constructions of youth and youth crime, it is impossible to simply characterise cultural shifts taking place. Human rights have a strong cultural presence as a focus of debate, as do debates specific to the troubles, such as campaigns around paramilitary punishment beatings of young people 'named and shamed' by ASBOs, street rioting and involvement of young people in street violence. There is not space to explore these complexities further here, but readers are directed to the Northern Ireland Commissioner for Children and Young People (NICCY) website and the extensive research conducted and underway by researchers at the Northern Ireland Universities (for example, Byrne, Conway and Ostermeyer 2005; Kilkelly et al. 2004; NICCY 2009).

What is clear in this brief cross-border discussion is that there will be no simple transference of the English symbolic production of youth and youth crime across the UK countries. Even in Wales, legislatively most tied to England, a 'socially inclusive, rights based approach' to youth justice is being promoted (Haines and Case 2007). Encouragingly, local particularities, different cultural traditions, active community and youth organisations, different modes of political will and different structures of feeling amongst the public characterise Britain in relation to youth and crime.

Culture, agency and structure in youth and youth crime
Young people's voices: (mis)representing youth in research

Alongside the (often contradictory) rhetorics, policies and representations that surround youth and youth crime which frame their public and legal definitions, young people's everyday experiences co-exist. Youth cultures continue to be produced and reproduced through music, style, dress, language and interaction; sub-(mass)media but hyper-mediated through talking, texting and telecoms (Epstein 1998). The exponential growth of the social web is producing endless varieties of communication and virtual alternatives for young people, (much to adults' consternation), which are 'cool spaces' and largely ungovernable without young people's consent (Brown 2005; Holloway and Valentine 2003; Skelton and Valentine 1998). However, young people as social agents are also bound by social structures, which they are hard pressed to challenge, not least because of their relative powerlessness in decision making and their relatively subdued collective voice.

This has a crucial bearing on the changing landscape of youth and youth crime. Work from within childhood studies has consistently argued that children, constructed by adults as dichotomously 'in trouble' or 'troubled', are responded to as though agency on their part can only be negative (Lee 2001). That is, children are either passive, innocent and victimised or active, dangerous and demonised. The notion of the child or young person as a positive agent, capable of authorship of their lives and with entitlement to that, is much rarer.

In fact, until the early 1990s children and young people *themselves* were rarely even asked about youth crime in the UK – either their commission of it or their experiences of it. In some senses, what followed was a double edged sword. Taking inspiration from the emergence of local adult crime surveys and 'new left realism' (Jones, Maclean and Young 1986; Kinsey 1985), came the concept of the *youth* crime survey. This was a largely well-intentioned attempt to extend the left realist principles of the victimisation survey to the young, who had never been allocated the status of credible victims of crime in *public* space. Pioneered in Edinburgh in 1988 by researchers based at Edinburgh University (Anderson *et al.* 1994) and followed in 1992–4 by similarly large scale projects in the north-east of England by a Teesside based team (Brown 1994, 1995), these first major studies (based on large systematic survey samples of 11–15-year-olds and in-depth qualitative work with sub-samples) revealed most startlingly the extent of victimisation of young people in public space, and the poor relations with police and some adults that prevented reporting of quite serious incidents by young people. They were followed by numerous smaller studies of a similar kind (see e.g. Hartless *et al.* 1995). In 1992 the British Crime Survey expanded its coverage to young people aged 12–15 for the first time (Home Office 1995) and found lesser, but still significant, amounts of youth victimisation.

However, politicians, policymakers and the media emphasised only particular aspects of the findings. The first of these was the extent to which young people were the victims of *other young people*, turning the 'problem' back into youth crime or, alternatively, 'bullying'. The second, and most damaging, was to fasten on to the relatively high proportions of young people admitting offending behaviour, including theft, drug and alcohol use, and violence in the previous twelve months. The argument from the researchers was that offending at low levels was so widespread as to be commonplace amongst young people, and thereby to 'normalise' it as part of growing up, and to emphasise the very *small* amount of serious offending. In retrospect this was devastatingly naive. Then and subsequently self-report surveys and adult attitude surveys have been used politically and ideologically to reinforce the notion that youth is 'out of control'. Interestingly, the figures from the early studies are very similar on most types of offence to those carried out in many subsequent studies, including a 2002 Joseph Rowntree Foundation-funded study and the Home Office Offending Crime and Justice Survey (Home Office 2008c) – all suggesting that levels of youth crime have remained fairly stable or have fallen. However, rather than enter into an extensive discussion of the now numerous sources of statistics on youth offending and victimisation here (which increasingly – in their very diversity–demand and deserve a painstaking scrutiny), I would like to turn to the question of young people's experiences of youth and liminality in everyday life, a little disputed *context* of both victimisation and offending.

Young people and experiences of crime: transitions, trajectories and social (in)justice

Here I am concerned with some interesting areas of overlap between the genres of youth studies and youth criminology. This has principally occurred where researchers have been concerned with understanding processes of structure and agency in the life course of young people, whether or not the principal focus was on offending. Examples include studies of social exclusion, transitions in the life course and homelessness. Broadly character-ised, such research has at its heart the problematic of social justice for young people.

The themes that emerge from these strands of research would indicate that social (economic, educational, cultural) exclusion occurs through child-hood difficulties and marginalisation from young ages, on to disrupted transitions after school – marginalities that do involve the agency of young people themselves in withdrawal from available systems and opportunities (schooling, training), but which are more shaped by structural exclusionary forces in the post-Fordist economy. Hence in research on Teesside it was found that whilst a history of chaotic or disturbing family or other close rela-tionship environments, negative life events (such as the death or loss of a parent), drug use or single parenthood, might make 'choices out' of economic marginality less likely, they were not the primary factors behind marginality (MacDonald and Marsh 2001). An economy of transient, temporary, casual, low-paid jobs makes unemployment the 'default position' for many young people in areas of multiple disadvantage (MacDonald and Marsh, pp.386–387). Many young people held conventional attitudes and aspirations, and did not feel especially 'culturally' excluded – but their choices were quite simply constrained by lack of sufficient quality of employment. Similar points have been made by McKendrick, Scott and

Sinclair in a study of children and young people in Drumchapel, Glasgow (2007).

This situation potentially impacts upon crime in a number of ways affecting young people. First, it makes the transition to independent adulthood and the possession of social capital (Barry 2006) – perhaps the strongest predictors of desistance from offending – more difficult to achieve. Second, it makes any transition out of involvement with the justice system and 'official' criminality extremely difficult to achieve. Thus Gray notes that Labour's emphasis on the need for the 'reintegration' of young offenders places the onus to achieve this on young offenders themselves, a 'personal moral responsibility...with limited acknowledgement of the structural barriers to reintegration that are posed by the unequal distribution of socio-economic resources' (Gray 2007, p.402). Interlocking social disadvantage, described by Carlen in her 'political criminology of youth homelessness' as a 'jigsaw', characterises many young offenders' lives. Carlen found that although a substantial majority of homeless respondents had been involved in offending, they had also been victims of crime and multiple disadvantage and abuse, and 'their fundamental concerns are the same as most people...the main difference between them and domiciled people is that they have to achieve [these objectives] outwith one of the major social props to self esteem *and* state acknowledgement of citizenship claims – the address' (Carlen 1996, p.124).

Barry's sensitive study of young people desisting (or not) from offending concludes that the social, economic, cultural and symbolic capital necessary for effective desistance was depleted by liminality, labour market marginality, lack of citizenship status, substance addiction, poor reputation, geographical immobility (having to remain in the neighbourhood for economic or family reasons), housing problems and involvement with the criminal justice system (Barry 2006, see also Farrall and Calverley 2006). These factors were also *gendered*, a dimension frequently missing from analyses of social exclusion and criminalisation. For young men, achieving masculinity was frequently a priority by any means (Barry 2006; see also Newburn and Stanko 1994), and for young women, the paths to desistance (or not) were structured by events such as children being taken into care, domestic or partner violence, and relationship and/or drug dependencies.

Whilst all of these barriers to desistance involve agency as well as structure, once established, they can become overwhelming because they profoundly disempower young people from a notion of citizenship. Hence Gray suggests that 'responsibilisation'-based youth justice policies, with their 'individualisation of social risks', 'have not fostered belonging (a precondition of citizenship), and have done little to change the self-esteem of young people or their material circumstances, and they have been made to feel that exclusion is down to their own deficiencies' (Gray 2007, p.410; see also Carlen 1996).

Because youth policies focus on criminalisation rather than social justice, moreover, young people outside the 'golden circle' (that is, the always-already included) who participate in youth councils and youth parliaments (the governmental concession to according formal citizen status to the young) are not constructed as citizens. Street children, those excluded from school, the homeless and offenders, are not 'citizens'. One final point to note here is the need to extend the notion of citizenship downwards to early and pre-teenage people. The focus on 'youth' in many studies has excluded children as agents even by researchers themselves. We know little about young children's experiences of liminality and marginality, and how economic and social marginality interact with their agency and interaction with 'crime'. The Offender, Crime and Justice Survey begins at age ten and the youth surveys discussed above typically begin at 11 or 12, and, as we have seen, there has been a growth in the construction of the child 'criminal'. Yet youth transitions studies and youth exclusion studies tend to be concerned with older young people, leaving younger children's lives to be analysed in terms of the ubiquitous 'risk factors'. Certainly, the impact of global issues on 'youth' criminology will soon make it inevitable to accord voices to younger children.

Globalisation, the (g)local and the changing landscape of youth and youth crime

Flows, borders and young people: future scanning

Finally, the landscape of youth and youth crime is being transformed in ways that are not yet fully grasped, by processes of globalisation and glocalisation (Featherstone, Lash and Robertson 1995): the macro shifts that have begun to subvert the insular definitions of youth and youth crime in the localised contexts of the countries and regions of the United Kingdom. These dynamics are the results of movements of peoples, cultural flows, trans-border crime, cyberspace or communications technology flows, and changes in the boundaries of legal discourses and jurisdictions, which taken together have both produced new challenges in understanding youth and crime, and have introduced questions of rights and autonomies that go to the heart of former preconceptions about youth itself. Not least, as noted above, UK youth and crime studies have tended to focus on teenagers, whereas many of the young people affected by (g)local issues are younger.

There is not space here to discuss the whole of the broader agenda for landscapes of youth and youth crime implied by global trends, which include (at least) issues facing children and young people who have entered the UK within the last ten years as asylum seekers, refugees or economic migrants from 'new' European countries; the effects of existing domestic policies on these young people; their constructions and experiences of uneven trajectories of 'integration' in relation to exclusion, crime and victimisation, and the issues for trafficked children and young migrants facing various forms of enforced labour, including sex work, and various forms of hate crime (Brown 2005). In the global electronic landscape the study of cybercrime against children and young people is somewhat more advanced (Brown 2005; Jewkes and Andrews 2007; and the websites www.iwf.org.uk; www.ecpat.net/eng/index.asp; www.wiredpatrol.org all provide starting points). Additionally, Muncie (2005, 2008) has written extensively on processes of neo-liberal convergences in youth and juvenile justice systems under conditions of globalisation, in particular focusing on the 'punitive turn' and the spread of both repressive practices and restorative practices in justice systems. Alongside this he notes, as does Brown (2005), the concomitant appeals to international conventions on rights for children, and it is on this aspect that I wish to focus next, for it has been at the heart of recent animated debates concerning young people and crime in the UK.

Contesting rights for children: conventions, laws and powers

The UK's record in the matter of the United Nations Convention on the Rights of the Child is deplorable. Having ratified the treaty in 1991, Britain has been chastised twice, in 1999 and 2002, for a continual abrogation of its obligations, on everything from misuse of child custody to violence against children, to freedom of association, to the right to be heard (Brown 2005). Finally in 2001 came the establishment of official Children's Commissioners, appointed in Wales in 2001, Northern Ireland and Scotland in 2004 and England in 2005, with a responsibility to 'oversee' the integration of the United Nations Convention on the Rights of the Child in domestic policy. The Commissioners have taken up the UK's poor record in meeting its obligations and in June 2008 the Commissioners for all British jurisdictions jointly published a report to the UN Committee, stating that concerns and recommendations made by the UN Committee in previous reports of Britain's failure to comply with the UNCRC had not been met, that in 2008 the position had worsened further and that 110 recommendations should be acted upon.

The advantage of a rights discourse is that it is capable of according children agency. However, it also encourages dependency, in that many 'rights' are in fact *protections*, which should not be so necessary if children's rights were actually taken seriously in the first place. To clarify, if the fundamental right for children to participate and be heard *in any matter which affects them* under Article 12 of the UNCRC were interpreted actively, many of the 'protective' rights would be rendered superfluous. In addition, there are other problematic complexities with rights discourses that I have discussed elsewhere (Brown 2005, pp.200–206), although there are numerous specific instances where the UNCRC and other international rights and legislative measures may prove useful both symbolically and legislatively if they can be mobilised. This latter point is the most important, for 'rights' discourses of any kind are abstract and universalising: they do not speak to the specific power structures and conflicts that produce the criminalisation or the victimisation of children and young people (Brown 2005; Gaete 1999). Any rights agenda for young people and access to justice must therefore: be articulated through concerted, specific organisational strategies (typically through the agency of the Third Sector and NGOs); be able to access international justice (to bring cases for example, to the European Court, since unlike the UNCRC, human rights issues under the European Convention on Human Rights are subject to the 1998 Human Rights Act); and occur in tandem with a strategy for social justice and the redistribution of agency and resources in favour of children and young people as citizens (Brown 2005; Carlen 1996; Gray 2007).

Conclusions

In Cornwall, recently, Redruth Police and Local Authority took highly 'effective' measures against youth crime: they simply banned young people from the streets in less affluent neighbourhoods in a 'voluntary' scheme (backed up by the threat of parental interventions in the event of non-compliance). 'Operation Goodnight' resulted in the removal of hundreds of teenagers from the streets from 9pm onwards over the summer holidays of 2008 (*Metro*, Friday, 25 July 2008) and the adults are still congratulating themselves at the time of writing six months later.

We are clearly a long way away from what Gray (2007) describes as a 'transformative rights' programme. Nevertheless, children and young people are finding their own agency despite adults through, particularly, inventive use of information and communication technologies; the third sector is relatively flourishing in the arena of social justice for young people; practitioners continue to subvert inequitable policies; localities continue to resist globalising punitive tendencies; and the UK government has been forced to respond, if in partial and somewhat cynical ways, to demands for official avenues of representation for children's rights. A rich seam of academic research exists and continues to be vigorously pursued in tandem with the willingness of the third sector to fund and publicise research as well as campaign. There are some prospects for resistance and change. We may yet see a time when we are able to speak positively about the changing landscape of youth and youth crime; when discussions of soaring crime rates, risk factors, and intensive intervention have been superseded by discourses of agency, participation and social justice, and effective rights for children in conflict with the law. In the meantime we need to remember what children repeatedly tell researchers when they are asked about their difficulties... 'it's adults. They just don't listen.'

References

Anderson, S., Kinsey, R., Loader, I. and Smith, G. (1994) *Cautionary Tales: Young People and Policing in Edinburgh*. Aldershot: Avebury.

Audit Scotland (2007) *Dealing with Offending by Young People: Performance Update*. Report prepared for The Auditer General for Scotland. Available at http://www.audit-scotland.gov.uk/docs/central/2007/nr_070823-youth-justice-update.pdf (accessed 29 May 2009).

BBC (2006) 'Looking back: Meadowell riots.' Available at http://www.bbc.co.uk/tyne/content/articles/2006/09/07/meadow_well_riots_feature.shtml (accessed 10 March 2009).

Barry, M. (2006) *Youth Offending in Transition: The Search for Social Recognition*. Abingdon: Routledge.

Bottoms, A. and Dignan, J. (2004) 'Youth justice in Great Britain.' *Youth Crime and Youth Justice: Comparative and Cross National Perspectives 31*, 21–183.

Brake, M. and Hale, C. (1992) *Public Order and Private Lives*. London: Routledge.

Brown, S. (1994) *Whose Challenge? Youth, Crime and Everyday Life in Middlesbrough*. Middlesbrough: Middlesbrough City Challenge Partnership.

Brown, S. (1995) 'Crime and safety in whose "community"?' *Youth and Policy 48*, 27–48.

Brown, S. (2003) *Crime and Law in Media Culture*. Buckingham: Open University Press.

Brown, S. (2005) *Understanding Youth and Crime: Listening to Youth?*, 2nd edn. Maidenhead: Open University Press.

Byrne, J., Conway, M. and Ostermeyer, M. (2005) *Young People's Attitudes and Experiences of Policing, Violence and Community Safety in North Belfast*. Belfast: Institute for Conflict Research.

Campbell, B. (1993) *Goliath: Britain's Dangerous Places*. London: Methuen.

Carlen, P. (1996) *Jigsaw – A Political Criminology of Youth Homelessness*. Buckingham: Open University Press.

Coles, B. (1995) *Youth and Social Policy: Youth Citizenship and Young Careers*. London: UCL Press.

Douglas, M. (1994) *Risk and Blame: Essays in Cultural Theory*. London: Routledge.

Downes, D. and Morgan, R. (2002) 'The Skeletons in the Cupboard: The Politics of Law and Order at the Turn of the Millenium.' In M. Maguire, R. Morgan and R. Reiner (eds) *The Oxford Handbook of Criminology*, 3rd edn. Oxford: Oxford University Press.

Epstein, J. S. (ed.) (1998) *Youth Culture: Identity in a Postmodern World*. Oxford: Blackwell.

Farrall, S. and Calverley, A. (2006) *Understanding Desistance from Crime*. Maidenhead: Open University Press.

Farrington, D. (2002) 'Developmental Criminology and Risk-focused Prevention.' In M. Maguire, R. Morgan and R. Reiner (eds) *The Oxford Handbook of Criminology*, 3rd edn. Oxford: Oxford University Press.

Featherstone, M., Lash, S. and Robertson, R. (eds) (1995) *Global Modernities*. London: Sage/TCS.

Gaete, R. (1999) 'The West, its Other, and Human Rights.' In T. Skelton and T. Allen (eds) *Culture and Global Change*. London: Routledge.

Goldson, B. (2000) *The New Youth Justice*. Lyme Regis: Russell House.

Goldson, B. (2004) 'Youth Crime and Youth Justice.' In J. Muncie and D. Wilson (eds) *Student Handbook of Criminal Justice and Criminology*. London: Cavendish.

Gray, P. (2007) 'Youth justice, social exclusion and the demise of social justice.' *Howard Journal 46*, 4, 401–416.

Haines, K. and Case, S. (2007) 'Individual differences in public opinion about youth crime and justice in Swansea.' *Howard Journal 46*, 4, 338–355.

Hall, S., Critcher, C., Jefferson, T., Clarke, J. and Roberts, B. (1978) *Policing the Crisis: Mugging, the State, and Law and Order*. London: Macmillan.

Hartless, J., Ditton, J., Nair, G. and Philips, S. (1995) 'More sinned against than sinning: a study of young teenagers' experiences of crime.' *British Journal of Criminology 35*, 1, 114–133.

Home Office (1995) *Young People, Victimization and the Police: British Crime Survey Findings on Experiences and Attitudes of 12–15 Year Olds*. Home Office Research Study 140. London: HMSO.

Holloway, S.L. and Valentine, G. (2003) *Cyberkids: Children in the Information Age*. London: Routledge.

Home Office (2003) *Respect and Responsibility: Taking a Stand Against Anti-Social Behaviour*. London: Stationery Office.

Home Office (2008a) *HM Government Youth Crime Action Plan 2008*. London: Stationery Office. Available at http://www.homeoffice.gov.uk/documents/youth-crime-action-plan/youth-crime-action-plan-08?view=binary (accessed 29 May 2009).

Home Office (2008b) 'New Measures Will Cut Red Tape in the Fight Against Knife Crime.' Home Office Press Release, 18 September. Available at http://press.homeoffice.gov.uk/press-releases/measures-cut-red-tape (accessed 29 May 2009).

Home Office (2008c) *Young People and Crime: Findings from the 2006 Offending, Crime and Justice Survey*. Home Office Statistical Bulletin 09/08, 15 July. London: Stationery Office. Available at http://www.homeoffice.gov.uk/rds/pdfs08/hosb0908.pdf (accessed 10 March 2009).

Hockey, J. and James, A. (1993) *Growing up and Growing Old: Ageing and Dependency in the Life Course*. London: Sage.

Hudson, B. (2008) 'Difference, Diversity and Criminology.' *Theoretical Criminology 12*, 3, 275–292.

James, A. and Prout, A. (eds) (1990) *Constructing and Reconstructing Childhood*. London: Falmer.

James, A. Jenks, C. and Prout, A. (eds) (1998) *Theorizing Childhood*. Cambridge: Polity.

Jewkes, Y. (2004) *Media and Crime*. London: Sage.

Jewkes, Y. and Andrews, C. (2007) 'The Problem of Child Pornography on the Internet: International Responses.' In Y. Jewkes (ed.) *Crime Online*. Cullompton: Willan.

Jones, T., Maclean, B. and Young, J. (eds) (1986) *The Islington Crime Survey*. Aldershot: Gower.

Kilkelly, U., Kilpatrick, R., Lundy, L., Scraton, P., Davey, C., Dwyer, C. and McAlister, S. (2004) *Children's Rights in Northern Ireland*. Belfast: Northern Ireland Commissioner for Children and Young People.

King, M. (1991) 'The Political Construction of Crime Prevention: A Contrast between the French and British Experience.' In K. Stenson and D. Cowell (eds) *The Politics of Crime Control*. London: Sage.

Kinsey, R. (1985) *First Report of the Merseyside Crime Survey*. Liverpool: Merseyside City Council.

Lee, N. (2001) *Childhood in Society: Growing Up in an Age of Uncertainty*. Maidenhead: Open University Press.

MacDonald, R. and Marsh, J. (2001) 'Disconnected youth?' *Journal of Youth Studies 4*, 4, 373–391.

McKendrick, J., Scott, G. and Sinclair, S. (2007) 'Dismissing disaffection: Young people's attitudes towards education, employment and participation in a deprived community.' *Journal of Youth Studies 10*, 2, 139–160.

MacWhirter, I. (2002) 'Is This How to Change a First Minister into a Basket Case?' *The Herald* (Glasgow) 19 June, p.14.

Marr, A. (2008) *A History of Modern Britain*. London: Pan Macmillan.

Muncie, J. (2004) *Youth and Crime*, 2nd edn. London: Sage.

Muncie, J. (2005) 'The globalization of crime control – the case of youth and juvenile justice: Neo-liberalism, policy convergence and international conventions.' *Theoretical Criminology 9*, 1, 35–64.

Muncie, J. (2008) 'The "punitive turn" in juvenile justice: Cultures of control and rights compliance in Western Europe and the USA.' *Youth Justice 8*, 2, 107–121.

Muncie, J., Hughes, G. and McLaughlin, E. (2002) *Youth Justice: Critical Readings*. London: Sage.

Murray, C. (1990) *The Emerging British Underclass*. London: Institute of Economic Affairs.

Newburn, T. (2002) 'Young People, Crime and Justice.' In J. Muncie and D. Wilson (eds) *Student Handbook of Criminal Justice and Criminology*. London: Cavendish.

Newburn, T. and Stanko, E. (eds) (1994) *Just Boys Doing Business? Men, Masculinities and Crime*. London: Routledge.

NICCY (2009) *Children's Rights: Rhetoric or Reality?*. Belfast: Northern Ireland
Commissioner for Children and Young People. Available at
http://www.niccy.org/article.aspx?menuId=467 (accessed 10 March 2009).

Pitts, J. (1988) *The Politics of Juvenile Crime*. London: Sage.

Pitts, J. (2001) *The New Politics of Youth Crime: Discipline and Solidarity*. London:
Routledge.

Redhead, S. (1995) *Unpopular Cultures: The Birth of Law and Popular Culture*.
Manchester: Manchester University Press.

Shearing, C. and Wood, J. (2007) *Imagining Security*. Cullompton: Willan.

Skelton, T. and Valentine, G. (1998) *Cool Places: Geographies of Youth Cultures*. London:
Routledge.

Soodin, V. (2008) 'Knife menace every 4 minutes.' *Sun*, 17 July. Available at
www.thesun.co.uk/sol/ homepage/news/article1434610.ece, accessed 19 March
2008.

Young, A. (1996) *Imagining Crime: Textual Outlaws and Criminal Conversations*. London:
Sage/TCS.

Zedner, L. (2007) 'Pre-crime and post-criminology?' *Theoretical Criminology 1*, 2,
261–281.

CHAPTER 3

Criminal Careers and Young People

Susan McVie

Introduction

In recent years we have seen a radical shift in both political and public discourses about youth offending and anti-social behaviour in Britain, as evidenced elsewhere in this volume. One of the main consequences of this shift has been an explosion in the number of policies, initiatives and crackdowns targeted at young people perceived to be at risk of offending and an increasing tendency to responsibilise young children in a seemingly desperate search for the solutions to the problem of crime (Muncie and Goldson 2006). Much Government policy has been based on evidence emerging from the field of developmental criminology and the argument that the propensity to become involved in criminal offending in adulthood is apparent from the earliest years of childhood (Farrington 2003; Loeber 1991; West and Farrington 1977). This chapter considers the relationship between age and crime, known universally as the 'age-crime curve' (Farrington 1986) and the emerging concept of the 'criminal career' (Blumstein *et al.* 1986).

The chapter starts with a review of the age-crime curve and highlights one of the biggest debates within the discipline of criminology. It then considers key dimensions of the criminal careers paradigm and summarises some of the research evidence contributing to this important field, paying particular attention to gender differences. The chapter concludes with some implications for policy and practice and argues that there is considerable evidence to support the criminal careers paradigm and good reasons for adopting a life-course approach to the study of crime. However, it is crucial not to overestimate the promise of prediction since anti-social tendencies in early childhood do not inevitably lead to criminal offending in adulthood and policy responses that target young children run the risk of irreversibly stigmatising and criminalising them.

The nature of the age-crime curve

The term 'age-crime curve' is used to describe a characteristic peak found in aggregate crime data when it is plotted against age. The first recorded example of such a curve was published in 1831 and since then the phenomenon has been replicated numerous times using various sources of data, making it one of the most studied aspects of criminology (Tittle and Grasmick 1997). Early studies focused largely on data collected by official criminal justice organisations (such as numbers of cautions, arrests or convictions), although the explosion of social surveys in the latter half of the last century has also provided strong substantiating evidence for this unimodal pattern using self-reported offending data (see Blumstein *et al.* 1986; Farrington 1986).

An illustration of the age-crime curve using recent official crime data is given in Figure 3.1. This graph is replicated from the most recently published data on criminal proceedings in Scottish courts (Scottish Government 2008) and shows the rate per 10,000 of the population, for males and females, against whom a charge was proved in Scotland in the year 2006/7 by age. These data are typical of a characteristic age-crime curve based on official convictions data and reveal a clear distinction between the sexes.

Figure 3.1 shows a sharp rise in the proportion of the male population convicted of a crime or offence in the Scottish courts between ages of 15 and 18, followed by a steep decline to about the mid 20s and a steadier decline thereafter. The pattern for females is similar, but the extent of the rise and decline in convictions amongst the female population is far less substantial than for the males. There is a rise in the proportion of the female population convicted between age 15 and 17, peaking at age 18, followed by a slowly tapering decline into late adulthood. The scale of the difference between

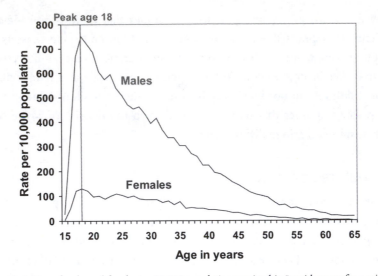

Figure 3.1: Rate of males and females per 10,000 population convicted in Scottish courts for a crime or offence in 2006/7
Source: Scottish Government (2008)

males and females appears greatest at age 18, the peak age for both sexes, when the ratio between the sexes in terms of proportion of the population with a conviction is around 6:1.

The exact ages at which these changes occur and the nature of the curve are subject to considerable variation over time and depending on what source of data is used. For example, an age-crime curve based on self-report offending data would be expected to display a similar profile, although the peak age of offending is generally younger than for convictions data and the scale of the difference between males and females is usually less extensive (see Farrington *et al.* 2003; Weis 1986).

The 'great debate' about the age-crime curve

Following a systematic review of the evidence, Hirschi and Gottfredson concluded that the form of the age-crime curve had remained so stable over different time periods, between different jurisdictions and within different demographic groups that it was one of the 'brute facts of criminology' (1983, p.552). However, the nature of the curve and its theoretical meaning has been subject to some of the most heated arguments in the discipline, described by Vold, Bernard and Snipes (1998) as the 'Great Debate'. The debate essentially centres around whether or not the aggregate age-crime curve accurately reflects individual patterns of behaviour, and whether the decline in offending after mid to late adolescence reflects a reduction in the *prevalence* or the *frequency* of offending. Before discussing the nature of the debate, it is useful to review what these two terms mean.

Prevalence of offending

The prevalence of offending is a macro-level measure of the proportion of the population that is involved in offending behavior, or the participation rate, usually expressed as a proportionate unit of the population. Prevalence rates tend to be highest during the mid to late teenage years and lower at other ages (Farrington 1986). This general pattern tends to be repeated for both males and females; however, participation in offending is almost always greater amongst males than amongst females (Junger-Tas, Terlouw and Klein 1994; Moffitt *et al.* 2001; Rutter, Giller and Hagel 1998). Research has indicated that sex differences in prevalence rates appear greater in official data sources because males are likely to be involved in more frequent and serious offending, resulting in greater likelihood of contact with criminal justice agencies (Hindelang, Hirschi and Weis 1979). There is also some evidence that selection effects within official systems may be gender biased, however, which means that males who offend in their teenage years are more likely to be drawn into youth justice services than females, even when the extent of their involvement in serious offending is controlled for (McAra and McVie 2005).

Frequency of offending

Also referred to as *incidence*, the frequency of offending is used to describe the total number of offences committed amongst those individuals who are active offenders, usually defined in terms of a certain time period. There are considerable practical problems associated with collecting reliable information on frequency of offending (Blumstein *et al.* 1986). Self-report data are subject to response bias, errors in recall, under or over-reporting and imprecise measurement tools. On the other hand, official data are likely to represent a relatively small proportion of the total number of offences committed since most crime never comes to the attention of the police (Weis 1986). Research indicates that there is a narrower difference between the sexes in terms of frequency of offending compared to prevalence (Blumstein *et al.* 1986), although evidence suggests that this varies by crime type. The greatest sex differences in frequency of offending tend to be found for violent crimes, while there are far smaller differences for drug and alcohol related crimes (Junger-Tas *et al.* 1994; Moffitt *et al.* 2001).

Prevalence versus frequency

Hirschi and Gottfredson (1983, see also Gottfredson and Hirschi 1990) argued that the relationship between age and crime was invariant; in other words all people, everywhere, increased their offending sharply during adolescence and then committed less crime as they grew older. They did not propose that individual propensity to offend was the same in all individuals; rather they argued that the *relationship* between age and crime was the same for all individuals. Thus, the decline in the age-crime curve following mid to late adolescence was explained by a reduction in the frequency of offending amongst offenders, rather than a reduction in the prevalence of offenders within the population. This has been fiercely contested by Farrington (1986) and Blumstein *et al.* (1986, 1988a, 1988b) who argued that the frequency of offending amongst offenders remained relatively constant over time, and that the shape of the age-crime curve was a manifestation of a change in the prevalence of offending within the population at different ages. In other words, the characteristic peak was caused by an increase in the number of people within the population starting to offend in early to mid adolescence, followed by an increase in the number of people stopping offending in mid to late adolescence.

Hirschi and Gottfredson's theory that age itself is somehow a causal factor in criminal offending has been criticised on the basis that age is not a personal characteristic but rather a stage of development, in which case it is important to study processes of development and their associated social meanings (Rutter 1989). However, arguments that the age-crime curve reflects change in prevalence of offending rather than frequency are also disputed (Nagin and Land 1993). Even amongst the most serious and chronic offenders, research has shown that frequency does tend to decline with age (Ezell and Cohen 2005; Laub and Sampson 2003). Hence, it is now commonly acknowledged that 'it is important to recognize that the aggregate crime rate is the result of the combined effect of participation and frequency' (Blumstein 1994, p.402).

Important implications emerge from this debate in terms of sentencing policy. If the age-crime curve is due to a change in frequency of offending, then increasing the prison rate will not necessarily reduce crime as the rate of crime should drop inevitably. Whereas, if change in prevalence of offending explains the age-crime curve, then an increase in the prison rate should reduce crime as long as the system targets the correct offenders. Arguably, however, it is futile to try to explain the aggregate pattern of the age-crime curve because it is essentially an amalgam of underlying micro-crime curves for different offence types that vary widely in shape, and may represent quite different combinations of change in terms of prevalence and frequency (Brame and Piquero 2003; McVie 2006).

The 'criminal careers' approach

Criminologists who adhere to the criminal careers perspective take a developmental or life-course approach to the study of criminal offending, which implies that changes in behaviour are related to age in an orderly or sequential way (Patterson 1993). Hence, criminal careers are conceived of as sequences of delinquent or criminal acts committed by individuals over the course of their lifespan, from childhood through adolescence and into adulthood. Exploring within-individual changes over time involves studying the trajectory or pathway of a person's criminal activity from their first offence through to their last, based either on their officially recorded criminal histories or their own self-reported offending (Piquero, Farrington and Blumstein 2007). This approach recognises that pathways may vary between individuals and that such variations may be caused by a range of different influences, from birth to old age. The focus on trajectories implies a strong connection between childhood and adulthood, although developmental criminologists do accept that life events may alter trajectories. In other words, it is not inevitable that the antisocial child will become an antisocial adult.

The notion of a 'criminal career' is a useful conceptual mechanism for considering an individual's offending history as a longitudinal sequence of criminal acts characterised by a variety of structural dimensions (Piquero, Farrington and Blumstein 2007). Most traditional theories are insufficient to explain crime, according to this perspective, because they are too 'static' and don't take account of developmental considerations or fully explain the various dimensions of the criminal career, such as when it starts, when it stops and how long it lasts. Blumstein *et al.* (1986) argued that it was vital to study these different components of an individual's criminal career in order to build up a bigger picture of individual offending trajectories and to properly understand how various factors and government policies could be adapted to prevent or reduce offending behaviour. Below are noted some of the dimensions of criminal careers typically studied by developmental criminologists and a summary of the research evidence underlying each. There are also other dimensions that could be included, such as seriousness, escalation and de-escalation (see Blumstein *et al.* 1986).

Age of onset

The age at which an individual commits their first criminal offence is often described as their *age of onset* or *career initiation*. This varies for different types of crime, so that forms of anti-social behaviour (such as minor property damage and generally disruptive behaviour) tend to have an earlier age of onset than more serious forms of criminal offending (including hard drug use). This pattern can vary, however, depending on the source of the data used to study career initiation. Self-report data tend to show an earlier age of onset than official data, and indicate a progression in the offence onset sequence from minor to more serious offences, as described above; whereas official records tend to show a later age of onset and indicate that serious offences tend to occur first and more minor offences are recorded later. The difference between data sources in the age of onset is most probably due to the fact that offenders are actively involved in crime for several years prior to their first conviction (Blumstein *et al.* 1986). The ambiguity in the sequencing of minor and more serious offences is probably an artefact caused by the greater likelihood of detection and conviction for serious crimes compared to minor crimes in the early career stages. Piquero *et al.* (2007) also note that the reliability of both prospective and retrospective self-reports of age of onset can be poor.

Individuals who exhibit an earlier age of criminal career initiation (under the age of 14) tend to get involved in more serious forms of offending and to accumulate many more convictions than those who start offending later (age 14 or over) (Piquero *et al.* 2007). Offenders with an early age of onset also tend to garner convictions for a wider variety of offence types, although evidence shows that one of the main factors that characterises the most frequent offenders is early onset of offending in childhood (Blumstein *et al.* 1986). On average, males tend to be more likely than females to start offending at an earlier age (Moffitt *et al.* 2001). However, like the research evidence on frequency, the difference in age of onset appears to be greatest for offences such as violence and theft (for which males start earlier), but far less for drug or alcohol related crimes.

Career length

There is strong evidence that age of onset is directly related to the *career length* or *duration* of an individual's criminal career, as studies have shown that the earlier the age of onset, the greater the probability of recidivism and, consequently, the longer the span of the criminal career (Blumstein *et al.* 1986). The duration of criminal careers varies widely according to different studies, especially since research tends to focus on a range of different populations at different ages and stages of their careers. The research literature in this area is sparse, but a summary of the evidence by Piquero *et al.* (2007) indicates that career lengths tend to be relatively short, ranging between 5 and 12 years. Research which has focused on more serious offenders, or has tracked people over a longer period of time, not surprisingly reveals that career length is more extensive. A recent study of serious offenders on parole in the US found that criminal careers ranged from 4 to 30 years, with an average of 17 years, although those with the earliest career initiation did have the lengthiest criminal careers (Piquero, Brame and Lynam 2004). Another US study which tracked a group of delinquent males into their 70s found that the average criminal career was around 26 years, although lower for violent offences than for property crimes (Laub and Sampson 2003). Studying the nuances of criminal career length is obviously important from a policy perspective, since criminal justice policies that encourage lengthy sentences of imprisonment for those with long prior histories of offending may neglect to take account of the diminishing trajectory in an individual's offending behaviour and, hence, waste time and resources (Piquero *et al.* 2004).

Persistence

The tendency for individual offenders to continue offending over a defined period of time is known as persistence or *chronicity*. Alongside the existence of the age-crime curve, another well known 'fact' within criminology is that a small proportion of the population (particularly young people) tend to be responsible for a disproportionately large number of criminal offences and are, therefore, a particularly problematic group (Laub 2004). Data from the Cambridge Study in Delinquent Development supports this proposition. Piquero *et al.* (2007) found that, compared to other offenders, chronic offenders (those who had been convicted five times or more) had the longest criminal careers, the greatest number of convictions, the highest level of involvement in violent offending and the broadest range of offending repertoires. Once again, however, it is important to consider age in the equation. Moffitt (1993, 2004) developed a taxonomy of offending, and identified two groups of offenders: a large 'adolescence-limited' group and a much smaller 'life-course persistent' group. Moffitt argues that the life-course persistent group are the most problematic offenders as they display a pattern of anti-social behaviour which is continuous throughout their lives, although it manifests itself in different ways at different ages. Conversely, the adolescence-limited group get involved in offending only for a relatively short period during the teenage years. According to this taxonomy, the two groups are difficult to distinguish around the peak age of offending, as they may be involved in similar levels of serious or frequent offending; however, the adolescence-limited group do not display persistent anti-social behaviour over the life-course. This theory has significant implications for policy, as it suggests that a 'one size fits all' approach to dealing with offenders during the peak offending years of the age-crime curve is neither necessary nor appropriate.

The issue of 'persistent young offenders' has been particularly high on the policy agenda under New Labour, and has formed the basis for a large raft of new legislative measures in recent years (see Chapters 2 and 4 in this volume). However, official records on offending represent only a fraction of the offences committed by many individuals, therefore official measures of persistence are generally crude and unreliable (Weis 1986). Equally, comparative measures of persistence are hugely problematic because criminal justice systems vary between jurisdictions and definitions of persistence may also differ. The UK is a case in point. Between 2003 and 2006 the Scottish Executive defined persistent young offenders as children aged between 8 and 15 with five or more offence referrals to the Children's Reporter within a six-month period (Scottish Children's Reporters Administration 2007). During the same time period, the official Home Office definition of a persistent young offender within England and Wales was a young person aged between 10 and 17 who was sentenced by a criminal court on three or more occasions for one or more recordable offences (Perrett and Bari 2006). Clearly, it is problematic from a practical perspective to label people according to arbitrary definitions of persistence, as sentencing policies based on such definitions may lead to unequal treatment in the criminal justice system (see Hagell and Newburn 1994).

Degree of specialisation

An important aspect of criminal careers research is the study of crime-type sequences to determine whether an offender specialises in one particular type of offending, such as particular types of property crime or sexual offending, or whether they are more versatile offenders who have a wide repertoire of offending. Research suggests that while some offenders do specialise in one particular type of offending, the majority of offenders – particularly young offenders – engage in a range of different types of offending behaviour (Farrington 1999; Farrington, Snyder and Finnegan 1988). Recent analysis of the 1953 birth cohort from the Offenders Index, containing data on offenders up to age 40 who were convicted of a crime in England and Wales, identified particular 'clusters' of offenders based on their patterns of offending (Francis, Soothill and Fligelstone 2004). Nine clusters were observed for males including six versatile groups and three specialised groups (vehicle theft, wounding and shoplifting). This compared to only three groups in total for females, only one of which was specialised (shoplifting). Patterns of offending varied markedly between males and females, with a much more coherent age profile and greater diversity in offending for male offenders compared to females.

Research in this area indicates that it is important to take both a short and a long-term approach to the study of criminal careers in order to understand continuity and change (Ezell and Cohen 2005). Offenders do not necessarily stick to the same patterns of offending across their life-course and, in fact, many tend to display 'switching' from one pattern of offending to another over time (Soothill, Francis and Fligelstone 2002). A focus on short-term patterns of offending has shown that offenders often specialise in certain types of offences for a period of time but, in the longer term, they shift in their preferences to other crime types, thus presenting a broader picture of versatility over the course of the criminal career (McGloin, Sullivan and Piquero 2009). Such research is important to policy as it highlights the importance of teasing out and studying changing sequences of behaviour over time, rather than simply treating offence histories as an aggregate measure. There also appears to be secular change in patterns of specialisation, as Soothill *et al.* (2008) indicate that, for males, versatile clusters of offending have increased over time while specialist clusters have declined. For females there has also been an increase in versatility and an increase in violence specialisation, but a decrease for those who specialise in shoplifting.

Co-offending

The tendency for young people to commit crimes together has long been recognised, and yet relatively little research has been carried out on this element of offending compared to some of the other dimensions listed here (Warr 1993). Understanding more about the reasons why young people offend together is important in both theoretical and policy terms, since it allows us to understand intersections in the criminal careers of different individuals and explore the consequences of criminal justice interventions on individuals operating within the same networks (Reiss 1986). A recent study found that co-offending was related to three key facets of the individual offender: their age, their recidivism rate and their propensity to be involved in violence (McCord and Conway 2005). These authors found that around 40 per cent of offenders committed most of their crimes with others, although co-offending was highest amongst those aged 13 and under. At this early age, those who were involved in co-offending had higher frequencies of offending and were more likely to be involved in violent offending. The authors conclude that early targeting of those known to offend with others may be an effective preventative strategy, particularly for development of later more serious violence. Into later adolescence and adulthood, the evidence suggests that offenders become less likely to co-offend. According to Piquero *et al.* (2007) this is due to a changing preference amongst male offenders to offend alone, rather than because the pool of potential co-offenders diminishes. However, co-offending does not disappear entirely, since a relatively small proportion of the offending population are dedicated solo offenders. Most of the research in this area has focused on males, so it is not entirely clear whether there are distinct sex differences in terms of co-offending patterns, although one study indicated that both male and female offenders tended to co-offend with males (Sarnecki 2001).

Desistance

Perhaps the most important of all the dimensions of the criminal careers approach is that of desistance from offending. Developmental criminologists tend to conceptualise desistance as a process rather than a specific event, since one can only be certain at the point of death that the most recent offence is the final one (Farrington 1997). Despite the proposition that those with a greater disposition towards offending tend to continue offending at a continuous pace throughout their lives (Farrington 1986), trajectories of offending studied by developmental criminologists, even amongst the most serious offenders, do appear to show evidence of an eventual decline in offending (Ezell and Cohen 2005; Laub and Sampson 2003).

Explanations for desistance from offending have tended to centre on changes in maturity and social bonds with peers and adults. Central to Moffitt's (1993) theory is that involvement in criminal behaviour amongst adolescence-limited offenders forms part of a normal struggle for independence during which they engage in uncharacteristic behaviour by emulating delinquent peers. Desistance, therefore, is indicative of a growth in maturity and represents a departure from the influence of such peers. Other authors have also suggested that desistance from offending is strongly linked to a reduction in time spent with peers, less exposure to delinquent peers and weakened loyalty to peers in later adolescence (Graham and Bowling 1995; Warr 1993). Much of this research has focused on desistance during the teenage years; however, Sampson and Laub (1993, also Laub and Sampson 2003) have taken a longer term approach to the study of desistance. They argue that desistance from offending in adulthood is the result of personal transformation and engagement with conventional social roles. They take a dynamic approach to explaining desistance, and argue that it coincides with key turning points in people's lives which involve the strengthening of social bonds between offenders and their families (partners and children), work colleagues (particularly for those who enter the military) and the wider community. Their research strongly supports policy initiatives that promote transitions into employment and provide support to strengthen family relationships, whereas punitive responses to crime are seen as creating social and structural barriers to desistance.

Broadly, the desistance literature indicates that most young people will 'mature' out of crime, although both social structure and social context play some role in whether young people successfully make this transition or not. Analysis of data from the Edinburgh Study of Youth Transitions and Crime by Smith (2006) showed that young people's ability to reduce their involvement in offending was inhibited by living in neighbourhoods contexualised by deprivation, disorder, social instability and high crime rates. It is likely that such contextual difficulties have a similar influence on the formation of social bonds, and hence the ability to desist, in adulthood. There is also evidence that desistance is greater amongst young people who manage to avoid the stigmatisation of intervention by the formal agencies of social control. Using the same Edinburgh Study data, McAra and McVie (2007) found that young people were subject to labelling processes which resulted in certain categories of young people being repeatedly recycled by the youth justice system, whereas other serious offenders escape such tutelage. Quasi-experimental analysis showed that the deeper a young person penetrated the formal system, the less likely they were to desist from offending. These findings have poignant policy implications, as those with responsibility for dealing with the 'problem' of youth crime must balance the needs of the young people (including their natural inclination to desist versus the contextual and structural barriers that may prevent such desistance) against the needs of the wider public.

Implications for policy and practice

The development of the criminal careers approach to the study of criminal offending has been of immense importance to the discipline of criminology and has already had a profound impact on both policy and practice in the UK. Over the last ten years or so Government policies have been driven by an evidence-based approach which is underpinned to a significant extent by research on criminal careers. Such policies are strongly committed to the Risk Factor Prevention Paradigm and are based on those risk factors identified as being the main causes, correlates and predictors of childhood offending and anti-social behaviour. In fact, developmental prevention forms one of the core strategic approaches to preventing and reducing crime in the UK (see Farrington 2007).

While the criminal careers approach offers much in the way of theoretical enlightenment and practical suggestions for intervention, there is an inherent danger that pre-emptive initiatives may be targeted at particular individuals early in life simply on the basis of a condition, a character or a mode of life, rather than on the basis of an offence that such individuals may have committed. Much light has been shed on criminal offending by developmental criminologists over the last 30 or so years, but much also remains to be explained (see Piquero et al. 2007). Haines and Case (2008) warn against the Risk Factor Prevention approach on the basis that defining and measuring risk factors is problematic, interpreting risk factor evidence is very difficult, early intervention programmes are not easy to implement in practice and there is little consensus about 'what works' in risk-focused crime prevention in any case. In addition, the accuracy of early childhood prediction leaves much room for improvement. For example, White et al. (1990) looked at how accurately they could predict anti-social behaviour at ages 11 and 15 from risk factors identified at ages 3 and 5. They correctly predicted 81 per cent of those at age 11 as anti-social or not, but by age 15 only 66 per cent of the children were correctly classified as delinquent or not. A much wider review of prediction models concluded that: 'the prediction literature that we have reviewed leads inescapably to the conclusion noted above: predictive accuracy is rather low' (Gottfredson and Gottfredson 1986, p.274).

To conclude, the relationship between age and crime is complex and there are many factors underlying the characteristic age-crime curve. Criminal careers research presents a valuable opportunity to understand the dynamics of this relationship as it takes into consideration the many dimensions of individual offending, including both stability and change over the life-course. Such an approach has the potential to contribute widely to the planning and development of robust and effective youth crime prevention policies. However, the potentially stigmatising and criminalising effect of youth justice interventions, highlighted by authors such as McAra and McVie (2007), make it imperative that policymakers and practitioners remain wary of the false promise of prediction.

References

Blumstein, A. (1994) 'Next Steps in Criminal Career Research.' In E.G.M. Weitekamp and H.-J. Kerner (eds) *Cross-National Longitudinal Research on Human Development and Criminal Behaviour.* Dordrecht, The Netherlands: NATO ASI Series D: Behavioural and Social Sciences – Volume 76.

Blumstein, A., Cohen, J., Roth, J.A. and Visher, C.A. (1986) *Criminal Careers and 'Career Criminals': Volume 1.* Washington: National Academy Press.

Blumstein, A., Cohen, J. and Farrington, D.P. (1988a) 'Criminal career research: It's value for criminology.' *Criminology 26*, 1–36.

Blumstein, A., Cohen, J. and Farrington, D.P. (1988b) 'Longitudinal and criminal career research: Further clarifications.' *Criminology 26*, 57–74.

Brame, R. and Piquero, A.R. (2003) 'Selective attrition and the age-crime relationship.' *Journal of Quantitative Criminology 19*, 107–127.

Ezell, M.E. and Cohen, L.E. (2005) *Desisting from Crime: Continuity and Change in Long-term Crime Patterns of Serious Chronic Offenders.* Oxford: Oxford University Press.

Farrington, D.P. (1986) 'Age and Crime.' In M. Tonry and N. Morris (eds) *Crime and Justice: An Annual Review of Research*, Vol. 7, 189–250. Oxford: Clarendon Press.

Farrington, D.P. (1997) 'Human Development and Criminal Careers.' In M. Maguire, R. Morgan and R. Reiner (eds) *The Oxford Handbook of Criminology*, 2nd edn. Oxford: Oxford University Press.

Farrington, D.P. (1999) 'A criminological research agenda for the next millennium.' *International Journal of Offender Therapy and Comparative Criminology 43*, 154–167.

Farrington, D.P. (2003) 'Advancing Knowledge about the Early Prevention of Adult Antisocial Behaviour.' In D.P. Farrington and J.W. Coid (eds) *Early Prevention of Adult Antisocial Behaviour.* Cambridge: Cambridge University Press.

Farrington, D.P. (2007) 'Childhood Risk Factors and Risk-focused Prevention.' In M. Maguire, R. Morgan R. and Reiner (eds) *The Oxford Handbook of Criminology*, 4th edn. Oxford: Oxford University Press.

Farrington, D.P., Jolliffe, D., Hawkins, J.D., Catalano, R.F., Hill, K.G. and Kosterman, R. (2003) 'Comparing delinquency careers in court records and self reports.' *Criminology 41*, 933–958.

Farrington, D.P., Snyder, H.N. and Finnegan, T.A. (1988) 'Specialization in juvenile court careers.' *Criminology 26*, 461–487.

Francis, B., Soothill, K. and Fligelstone, R. (2004) 'Identifying patterns and pathways of offending behaviour: A new approach to typologies of crime.' *European Journal of Criminology 1*, 1, 47–87.

Gottfredson, S.D. and Gottfredson, D.M. (1986) 'Accuracy of Prediction Models.' In A. Blumstein, J. Cohen, J.A. Roth and C.A. Visher (eds) (1986) *Criminal Careers and 'Career Criminals': Volume 2*. Washington: National Academy Press.

Gottfredson, M.R. and Hirschi, T. (1990) *A General Theory of Crime*. Stanford, Calif.: Stanford University Press.

Graham, J. and Bowling, B. (1995) *Young People and Crime*. London: Home Office Research Study 145.

Hagell, A. and Newburn, T. (1994) *Persistent Young Offenders*. London: Policy Studies Institute.

Haines, K. and Case, S. (2008) 'The rhetoric and reality of the "Risk Factor Prevention Paradigm" approach to crime prevention.' *Youth Justice 8*, 5–20.

Hindelang, M.J., Hirschi, T. and Weis, J.G. (1979) 'Correlates of delinquency: The illusion of discrepancy between self-report and official measures.' *American Sociological Review 44*, 995–1014.

Hirschi, T. and Gottfredson, M. (1983) 'Age and the explanation of crime.' *American Journal of Sociology 89*, 552–584.

Junger-Tas, J., Terlouw, G-J. and Klein, M.W. (1994) *Delinquent Behaviour among Young People in the Western World: First Results of the International Self-report Delinquency Study*. Amsterdam: Kugler Publications.

Laub, J.H. (2004) 'The life-course of criminology in the United States: The American Society of Criminology 2003 Presidential Address.' *Criminology 42*, 1–26.

Laub, J.H. and Sampson, R.J. (2003) *Shared Beginnings: Divergent Lives: Delinquent Boys to Age 70*. Cambridge, Mass.: Harvard University Press.

Loeber, R. (1991) 'Antisocial behavior: More enduring than changeable?' *Journal of the American Academy of Child and Adolescent Psychiatry 30*, 3, 393–397.

McAra, L. and McVie, S. (2005) 'The Usual Suspects? Street-life, young offenders and the police.' *Criminology and Criminal Justice 5*, 1, 5–36.

McAra, L. and McVie, S. (2007) 'Youth justice? The impact of system contact on patterns of desistance from offending.' *European Journal of Criminology 4*, 3, 315–345.

McCord, J. and Conway, K.P. (2005) *Co-offending and Patterns of Juvenile Crime*. National Institute of Justice Research in Brief. Washington: US Department of Justice.

McGloin, J.M., Sullivan, C.J. and Piquero, A.R. (2009) 'Aggregating to versatility?:
    Transitions among offender types in the short term.' *British Journal of Criminology*
    49, 2, 243–264.
McVie, S. (2006) 'Patterns of deviance underlying the age-crime curve: The long term
    evidence.' *British Society of Criminology E-Journal 7*. Available at
    www.britsoccrim.org/volume7/007.pdf (accessed 11 March 2009).
Moffitt, T.E. (1993) '"Life-course persistent" and "adolescent-limited" anti-social
    behaviour: A developmental taxonomy.' *Psychological Review 100*, 674–701.
Moffitt, T.E. (2004) 'Adolescence-limited and Life-course Persistent Offending: A
    Complementary Pair of Developmental Theories.' In T.P. Thornberry (ed.)
    *Advances in Criminological Theory Volume 7: Developmental Theories of Crime and
    Delinquency*. New Brunswick, NJ, and London: Transaction.
Moffitt, T.E., Caspi, A., Rutter, M. and Silva, P.A. (2001) *Sex Differences in Antisocial
    Behaviour: Conduct Disorder, Delinquency and Violence in the Dunedin Longitudinal Study*.
    Cambridge: Cambridge University Press.
Muncie, J. and Goldson, B. (2006) 'England and Wales: The New Correctionalism.' In
    J. Muncie and B. Goldson (eds) *Comparative Youth Justice: Critical Issues*. London:
    Pine Forge Press.
Nagin, D.S. and Land, K.C. (1993) 'Age, criminal careers and population
    heterogeneity: specification and estimation of a non-parametric, mixed poisson
    model.' *Criminology 31*, 3, 327–362.
Patterson, G.R. (1993) 'Orderly change in a stable world: the antisocial trait as a
    chimera.' *Journal of Consulting and Clinical Psychology 61*, 329–335.
Perrett, J. and Bari, F. (2006) *Statistics on Persistent Young Offenders*. National Statistics:
    Department of Constitutional Affairs Statistical Bulletin 03/2006. London:
    Ministry of Justice Statistical Bulletin.
Piquero, A.R., Brame, R and Lynam, D. (2004) 'Studying criminal career length
    through early adulthood among serious offenders.' *Crime and Delinquency 50*, 412.
Piquero, A.R., Farrington, D.P. and Blumstein, A.(2007) *Key Issues in Criminal Career
    Research: New Analyses of the Cambridge Study in Delinquent Development*. Cambridge:
    Cambridge University Press.
Reiss, A.J. (1986) 'Co-offender Influences on Criminal Careers.' In A. Blumstein, J.
    Cohen, J.A. Roth and C.A. Visher (eds) (1986) *Criminal Careers and 'Career
    Criminals': Volume 2*. Washington: National Academy Press.
Rutter, M. (1989) 'Age as an ambiguous variable in developmental research: Some
    epidemiological considerations from developmental psychopathology.'
    International Journal of Behavioural Development 12, 1–24.
Rutter, M., Giller, H. and Hagell, A. (1998) *Antisocial Behaviour by Young People*.
    Cambridge: Cambridge University Press.
Sampson, R.J. and Laub, J.H. (1993) *Crime in the Making: Pathways and Turning Points
    through Life*. Cambridge, Mass.: Harvard University Press.
Sarnecki, J. (2001) *Delinquent Networks: Youth Co-offending in Stockholm*. Cambridge:
    Cambridge University Press.

Scottish Government (2008) *Criminal Proceedings in Scottish Courts 2006/07*. Edinburgh: Scottish Government.

Scottish Children's Reporters Administration (2007) *Persistent Young Offenders: A Study of Children Identified as Persistent Young Offenders in Scotland (2003–04, 2004–05 and 2005–06)*. Stirling: SCRA.

Smith, D.J. (2006) *Social Inclusion and Early Desistance from Crime*. Edinburgh: Edinburgh Study of Youth Transitions and Crime, Research Digest No. 12.

Soothill, K., Francis, B., Ackerley, E. and Humphries, L. (2008) 'Changing patterns of offending behaviour among young adults.' *British Journal of Criminology 48*, 75–95.

Soothill, K., Francis, B. and Fligelstone, R. (2002) *Patterns of Offending Behaviour: A New Approach*. London: Home Office Research Study 171.

Tittle, C.R. and Grasmick, H.G. (1997) 'Criminal behaviour and age.' *Journal of Criminal Law and Criminology 81*, 309–342.

Vold, G.B., Bernard, T.J. and Snipes, J.B. (1998) *Theoretical Criminology*. New York: Oxford University Press.

Warr, M. (1993) 'Age, peers and delinquency.' *Criminology 31*, 17–40.

Weis, J.G. (1986) 'Issues in the Measurement of Criminal Careers.' In A. Blumstein, J. Cohen, J.A. Roth and C.A. Visher (eds) (1986) *Criminal Careers and 'Career Criminals': Volume 2*. Washington: National Academy Press.

West, D.J. and Farrington, D.P. (1977) *The Delinquent Way of Life*. London: Heinemann.

White, J.L., Moffitt, T.E., Earls, F., Robins, L. and Silva, P.A (1990) 'How early can we tell? Predictors of childhood conduct disorder and adolescent delinquency.' *Criminology 28*, 507–533.

CHAPTER 4

Children and Young People: Criminalisation and Punishment

Rod Morgan

Introduction

This chapter aims to cover four issues relating to children and young people. First, the meaning of criminalisation and the extent to which interventions serving to criminalise are accompanied by punishment. Second, current trends regarding criminalisation and punishment. Third, what we know about the children and young people so dealt with. Fourth, the effectiveness of that which is done. With regard to all these questions my focus will be on England and Wales, there not being space to consider the considerable differences in the Scottish and Northern Irish systems.

Criminalisation and punishment

Until the post-war period the criminalisation of juveniles, as children and young people were then termed, was not an issue. Most offending, if detected, was dealt with informally even if it came to the attention of the police. But if children were of the age of criminal responsibility, which in England and Wales, as in Scotland, then meant eight years, they might be prosecuted, which involved being brought before the court, the juvenile court after the Children Act 1908. Here the procedure might be marginally less formal. But the juvenile court remained a criminal court not very different from an adult court. Moreover, though the available penalties were gradually differentiated from those for adults, they were not intrinsically very different: fines, supervision in the community, custody, albeit in designated institutions for juveniles.

Today the criminalisation and punishment of children is more complex. Euphemisms and contested rationales apply. Youth justice discourse abounds with references to 'interventions', the justification for which is variously said to be prevention, child protection, welfare, control, safeguarding, risk-reduction, rehabilitation and punishment. Most offences committed by children and young people almost certainly continue to be dealt with informally – in the family, the neighbourhood, the school or the workplace – but a growing number, if detected, are being drawn into the criminal justice system. Approximately one half of all criminalised children and young people are brought before the court, the first tier of which is now called the youth court. The remainder are subjected to out-of-court summary justice for criminal cases, or civil instead of criminal proceedings. This pattern represents a general approach first introduced for children and young persons, but for reasons somewhat different from those being given today.

Policing involves substantial discretion to ignore offending behaviour or deal with matters informally without invoking the law (for general discussion see Newburn 2005). The practice of issuing informal or formal warnings, 'cautions' as they came to be termed, was employed, though not always approved, from the beginning of modern policing (Steer 1970, pp.54–5). In the 1960s, however, use of formal police cautions for juveniles was encouraged by the Children and Young Persons Act 1969 on the grounds that it reduced the likelihood of re-offending. The child had been caught – the important issue for deterrence theorists (Von Hirsch *et al.* 1999) – and warned not to repeat the behaviour, but not stigmatised by having to appear in court. By the early 1990s, by which time use of cautions had become widely applied for minor offences for adults also, criticisms were being expressed about the practice of repeat cautioning of children and young persons. It was argued that the deterrent impact of the law was being eroded, that the factors associated with offending were typically not being addressed and re-offending was happening with impunity (Audit Commission 1996).

The Crime and Disorder Act 1998 s.65–66 introduced new cautioning arrangements for children and young persons, leaving those for adults in place. Henceforth 10–17-year-olds, the age of criminal responsibility having been raised to ten years in 1963 (in Scotland it remains eight years), might receive a 'reprimand' and then a 'final warning' if their offences were relatively minor. The doctrine of *doli incapax* – the rebuttable common law presumption that a child aged 10–13 does not know the difference between right and wrong and therefore cannot be convicted – was abolished, thereby emphasising the responsibility of children (whose parents might also be responsibilised with parenting orders). A final warning, moreover, was to be final: thereafter children and young people have to be brought before the court no matter how minor the subsequent offence, unless there is a substantial lapse of time.

Since 1998 a sea change has overtaken the meaning of summary justice. Whereas the term used to describe the business of lower, magistrates' courts (in Scotland the Sheriff Court) with the debate focused on which cases should go to the higher courts (Royal Commission on Criminal Justice 1993), the centre of gravity has shifted. The discussion today is about out-of-court summary justice, that is, which cases need to come before the court at all (Morgan 2008).

New Labour made it a key objective to develop 'simple, speedy, summary justice' whereby offenders who admit their offences are dealt with by the police and Crown Prosecution Service (CPS), most commonly by a fine, without need for court appearances. New Labour boasts that their criminal justice achievements involve circumventing the traditional, Dickensian, overly complex, slow and expensive criminal justice procedures (see Blair 2005, 2006; Falconer 2006; Home Office 2006a). The Government argues it is emulating what is done in other jurisdictions, which include Scotland, where the out-of-court powers of the Procurator Fiscal are widely used (see McDonald 2005; McInnes Report 2004). The magistrates' courts are said to be better able now to get on with the more serious business requiring their attention.

Thus, in addition to *cautions*, we now have: *fixed penalty notices* (FPNs), introduced in the 1980s for minor traffic offences, and since extended to relatively serious traffic offences; *penalty notices for disorder* (PNDs) which, contrary to the title, have been extended to offences such as retail theft which generally do not involve disorder; *cannabis warnings*, for possession of small quantities of the drug, and *conditional cautions*, whereby the offender, on the decision of the CPS, agrees to a caution given on condition that he or she undertakes to do something, usually make reparation to the victim or participate in some programme designed to reduce the risk of re-offending. Consultation is ongoing about the general introduction of further out-of-court sanctions, namely *deferred PNDs* and *youth restorative disposals* (YRs) (Home Office 2006b).

Both the latter proposals are made with children and young people in mind. They illustrate the fact that out-of-court summary justice developments have greatly muddied the ostensible clarity of the 1998 youth justice reforms. In addition to *reprimands* and *final warnings*, FPNs and PNDs can be issued to 16 and 17-year-olds, PNDs are being piloted for 10–15-year-olds and a *youth conditional caution* was introduced in April 2009. *Deferred PNDs* are being piloted for 10–15-year-olds and *YRs* for 10–17-year-olds. Finally, and most controversially, has been the introduction of the civil anti-social behaviour order (ASBO), originally designed for noisy 'neighbours from hell' (Labour Party 1996) but 45 per cent of which have been imposed on children and young people (Morgan 2006). Breach of an ASBO, which can be sought by local government officials as well as the police, is a criminal offence the maximum punishment for which is custody.

The point is this. New Labour's 1998 reforms were grounded on the proposition that young offenders would henceforth be dealt with by multi-disciplinary, local authority youth offending teams (YOTs). There was to be joined-up decision making and intervention to reduce offending. Whenever a young person came to the attention of the police and the CPS with a view to criminalisation, the matter would be referred to the YOT, a risk assessment made and an appropriate disposal determined or recommended to the court. It was perhaps inevitable that inefficiency would result in YOTs not always being consulted by the police and the CPS before some *reprimands* or *final warnings* were issued. But the widespread application to children and young people of FPNs and PNDs, the alleged merit and essence of which is their being if not on-the-spot decisions then certainly simple, speedy and summary, is inimical to the process of referral, consultation, assessment and deliberation. ASBOs, moreover, were in the early days most frequently sought by new, local authority, anti-social behaviour units which, it became apparent, had little confidence in YOTs and frequently failed to inform, let alone consult, them. It took behind-the-scenes arm wrestling between the Home Office and the Youth Justice Board (YJB, which oversees the youth justice system in England and Wales) before there was published guidance emphasising that application for an ASBO should be the last rather than a first resort (measures such as visits to parents, use of warning letters, the issuing of acceptable behaviour contracts (ABCs), etc., should first be considered) and the YOT should be an active party to the decision to seek an ASBO (Youth Justice Board/ACPO/Home Office 2005).

The proportionality of youth justice has thus been made questionable. A youth may be brought before the youth court for a very minor offence – in circumstances where an adult aged 18 or over might receive a repeat caution or cannabis warning – merely because s/he has previously received a *final warning*. By contrast, another youth might first come before the court already subject to an ASBO (which can be imposed by non-youth court magistrates in civil proceedings) and having had one or more FPNs or PNDs.

The risk of inappropriate decision making has further been heightened by the application of managerialist principles to criminal justice generally. Labour's 1997 Election Manifesto bewailed the 'justice gap', the disparity between the number of offences committed and recorded by the police and those for which offenders are brought to book (Labour Party 1997). Closing it became the policy priority. A numerical target for increasing the number of 'offences brought to justice' (OBTJ) by being cautioned, convicted or otherwise sanctioned was set. OBTJs were counted without regard to the seriousness of the offence or the age of the offender. The target was easily exceeded and this achievement, if achievement it be, relied not on an increase in the number of serious offences convicted and sentenced in court but substantial growth in the use of the expanding range of out-of-court sanctions (Morgan 2008). Children and young people figured prominently among the criminalised.

For a child or young person to receive a reprimand or final warning, both of which count as OBTJs, there must be sufficient evidence to prosecute and an admission of guilt. The consent required of an adult to receive a caution does not apply. In the case of PNDs, most frequently used for 'notifi-able' offences which count as OBTJs, a youth will have had his fingerprints, photograph and a DNA sample taken. The young person now has a criminal record which can be cited in any subsequent criminal proceedings and may prejudice future educational or employment prospects.

Concerns have always existed about the use of police cautions: young people may be tempted to admit offences for which they would not be likely to be convicted in order to avoid a delayed and potentially more serious and damaging outcome (Steer 1970). There is good evidence that the law regarding their use is not always complied with (see Sanders and Young 2006). But the considerable expansion of police powers, both in terms of who they may stop or search and now who, together with the CPS, they can formally sanction out-of-court, has excited the concerns of the judiciary and civil libertarians as well as youth justice commentators (see Morgan 2008; Young 2008). The concerns are various: the relative invisibility and unaccountability of out-of-court decision making; the risk that vulnerable subjects, of which children and young people are clear candidates, will agree to apparently more lenient outcomes; and net widening, the prospect that informal social controls and cases resulting in 'no further action' are being displaced by criminalising interventions.

These issues lie at the heart of the youth justice debate. The critics' 'net widening' is the Government's 'closing the justice gap'. Out-of-court summary justice may serve to 'nip unacceptable behaviour in the bud' (Home Office 2006b, p.3) or despoilingly drag an expanding cohort of young people into the criminal justice system with the increased risk, citing the most recent longitudinal evidence (McAra and McVie 2005, 2007), that they will not so readily 'grow out of crime' (Rutherford 1986).

Finally, we should briefly review the sentencing options available to the youth court. (For summaries of the origins and development of current sentencing options in England and Wales, and how they differ from those available in Scotland and Northern Ireland, see Bottoms and Dignan 2004; Morgan and Newburn 2007; Smith 2003.)

Though the new, restricted cautioning system introduced by the Crime and Disorder Act 1998 stipulates 'two strikes and you're out', other measures were taken designed to prevent up-tariff responses to youth crime. Upstream were various initiatives to promote early prevention in the community with youngsters held to be at risk of offending (see Morgan and Newburn 2007). Downstream is the referral order, introduced by the Youth Justice and Criminal Evidence Act 1999. The order may be for 3 to 12 months depending on the seriousness of the case, is mandatory for 10–17-year-olds pleading guilty to an imprisonable offence and convicted for the first time, unless the crime is serious enough to warrant custody or the court orders an absolute discharge. It involves referring the young offender to a youth offender panel. The panel provides a forum away from the formality of the court, a concept originating with the Scottish Children's Hearings system, the experience of family group conferencing, the experience of victim–offender mediation and restorative cautioning. The order *is* the sentence (though it can be combined with certain ancillary orders, including those for costs) and, as such, substitutes for action plan, reparation and supervision orders.

Panels comprise one YOT member and at least two community volunteers, one of whom leads the panel. Parents of offenders under 16 are expected to attend panel meetings. The offender can also nominate an adult to support them, but legal representatives do not participate. To encourage the restorative nature of the process a variety of other people, particularly victims, may be encouraged voluntarily to attend given panel meetings. The aim of the initial meeting is to devise a 'contract' and, where the victim chooses to attend, for them to meet and talk about the offence with the offender. The contract should always include reparation to the victim or wider community and a programme of activity designed primarily to prevent further offending.

The action plan order was designed to be the first option for young offenders whose offending is serious enough to warrant a community sentence. *No More Excuses* described the order as, 'a short, intensive programme of community intervention combining punishment, rehabilitation and reparation to change offending behaviour and prevent further crime' (Home Office 1997).

Reparation orders require reparation to either a specified person or persons or 'to the community at large'. The Government made a concerted effort to make both victims' views and reparation more central aspects of youth justice than previously had been the case. However, Dignan (1999, p.8) was undoubtedly correct when he argued that these 'reforms hardly amount to a "restorative justice revolution", let alone the "paradigm shift" that some restorative justice advocates have called for'.

In addition to discharges, fines and supervision orders New Labour introduced, from April 2000 onwards, a new, generic custodial sentence, the Detention and Training Order (DTO). The orders are from 6 to 24 months, half the sentence being served in custody and half in the community. DTOs, available to the youth court, sit alongside continued provisions whereby grave offences – in the case of murder, mandatorily – are committed to the Crown Court and liable to 'long-term detention' (to distinguish the sentence from a DTO) for which the maximum period is the same as if the child or young person were an adult. These long-term detention cases are known as section 90 or 91 cases (Powers of the Criminal Courts (Sentencing) Act 2000). Following the Criminal Justice Act 2003 (s.226 and 228) they were supplemented by the Indeterminate Sentence for Public Protection (IPP), in effect a life sentence but, unlike the traditional life sentence, available for a huge, heterogeneous list of offences for which the tariff, as just desert, can be as little as two years.

The DTO represented an increase in the powers of the youth court to impose custodial sentences. Whereas the maximum period of detention in a YOI for 15–17-year-olds had been six months for a single offence, the DTO has a maximum of two years. Further, though the pre-existing secure training order for 12–14-year-olds already provided for a two-year maximum, New Labour replaced the strict criteria for offenders under 15 relating to 'persistence' with the provision that the sentence be available where the court 'is of the opinion that he is a persistent offender'. The courts, including the Court of Appeal, have interpreted this power rather broadly (see Ball, McCormack and Stone 2001).

The counterpoint to these potentially expansive custodial provisions has been the YJB's investment of considerable resources in Intensive Supervision and Surveillance Programmes (ISSP) as the principal alternative to custodial remands and sentences in cases where that outcome is likely. ISSP can be used as a condition of bail or as an adjunct to a community or custodial sentence for serious or persistent young offenders who have previously been charged, warned or convicted on four or more separate occasions in the preceding 12 months and have previously received at least one community or custodial sentence. An ISSP runs for a maximum of six months with intensive supervision (including electronic tagging or tracking) and engagement (education or vocational training, offending behaviour programmes, recreational activities, etc.) for 25 hours a week for the first three months. ISSP was launched in July 2001 and extended to all areas in October 2003.

Finally, the sentencing of children and young people is to undergo significant change in 2009 following passage of the Criminal Justice and Immigration Act 2008. This brings the sentencing of youths into broad line with that for adults (following the Criminal Justice Act 2003) as far as sentencing purposes are concerned and introduces a single, generic, community sentence to which various requirements can be attached, along the lines of the Community Order for adults.

The principal statutory aim of the youth justice system is 'to prevent offending and reoffending'. The fact that children and young people are involved is reflected in the requirement that the courts have regard to 'the welfare of the offender' but the purposes of sentencing are, as with adults: punishment, reform and rehabilitation, protection of the public and reparation to persons affected by offences.

All second tier community sentences will be replaced by the generic Youth Rehabilitation Order (YRO) which will be used for the majority of youth offenders. A portfolio of no fewer than 18 requirements can be attached to a YRO. They include engaging in or refraining from an activity, curfews and exclusions, residence, drug testing and participation in drug treatment or other programmes, undertaking unpaid work, electronic tagging, intensive fostering and intensive supervision and surveillance – providing a statutory foundation for ISSP.

Other important changes include extending the circumstances in which a Referral Order may be made (where the offender has had one previous conviction but did not then receive a referral order or when the offender has previously been bound over to keep the peace or previously received a conditional discharge or, in exceptional circumstances, on the recommenda- tion of the YOT). Further, the court will have discretion to discharge Referral Orders early for good behaviour or extend them for up to three months on the recommendation of the YOP when dealing with breaches.

Finally, the Youth Conditional Caution (YPC) will be introduced as a higher-tariff pre-court disposal with the aim of reducing court appearances for low-level offences, though it will not be available for a youth who has already been convicted. The conditions, which may include a fine and/or an attendance requirement (which might include completion of a specified activity, but cannot exceed 20 hours), must be approved by the CPS.

Trends in criminalisation and punishment

As far as the long established balance between cautions (reprimands and final warnings) and prosecutions is concerned, Figure 4.1 shows that the proportionate decline in the use of cautions prompted by the Crime and Disorder Act 1998 has now gone into reverse. In 2006 42 per cent of all children and young people were prosecuted, whereas in 2002 and 2003 the majority were. This is still a long way short of the position a decade or more ago when only one third of all youth offenders were prosecuted. However, whereas criminalisation without prosecution then generally signified non-intervention, this is no longer the case. Now it more often signifies punishment without prosecution. As our discussion of the developing realm of out-of-court summary justice revealed, Figure 4.1 now provides an incomplete picture of what is happening. In 2006, in addition to cautions, 19,598 PNDs were imposed on 16 or 17-year-olds (Ministry of Justice 2007). The rate of growth in the use of PNDs for youths is striking.

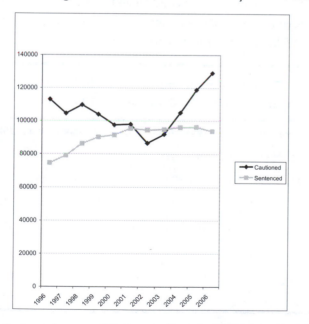

Figure 4.1: Cautions and sentences of 10–17-year-olds, England and Wales, 1996–2006
Source: Ministry of Justice (2007b): Tables 3.3 and 3.8

In 2004 they represented 6 per cent of all PNDs issued; in 2005 and 2006 the proportions were 8 and 10 per cent respectively. If PNDs, cautions and prosecutions are aggregated then only 39 per cent of all youths criminalised are prosecuted, a trend which might be seen as a return to the diversionary practice encouraged by the Children and Young Persons Act 1969. That would be the case were criminalisation being resorted to parsimoniously. However, the available evidence suggests the opposite. All the analyses so far undertaken to examine the implications of the growth in out-of-court summary justice (Amadi 2008; Bateman 2008; Morgan 2008; Solomon *et al.* 2007; Young 2008) conclude that it has had substantial net-widening conse-quences with many more young people, and even more so children, being criminalised.

Whereas, since 2003, successive sweeps of the British Crime Survey (BCS) and the Offending Crime and Justice Survey show reductions in volume crime and stability in self-reported delinquency, the number of children and young people criminalised in the period 2003–6 rose by 31 per cent. The International Convention on the Rights of the Child, Article 37, of which the United Kingdom is a signatory, states that the 'arrest' as well as the 'detention and imprisonment' of a child 'shall be used only as a last resort': the recent growth in the criminalisation of children and young people in England and Wales does not square with that obligation.

Table 4.1 Proportionate use of different sentences (%), England and Wales, 1996–2006

Sentence	1996	1997	1998	1999	2000	2001	2002	2003	2004	2005	2006
Discharge	32	32	31	30	25	18	15	15	13	13	10
Fine	23	23	24	23	23	23	16	15	15	15	12
Referral orders	–	–	–	–	1	2	20	27	27	31	32
Community orders excl. ROs	34	34	34	34	39	43	37	32	32	32	33
Custody	9	9	8	8	8	8	8	7	7	6	6
Others	2	2	2	2	4	4	6	4	5	3	6

Source: Ministry of Justice 2007b

Table 4.1 shows how the proportionate use of different sentences has changed during the period 1996–2006. It is apparent that the major New Labour sentencing innovation has been the referral order. It has substantially displaced discharges and fines and there has been a modest reduction in the proportionate use of custody. What is not represented in these figures is the increased number of conditions attached to community sentences, of which the extreme case is ISSP.

What of the number of children and young people in custody? Table 4.2 provides an overview of the numbers by type of institution. There are 15 Secure Children's Homes (SCHs), all but one of which are run by the local authorities and which cater mostly for children under 15; four secure training centres (STCs), all run by commercial security companies and catering mostly for medium aged adolescents, and 13 YOIs, two of which are run by commercial companies and the remainder by the Prison Service, accommodating 15–17-year-olds.

Table 4.2 Children and young persons in penal custody, England and Wales, 1995–2007

Type of custody	1995	1997	1999	2001	2003	2005	2007
Secure Children's Homes	80	95	90	258	292	238	226
Secure Training Centres	–	–	55	118	185	248	257
Young Offender Institutions	1675	2479	2422	2415	2267	2339	2431
Total in custody	1755	2574	2567	2791	2744	2825	2914

Source: Youth Justice Board 2008a, p.38

If the proportionate use of custody has fallen, why has the total number of children and young persons in custody risen so dramatically during the last ten years? Three factors explain the record high population. First, the proportionate use of custody may have fallen but the number of youths drawn into the criminal justice system and, even more importantly, sentenced by the courts has not: on the contrary. Second, there has been a modest increase in the length of determinate sentences passed (Ministry of Justice 2007b, Table

2.4). Third, there is a growing number of indeterminate sentence length young prisoners, including IPPs, who are not included in the average sentence length statistics. In 2006/7 the YJB reported that there were no fewer than 510 children and young people in custody subject to either s.90/91 or s.226/228, and a growing proportion of these were serving indeterminate sentences. Further, the young prisoner estate normally accommodates 300–400 young people aged 18 or over because the YJB, which is responsible for commissioning custodial facilities and allocating young offenders to them, has humanely adopted the policy of not transferring DTO prisoners to adult facilities if they attain the age of 18 during the later stages of their sentence. The result is an occupancy rate of 95 per cent (Youth Justice Board 2008, p.39) or more. This system crowding is seriously undermining what the system is able to achieve.

The characteristics of young offenders

There is an abundant epidemiological and wider literature on the characteristics of children and young people who offend or, more commonly, are criminalised. Further, the youth justice literature is replete with discussions of the methodological confusion surrounding use of the terms 'risk' and 'protective' factors, 'predictors' and 'causes' of youth anti-social and criminal behaviour. Policy statements are full of simplistic statements regarding the apparent ease with which early preventive effort might effectively be targeted at readily identifiable, young, at-risk children, or interventions focused on relatively small numbers of persistent or prolific offenders responsible for the majority of youth crime. Identifiable associations or indicators are not necessarily causes and causes are not necessarily universal. Whatever definition of persistence is adopted it results in the identification of groups whose membership is far from stable. And it is one thing to identify the early characteristics of adults whose career has been characterised by repeated crime and convictions, it is another matter entirely to focus efforts on every child with those same characteristics.

The YJB has adopted a 'risk' and 'protective' factors approach (YJB 2005) with a view to promoting programmes to be used by YOTs which will mitigate the former and enhance the latter. This is based on the advice of Farrington and others and is derived from their research (Farrington 2007). A risk assessment tool, ASSET, is used for all children and young people who come within the ambit of YOTs. By this means, the profile of the YOT caseload, which includes six to seven boys for every girl (though the number of girls is increasing at a much higher rate than that for boys) has been described in the following terms:

- Living arrangements – only 30 per cent living with both parents.

- Education – 25 per cent with special needs; 60 per cent with a special educational needs statement; 15 per cent currently excluded from school and 32 per cent having had fixed term exclusions during the past year; 41 per cent regularly truanting and 42 per cent underachieving at school.

- Peer affiliations – 40 per cent assessed as having pro-criminal peers, nearly 20 per cent as having a lack of age-appropriate friends and 25 per cent as having friends who were offenders.

- Drug use – 75 per cent regularly using tobacco and alcohol, over half recorded as having used cannabis and 13 per cent known to have used a Class A drug such as heroin and cocaine.

- General thinking and behaviour – three-quarters considered impulsive and acting without thinking; 44 per cent assessed as easily bored/needing excitement, with a similar proportion assessed as giving in easily to pressure from others.

- Vulnerability – 20 per cent considered vulnerable to the behaviour of others, specific events or circumstances; 25 per cent considered vulnerable because of their own behaviour with 9 per cent judged at risk of self-harm or suicide (15 per cent in the case of girls) (Baker *et al.* 2005).

This is not to say that significant proportions of the caseload are not characterised by positive factors also. Nevertheless, whatever view one takes of the risk and protective factor approach, whether the identified factors are causal or merely associated with either offending behaviour and/or being criminalised, it is clear from the epidemiological surveys that the YOT caseload comprises children and young people who typically are multiply disadvantaged in terms of: the neighbourhoods and income group from which they are drawn; their families and peer group associates tend to have histories of criminality; they are generally educational under-achievers; they are often engaged in precocious sexual activity and use of drugs and alcohol and significant numbers have poor physical or mental health.

These features are found in often acute form among the population in custody. Of the almost 3000 children and young people in custody in 2007, 93 per cent boys and 7 per cent girls, only 1.4 per cent were under 14 years, 20 per cent were aged 14 or 15, 28 per cent were aged 16 and exactly half were aged 17. Among this population histories of self-harm are relatively common. Almost one third have identifiable mental health problems and over half have significant or borderline learning difficulties (Harrington and Bailey 2005). It is difficult to say to what extent the latter reflects intrinsic learning difficulties or an absence of intellectual stimulation. Two-thirds of DTO detainees have been excluded from education, 4 in 10 have at some stage been in the care of a local authority and 17 per cent on a child protection register (Hazell *et al.* 2002; HMIP 2005). The result is that children in custody typically have literacy and numeracy ages some four to five years below their chronological ages. These problems are often compounded by substance abuse, with around one third reporting that they have taken drugs not to get high but just to 'feel normal', or to 'forget everything' or 'blot everything out' (Galahad SMS Ltd 2004), i.e. as a form of self-medication.

It is implausible that some of these chronic needs and deficits, the result of overlapping and mutually reinforcing patterns of social deprivation and exclusion (Social Exclusion Unit 2002), could be remedied within a youth justice system whose primary functions include punishment, reparation and public protection. But this is the backcloth to the programmes that the YOTs provide locally and the YJB seeks to encourage and, to a limited extent, fund centrally.

What works?

This apparently simple question is fiendishly complex and capable of being answered in many ways, most of them outside the scope of this chapter. Is the incidence of youth crime or re-offending rates falling? What do the evaluation data have to say about the effectiveness of particular programmes? Do the public have confidence in the youth justice system? And if the public do have confidence, or if crime or re-offending rates are falling, to what extent can those outcomes be attributed to anything the youth justice system is doing?

A key problem is that the threshold for entry to the youth justice system appears to be shifting. In the Government's periodic spending reviews, the YJB may succeed in persuading the Treasury that cost beneficial outcomes, in terms of reducing numbers of first-time entrants to the system, or reduced re-offending rates, will probably result from greater investment in community-based early prevention programmes or more intensive work with young people subject to community-based court orders. But those outcome calculations will be set at nought if the criminalisation threshold is significantly lowered and, all other things being equal, YOT caseloads are swamped.

We will concentrate on the big questions and numbers, some of which also constitute targets set by the youth justice system itself. We will rely principally on surveys of self-reported youth crime and the BCS, on the annual reports of the YJB and on two major independent assessments of the youth justice system, those carried out by the Audit Commission in 2004 and the Centre for Crime and Justice Studies, King's College, London, in 2008.

The incidence of youth crime

Though difficult to assess because of the shortcomings of the measures, it is generally agreed, on the basis of self-report and victim surveys, that the overall level has remained fairly constant since the mid 1990s, albeit there may have been some increase in certain categories of violent crime for which an increased number of young people have also been convicted (Audit Commission 2004; Roe and Ashe 2008; Solomon and Garside 2008). There have been reductions in the number of young people convicted for vehicle crime and burglary, but these falls mirror the reductions in the number of the same crimes recorded by the police and reflect a longstanding trend, the onset of which preceded the youth justice reforms (Nicholas, Kershaw and Walker 2007). There is no persuasive evidence that the overall incidence of youth crime has been materially influenced by the youth justice reforms.

First-time entrants to the youth justice system

In 2005 the YJB set a target to reduce the number of first-time entrants to the youth justice system by 5 per cent by 2008. The latest data published by the Board suggest that this target has been greatly exceeded and a 10 per cent reduction achieved (Youth Justice Board 2008b) However the Board's definition of first-time entrants inexplicably excludes PNDs of which there are now more than 19,000 issued to young persons per annum of whom, it seems likely, a high proportion are first-time entrants. Were PNDs to be included it seems probable that most if not all of the 10 per cent reduction would be wiped out.

Public confidence in the youth justice system

The YJB, somewhat surprisingly given the importance the Government attaches to public confidence in policing and the criminal justice system generally, does not have a target related to public confidence in the youth justice system. The issue was explored in 2004 by the Audit Commission, however, and has received some attention in recent sweeps of the BCS. The Audit Commission reported that public confidence in and knowledge about the youth justice system had fallen since 1996 (Audit Commission 2004). Further, the most recent sweep of the BCS has found that public confidence in the way the system deals with young offenders is no higher today than when the BCS first investigated the matter five years earlier and found it to be very low (Nicholas *et al.* 2007). This may reflect a high level of public ignorance about a system that is relatively complex, which has in recent years undergone substantial change and with which most members of the public are unlikely to have had contact. Nevertheless, public confidence is low and has not improved.

Youth re-offending and reconvictions

There is a good deal of official spin regarding the manner in which this issue is now treated. The Ministry of Justice and the YJB repeatedly refer to evidence of youth re-offending when they are in fact referring to youth offender reconvictions, a very different matter. Despite being chided over their misuse of language (see Solomon and Garside 2008, pp.49–52) they continue mystifying the issue and the statistics. Ministry of Justice reconviction estimates do not include the increasingly numerous PNDs despite the fact that their greater use is justified on the grounds that they displace court business. Their omission therefore calls into question the reported absolute reduction in reconvictions and, just as importantly, their frequency and seriousness, for juveniles aged 10–17 included in the 2000 and 2006 cohorts (Ministry of Justice 2008). When changes in offender characteristics are controlled for, the resulting fall in the 're-offending' rate, actually the reconviction rate, is reported to be 0.3 per cent. Whether this 'success', together with the decline in frequency and seriousness, would survive inclusion of those reconvictions that have been omitted is not known.

Use of custody and children and young people in custody

The YJB has from its inception aimed to so influence supervision of offenders in the community by YOTs and sentencing that the number of children and young people in custody is reduced. The Board has chosen to express this aim in targets relating to the average number of children in custody. The Board's most recent target was to reduce the custodial population by 10 per cent between March 2005 and 2008 (Youth Justice Board 2007b). In this the Board has clearly failed as Table 4.2 demonstrates. However, it might be argued that in so far as the proportionate use of custodial sentences by the courts has marginally fallen (see Table 4.1) the Board has succeeded, a viewpoint to which Solomon and Garside (2008) give no acknowledgement. The problem is that it can reasonably be argued that the fall in the proportionate use of custody is no great achievement given the rising tide of children and young people being criminalised, many of them for relatively minor offences. England and Wales has both the highest number and proportion of children and young people in penal custody of any country in Western Europe and the reformed youth justice system has singularly failed to reverse that position.

Conclusion

In the wake of the King's College Centre for Crime and Justice Studies audit of *Ten Years of Labour's Youth Justice Reforms* (Solomon and Garside 2008) the Chair of the YJB wrote to the authors expressing her concern about their analysis, protesting that it was 'methodologically flawed', lacked 'analytical rigour' and reached 'unjustified conclusions', charges to which the authors replied, equally vigorously. The YJB Chair argued that the reformed system has many merits to which the Audit Commission drew attention in 2004 and of which the CCJS analysis made no mention. This is true. The reformed system, it is generally acknowledged (see Morgan and Newburn 2007), has many characteristics which arguably have considerable merit. The system is devolved, thereby ensuring that local arrangements are devised to suit local circumstances. The YJB exercises only light touch guidance from the centre. The YOTs are multi-disciplinary teams whose members were originally drawn from all the key child-related services – social services, probation, the police, education and health. There are as many community volunteers engaged in the delivery of services as there are full-time professionals and many programmes are contracted out to voluntary sector organisations. Further, several programmes which the YJB has pioneered have been independently evaluated and show much promise (for a review see Morgan and Newburn 2007).

In their defence the CCJS authors protested that they could scarcely be criticised for not doing something they never set out to do. They had taken the YJB's targets seriously, at face value. They had focused on the key measures, the bottom line. They might equally have said in their defence that they did not mention aspects of the reformed youth justice system of which the Audit Commission had been highly critical in 2004: the fact that the level of supervision engagement with young offenders was, at roughly an hour a week, in 2004 no greater than was delivered in 1996, or the substantial over-representation of minority ethnic young people in the system, a major concern which the evidence suggests reflects institutional racism (see Feilzer and Hood 2004).

In this chapter also I have focused on the bottom line, which is that in England and Wales we are criminalising many more children and young people; if they come before the courts we are subjecting them to more and more requirements which, if breached, are leading to greater sanctions, including custody; the average number of children and young people in custody is rising rather than falling; and there is no evidence that any of this reliance on criminal justice solutions is having an impact on the incidence of youth crime.

None of this will surprise students of the subject. The life chances of young offenders are not generally enhanced by their being criminalised and the solutions to youth crime have little to do with decisions made in the youth court. They have more to do with the agenda nobly set out in *Every Child Matters* (HM Treasury 2003) and the Children Act 2004. Here, five outcomes for children are identified: 'being healthy'; 'staying safe'; 'enjoying and achieving'; 'making a positive contribution' and 'achieving economic well-being'. These outcomes are largely determined by mainstream child-related services, not youth justice. Regrettably, the hard evidence is that when the individual and social characteristics of criminalised and punished young offenders are closely examined and we track what happens to them within the youth justice system, it appears that these children do not greatly matter despite the best intentions and efforts of most of those who work within the system.

References

Amadi, J. (2008) *Piloting Penalty Notices for Disorder on 10– to 15-year-olds: Results from a One Year Pilot.* London: Ministry of Justice.

Audit Commission (1996) *Misspent Youth: Young People and Crime.* London: Audit Commission.

Audit Commission (2004) *Youth Justice 2004: A Review of the Reformed Youth Justice System.* London: Audit Commission.

Baker, K., Jones, S., Roberts, C. and Merrington, S. (2005) *The Evaluation of the Validity and Reliability of the Youth Justice Board's Assessment for Young Offenders: Findings from the First Two Years of Use of ASSET.* London: Youth Justice Board.

Ball, C., McCormack, K. and Stone, N. (2001) *Young Offenders: Law, Policy and Practice,* 2nd edn. London: Sweet and Maxwell.

Bateman, T. (2008) '"Target practice": sanction detection and the criminalization of children.' *Criminal Justice Matters 73,* 2–5.

Blair, T. (2005) 'Speech to launch a Respect and Parenting Order Task Force.' 2 September, Hertfordshire.

Blair, T. (2006) 'Our nation's future: Criminal justice', Speech delivered at University of Bristol, 23 June.

Bottoms, A.E. and Dignan, J. (2004) 'Youth Justice in Great Britain.' In M. Tonry and A.N. Doob (eds) *Youth Crime and Youth Justice: Comparative and Cross-National Perspectives.* Chicago: University of Chicago Press.

Dignan, J. (1999) 'The Crime and Disorder Act and The prospects for restorative justice.' *Criminal Law Review,* 48–60.

Falconer, Lord (2006) *Doing Law Differently.* London: Department for Constitutional Affairs.

Farrington, D. (2007) 'Childhood Risk Factors and Risk-focused Prevention.' In M. Maguire, R. Morgan and R. Reiner (eds) *The Oxford Handbook of Criminology.* Oxford: OUP.

Feilzer, M. and Hood, R. (2004) *Differences or Discrimination: Minority Ethnic Young People in the Youth Justice System.* London: Youth Justice Board.

Galahad SMS Ltd (2004) *Substance Misuse and the Juvenile Secure Estate.* London: Youth Justice Board.

Harrington, R. and Bailey, S. (2005) *Mental Health Needs and Effectiveness of Provision for Young Offenders in Custody and in the Community.* London: YJB.

Hazell, N., Hagell, A., Liddle, M., Archer, D., Grimshaw, R. and King, J. (2002) *Detention and Training: Assessment of the Detention and Training Order and its Impact on the Secure Estate across England and Wales.* London: YJB.

HMIP (2005) *Juveniles in Custody 2003–4: An Analysis of Children's Experiences of Prisons.* London: HM Inspectorate of Prisons and YJB.

HM Treasury (2003) *Every Child Matters.* Cm 5860. London: Stationery Office.

Home Office (1997) No More Excuses – a New Approach to Tackling Youth Crime in England and Wales. Cm 3809. London: Home Office.

Home Office (2006a) *A Five Year Strategy for Protecting the Public and Reducing Offending.* Cm 6717. London: Stationery Office.

Home Office (2006b) *Strengthening Powers to Tackle Anti-Social Behaviour: Consultation Paper.* London: Home Office.

Labour Party (1996) *Protecting Our Communities: Labour's Plans for Tackling Criminal, Anti-social Behaviour in Neighbourhoods.* London: Labour Party.

Labour Party (1997) *Labour Party Election Manifesto: Labour Because Britain Deserves Better.* London: Labour Party.

McDonald, K. (2005) 'The Cripps Inaugural Lecture.' Howard League Centre for Penal Reform, 17 November, unpublished.

McAra, L. and McVie, S. (2005) 'The usual suspects? Street-life, young people and the police.' *Criminal Justice 5,* 5–35.

McAra, L. and McVie, S. (2007) 'Youth justice? The impact of system contact on patterns of desistance from offending.' *European Journal of Criminology 4,* 3, 315–345.

McInnes Report (2005) *The Summary Justice Review Committee: Report to Ministers.* Edinburgh: Scottish Government.

Ministry of Justice (2007a) *Criminal Statistics 2006 England and Wales.* London: National Statistics.

Ministry of Justice (2007b) *Sentencing Statistics 2006.* RDS Statistical Bulletin. London: Ministry of Justice.

Ministry of Justice (2008) *Reoffending of Juveniles: Results from the 2006 Cohort.* Ministry of Justice Statistical Bulletin. London: Ministry of Justice.

Morgan, R. (2006) 'With Respect to Order, the Rules of the Game Have Changed: New Labour's Dominance of the "Law and Order" Agenda.' In T. Newburn and P.

Rock (eds) *The Politics of Law and Order: Essays in Honour of David Downes.* Oxford: Clarendon Press.

Morgan, R. (2008) *Summary Justice: Fast − but Fair?* London: Centre for Crime and Justice Studies, King's College.

Morgan, R. and Newburn, T. (2007) 'Youth Justice.' In M. Maguire, R. Morgan and R. Reiner (eds) *The Oxford Handbook of Criminology.* Oxford: OUP.

Newburn, T. (ed.) (2005) *Policing: Key Readings.* Willan: Cullompton.

Nicholas, S., Kershaw, C. and Walker, A. (2007) *Crime in England and Wales 2006/7.* London: Home Office.

Roe, S. and Ashe, J. (2008) *Young People and Crime: Findings from the 2006 Offending Crime and Justice Survey.* RDSD Statistical Bulletin 9/8. London: Home Office.

Royal Commission on Criminal Justice (1993) *Report.* Cmnd. 2263. London: HMSO.

Rutherford, A. (1986) *Growing Out of Crime: Society and Young People in Trouble.* Harmondsworth: Penguin.

Sanders, A. and Young, R. (2007) *Criminal Justice,* 3rd edn. London: Butterworths.

Smith, R. (2003) *Youth Justice: Ideas, Policy, Practice.* Cullompton: Willan.

Social Exclusion Unit (2002) *Reducing Re-offending by Ex-prisoners.* London: Office of the Deputy Prime Minister.

Solomon, E., Eades, C., Garside, R. and Rutherford, M. (2007) *Ten Years of Criminal Justice under Labour: An Independent Audit.* London: Centre for Crime and Justice Studies, King's College.

Solomon, E. and Garside, R. (2008) *Ten Years of Labour's Youth Justice Reforms: An Independent Audit.* Centre for Crime and Justice Studies, King's College. Available at www.crimeandjustice.org.uk/opus647/youthjusticeaudit.pdf, accessed 30 June 2009.

Steer, D. (1970) *Police Cautions − a Study in the Exercise of Police Discretion.* Oxford University Penal Research Unit, Occasional Paper no. 2. Oxford: Basil Blackwell.

Von Hirsch, A., Bottoms, A.E., Burney, E. and Wikstrom, P.O. (1999) *Criminal Deterrence and Sentence Severity: An Analysis of Recent Research.* Oxford: Hart Publshing.

Young, R. (2008) 'Street Policing after PACE: The Drift to Summary Justice.' In E. Cape and R. Young (eds) *Regulating Policing: The Police and Criminal Evidence Act 1984, Past Present and Future.* Oxford: Hart Publshing.

Youth Justice Board/ACPO/Home Office (2005) *Anti-Social Behaviour: A Guide to the Role of Youth Offending Teams in Dealing with Anti-social Behaviour.* London: Youth Justice Board.

Youth Justice Board (2005) *Risk and Protective Factors.* London: Youth Justice Board.

Youth Justice Board (2007a) *Annual Report and Accounts 2006/07.* London: Youth Justice Board.

Youth Justice Board (2007b) *Corporate and Business Plan 2006/7−2008/9.* London: Youth Justice Board.

Youth Justice Board (2008a) *Youth Justice Annual Workload Data 2006−7.* London: Youth Justice Board.

Youth Justice Board (2008b) *First-time Entrants.* London: Youth Justice Board.

CHAPTER 5

Youth Justice Policy and its Influence on Desistance from Crime

Monica Barry

Introduction

Tackling youth crime has become a prime concern of Government policy relating to children and young people. However, the arena in which such policy is played out remains predominantly within the confines of the youth justice system rather than in wider policy initiatives. As has been seen in other chapters in this book, this has resulted in the increasing criminalisation and stigmatisation of young people, with less emphasis on their status as 'troubled' and more emphasis on their label as 'troublesome'. Although only a small minority of young people offend with any conviction, in both senses of the word, these young people are seen to justify the majority of youth justice funding, policy and practice initiatives. Thus a smaller group is being targeted for a wider and more punitive level of intervention, resulting in 'substantial penal expansion and concomitant growth in the population of child prisoners' (Goldson 2005, p.77).

Desistance for young people embroiled in the youth justice system is arguably made more difficult *because* of such intervention, not least because what young offenders feel may help them stop offending runs counter to the policy rhetoric. The rhetoric is about punishing or correcting the young offender, whereas the young person's experience is of social and structural barriers to change and participation in society.

This chapter briefly explores the literature on desistance as well as current policy statements relating to reducing or preventing re-offending. It then draws out the views of young offenders about what helps and hinders them in the process of desistance, to further explore the tensions and dissonances between the commentaries of young people versus policymakers on youthful offending and youth justice.

The road to desistance

One cannot reduce offending, from an interventionist viewpoint, without first understanding what young people themselves think about offending, the desistance process and what the alternatives to offending actually are. Youth justice policy based on political posturing or media soundbites is unlikely to be effective in reducing offending amongst young people unless there is also some weight given to the theoretical and empirical research evidence about desistance. This section therefore outlines the broad theories of desistance before looking more closely at the extent to which youth justice policy reflects the research 'evidence'.

There are two types of desistance theory which relate to young people and these can be differentiated as follows: one type sees the desistance process as being initiated by the young offender him/herself; the other sees the desistance process as being initiated by social factors (namely policies and structural opportunities for meaningful integration of [ex-]offenders). Both are summarised below:

Desistance and human agency

There are two broad theories of desistance which function at the level of personal agency through their focus on the maturation and rationality of offenders. The first theory emphasises the inevitability of maturation in reducing or stopping offending behaviour in youth (Glueck and Glueck 1940; Rutherford 1986), but such theories tend to operate in a vacuum, devoid of external influences such as schooling, employment, relationships and the social status of young people in transition. Theories of maturational reform also imply that interventions to reduce offending may be counterproductive, given that young people will naturally grow out of crime. Nevertheless, young people are still disproportionately discriminated against because of their age and the assumption in policy circles, however misguided, that crime is *not* a natural and developmental phenomenon and that young people will *not* stop offending unless external measures are put in place to make them.

The second theory, Rational Choice Theory (Cornish and Clarke 1986), stresses the decision making capacities of individuals not only to start, but also to stop offending, the latter because of the possible 'burn out' or deterrence effect of the youth and criminal justice systems and/or a rational reassessment of the costs and benefits of crime, not least in the transition to adulthood. However, 'rational' decision making could arguably straddle both individual and structural theories of desistance since structural opportunities and constraints will undoubtedly influence rational choice.

The Rational Choice approach in its pure form has been manipulated by policymakers who argue that young people will not stop unless their cognitive skills are improved and their behaviour modified. This suggests a 'deficit' model of youth offending – that young people are solely to blame for their own behaviour because of their own failings. Government policy argues that such deficits can only be remedied by making young people more responsible for their actions and their consequences, referred to as the 'responsibilisation' model of youth offending (Gray 2005). Gray describes responsibilisation of young offenders as: 'challenging perceived deficits in their moral reasoning' (ibid., p.938). Current practice thus focuses on criminogenic needs (principally though not exclusively concerned with deficient moral reasoning) which can be addressed through cognitive-behavioural intervention, and emphasises equality of *opportunity* rather than structural and economic redistribution per se. Not only are young people made solely responsible for their actions, they are also expected to take prime responsibility for the remedies. Bennett (2008) argues that offending behaviour programmes make individuals responsible for their own rehabilitation and desistance, and that where they fail to take such responsibilities, punishment will be justified.

Desistance and structural change

The structural factors which may influence desistance mainly include social bonds, employment and marriage. Hirschi (1969) defined social bonds as having emotional ties to others, an investment in relationships, access to legitimate activities and a commitment to the rule of law. Structural opportunities are less available for young people in the transition to adulthood who are confined to school and largely dependent on adults for their livelihood. Structural theories relating to relationships and other social bonds (rather than employment and marriage per se) have proved relatively successful in understanding gender differences in the desistance process amongst young people, in that young women with commitments to partners and children are more likely to desist from crime than young men. Graham and Bowling (1995) found that young women were more likely to make a successful and speedier transition to adulthood, with more opportunities for independent living and less peer pressure to offend. Young women may also have greater access to social and other forms of capital which may enable an earlier progress towards desistance (Barry 2006a).

In respect of young adults, several theorists suggest that conventional opportunities such as marriage and employment are crucial factors in the desistance process (Sampson and Laub 1993; Shover 1996). However, many individuals are both married and employed but still persist in offending behaviour and, in respect of young people, relationships and employment can often exacerbate offending because of the transience and instability of such arrangements at that age. As a result of this anomaly it is often stressed that it is the *quality* of such bonds or opportunities rather than the bonds or opportunities themselves that is important in encouraging desistance (Rutter 1996; Sampson and Laub 1993). 'Turning points' – often linked to developing social bonds – may promote desistance by encouraging the revision of personal values about offending and conformity (Farrall and Bowling 1999; Leibrich 1993), although more often than not, such revised values come from within (e.g. the 'burn out' effect mentioned in the previous section or the powerfully felt importance of a new relationship or role) rather than from external influences such as the all-too-rare experience of being trusted with responsibilities or recognised for one's skills and abilities (Barry 2006a; Maruna 2001).

The impact of the youth justice system on desistance

As has been suggested by Rod Morgan in the preceding chapter, the youth justice system in England and Wales now has a primary focus on punishment and containment, and as Goldson (2005, p.84) has pointed out: 'the priority role of staff is to maintain discipline, order and institutional security…the care principle is always relegated to a secondary status'. Punishment and discipline are approaches allied very much with desistance at the agency level rather than the structural level, focusing on responsibilisation and individualisation. There is usually an element, however tokenistic, of welfare within the youth justice system in the form of education, training and employment opportunities, but Kemshall (2002) has suggested that the individualisation of the social context of youth crime makes young offenders responsible for negotiating and seizing such opportunities themselves.

This individualisation of risk (Gray 2005) is evident in both the current Scottish and English action plans for youth crime (HM Government 2008; Scottish Government 2008). In Scotland, the policy document – *Preventing Offending by Young People: A Framework for Action* – accepts that the 'deeds' of young offenders can only be addressed in tandem with their needs and that youth justice provision on its own cannot deal effectively with youth crime. To that end it talks of investing in educational, cultural and leisure opportunities for young people through a partnership of children's, educational and youth justice services. Nevertheless, the emphasis remains on building the capacity of young people, their families and communities 'to secure the best outcomes *for themselves*' (para 3.6, emphasis added). With persistent young offenders, the Government wants to 'challenge and change that behaviour and provide the support that will *enable these young people to turn their lives around*' (para 3.18, emphasis added), again stressing the responsibilisation model of tackling youth crime, rather than making available to young people the structural opportunities and community-generated supports that might help them in that process.

The *Youth Crime Action Plan* for England and Wales (2008) combines a somewhat unhealthy and incongruent mix of seemingly proactive welfare measures with overt reactive and punitive measures. On the one hand, it offers 'support for those who *make an effort* to try to turn their lives around' (p.5, emphasis added), it suggests expanding youth work provision, and offers resettlement opportunities to those previously in custodial care. On the other hand, it talks of 'tough penalties' for those young people who are 'going astray' or who 'blight' their communities' (p.4), of challenging parents 'to meet their responsibilities' (p.4), of young offenders being seen to repay their communities, and 'making young offenders feel the consequences of their actions' (p.7).

In so doing, the Action Plan adopts a 'triple track approach' with three key objectives:

- enforcement and punishment
- non-negotiable support and challenge
- better and earlier intervention.

However, the emphasis in this Action Plan is very much on managing individual offenders rather than on addressing wider socio-economic constraints. It epitomises the deficit model of youth offending, where the carrot of 'support' is secondary to the stick of 'punishment', and where such support is 'non-negotiable' – an oxymoron par excellence. Such language may be lost on young offenders, but the tone of the argument will be all too familiar to them.

The following section illustrates this point by highlighting the views of young offenders themselves about what helps and hinders them in the process of desistance. This chapter illustrates the dichotomy between young offenders' views and those of policymakers by superimposing the views of young offenders in Scotland, which has a more welfare-oriented youth justice system, onto the policies currently emanating from England and Wales, which espouse neo-correctionalist principles (Cavadino and Dignan 2006). Because incarcerated or accommodated young people in Scotland are arguably treated more humanely than their counterparts south of the Border as a result of the different principles applied in both jurisdictions, their views about punishment, enforcement and coercion are all the more pertinent when set against the backcloth of the neo-liberal system in England and Wales.

Young offenders' views on the desistance process

Much desistance research, whether of the individual or the structural school, suggests a common outcome for young people, namely the social integration that comes with improved status, responsibilities and rights associated with conformity in adulthood. However, for many young people, not least those who are 'looked after and accommodated' because of their troubled backgrounds or troublesome behaviour, the transition to adulthood and conformity is often elusive.

This section draws on the views of such young people, elicited through two research studies undertaken by Who Cares? Scotland in collaboration with the author (Barry and Moodie 2008; Cruickshank and Barry 2008). Who Cares? Scotland is a charity providing independent advocacy for Scotland's looked after children and young people, and which undertakes research on their views and experiences. In total 103 young people were interviewed, participated in focus group discussions or completed question- naires, comprising 73 young men and 30 young women between the ages of 11 and 21. The sample was drawn from residential units, residential schools, secure units and young offender institutions across Scotland, and the fieldwork was undertaken during the period November 2006–August 2007.

Whilst one of the studies focused particularly on persistent offending behaviour by young people who were, or had been, looked after and accom- modated, the other study sought their perceptions and experiences more generally of residential and secure care, including offending and the use of sanctions for infringement of rules whilst looked after and accommodated. The following analysis is therefore taken from both studies where views and experiences of offending and punishment were noted.

In terms of desistance from crime in youth, the majority of respondents mentioned that they, or other young people, might be encouraged to stop offending if there were more constructive opportunities for them to occupy their time. These included leisure activities, education and employment op- portunities, and as one 15-year-old young man suggested: 'something better to do than steal'. For the younger age group, leisure activities in their own communities to relieve boredom and to avoid admission to care were an essential ingredient in the desistance process, not least for young people who felt marginalised from mainstream activities:

There's no community centres. In any of the community centres you go in…they chuck you back out because you're a young one. You can only hang about the streets in groups of five and, even in groups of five, you get lifted. It's stupid… If there were more things in the community for us to do…if there was fighting classes like kick boxing or something, then we could do it to each other, rather than go out and batter random people, but there's no. There's nothing for us to do. (15-year-old female)

There was nothing to do but hang about street corners… If you put in more football parks and youth clubs in your areas, that would help you sort out offending. That's what I would do a couple of days a week, sit in there and play pool instead of going out fighting. (15-year-old male)

The fear of escalating offending resulting in harsher penalties as they get older was also a prime concern for many young people, not least because young people under the age of 16 in Scotland tend to equate the Children's Hearings system with a more 'welfare' ethos, whereas once they reach the age of 16, they may be treated more harshly by the criminal justice system. However, definitions of 'persistent offending' have become more stringent over the years and have resulted in a higher number of young people escalating through the youth justice system as a result of such labelling, especially young people who are looked after and accommodated.

There are numerous reasons for and ways of measuring persistent offending based on seriousness, frequency, prevalence and legal definition of offending. The Home Office, for example, defines persistent young offenders as those who have been dealt with by the court on three or more occasions and who commit another offence within three years of last appearing before a court (Moore *et al.* 2006). In Scotland, the definition of persistent offending is five 'episodes' of offending within a six-month period which result in referral to the Children's Hearings system. A report produced by Edinburgh City Council (2007) recommended that the Scottish Government re-examine its current definition because of concerns that:

An individual who commits three or four serious episodes over a period of a year falls outwith the definition, but someone who commits five or more minor episodes will be included despite the fact that they may be considered to be at a much lower risk of future offending… The definition is more likely to include children in local authority care, as minor offences are more likely to involve the police rather than being dealt with by families in the home.

Several studies have suggested that children and young people looked after and accommodated are more likely to come to the attention of the police as a result of 'incidents' occurring within the care environment. The Home Office (2004) highlighted the issue of residential care staff over-reporting to the police young people who were disruptive, thus potentially escalating their movement through the youth and criminal justice systems. Equally, Nacro (2005) has suggested that looked after young people's contact with the police is above average compared with young people generally, and that they are more likely to be reported, warned and prosecuted for relatively minor offences committed within residential care establishments. In Scotland Hill *et al.* (2005, p.21) identified a greater escalation of offending incidents for young people in residential care which were 'very specific to their living situation…compounded [by] cramped conditions in establishments or staff difficulties in managing young people with a variety of different needs'.

As will be seen in the following section, the use of sanctions for often minor misdemeanours in residential care can often result in young people being labelled as persistent offenders and dealt with accordingly. In focus group discussions many of the young people were critical of the Scottish Government's definition of persistent offending (PA Consulting 2004) because five episodes of offending in a six-month period were fairly easy to accrue within the residential care setting, which may result in more young people who are looked after being labelled as persistent offenders.

Nevertheless, a minority of young people felt that being in residential care created a disincentive to accrue more offences because it removed them from the bad influences of peers, drugs and alcohol, and also gave them time to think about their current circumstances and the consequences of offending:

> I think these places [secure units and young offender institutions] give you time to reflect on your behaviour when you're sober, straight and have a clear head. You think: 'that's no the way things are done and you never go anywhere in life if you act like that', and I realise that now. (17-year-old man)

Several young people also commented on encouragement given by professionals as being important in the desistance process, not least if such 'adults' were more willing to trust and respect young people. Positive relationships with professionals have been cited in other desistance literature (see, for example, Barry 2000; McNeill, Chapter 8, this volume; McNeill 2006) and yet the current approach within the youth justice system tends to downplay such constructive and reciprocal engagement between worker and client. The 'triple track' approach of the Youth Crime Action Plan is a case in point, where punishment, coercion and non-negotiable support are the overarching factors in the worker/client relationship. In the following section the views of these respondents are grouped under the three prongs of the current UK Government's initiative to tackle youth crime in England and Wales, as cited above, namely enforcement/punishment, non-negotiable support/challenge and better/earlier intervention.

Young people's attitudes to enforcement/punishment

There is some ambiguity in definitions of, and the resulting balance between, 'care' and 'control' in the lives of young people who are looked after and accommodated — not least if they are accommodated because of their offending behaviour. Children and young people have a right to be 'safe' when accommodated, but likewise the public have a right to protection from crime. Secure care is usually used for more troubled and troublesome young people who are at a high risk of posing a danger to themselves or others if left in their own communities.

Although many of the respondents said they felt safe in secure care, and that it was a justifiable response to their previous behaviour, many also suggested that the environment proved more 'controlling' than 'caring' when it came to the use of sanctions: namely, single separation and restraint. Single separation — where the young person is locked in his/her room to calm down — was said to result from being cheeky, causing damage or fighting with staff or other residents. On occasions, and presumably depending on the mental state of the young person, items would be removed from the room, including mattresses, televisions and writing implements, to ensure that the young person 'reflected' on the incident and apologised before being able to rejoin the group setting. However, this isolation tended to make young people more, rather than less, agitated, thus proving counterproductive in the longer term:

> You are asked to go to your room. If you refuse the staff there will try and get you to your room. If they can't...you are dragged... How would you

feel with your room emptied and your toilet locked, stuck in a cell basically? You go off your head 'cos you can't get out. (14-year-old male)

It's a punishment. It should be a last resort, but some staff just stick you
in your room right away... It doesn't work, it makes you worse. There is
nothing to keep you busy, no TV, no radio, can't even draw. You get
nothing, no power in your room... If the staff are in a good mood, you
can be in your room for ten minutes. If the staff are in a bad mood, then
you can be in your room for two hours. (14-year-old male)

Whilst some young people felt in retrospect that staff had encouraged them
to calm down afterwards and that this had been effective, in many respondents' opinion the ultimate aim of single separation was primarily to admit
defeat and to apologise to staff, and several commented that this was unfair
and often counterproductive: 'Sometimes you don't agree with their views
and this can kick you off again' (17-year-old male).

Restraint practices result where a young person is becoming increasingly
aggressive and has to be held down by staff for their own protection and the
safety of others in the unit. Restraint was often used prior to single separation,
and again tended to be seen by respondents as a punishment which would
exacerbate rather than diffuse a situation, not least if staff caused undue pain
or anxiety for the young person being restrained: 'It definitely makes you
worse being restrained. It takes you ages to calm down' (15-year-old female).

Four guys lying on top of you, it's not done right... It doesn't help you,
it only makes matters worse...you're in your room after, pure raging,
dying to get back out there and start again... Sometimes they take you
down wrongly, they hurt you...carpet burns on the face and that. Then
the staff say you've been self-harming, but it's not. It's those bastards
and the way they put you down. (14-year-old male)

For many young people who are caught up in the youth justice system, there
is a lack of clarity – not least for them, but also arguably for practitioners –
about the balance required between care and control and enforcement and
punishment. This is by no means the first study of young offenders' views
which has elicited their criticisms about coercive or punitive measures which
they perceive to be harsh or unjustifiable. Coupling these views with their
equally common criticism that their views are not taken into account suggests

that the Government's triple track approach may prove counterproductive in effecting a change of attitude or behaviour amongst young offenders. The second element of this triple track approach – 'non-negotiable support' – is now explored below from a young person's perspective.

Young people's attitudes to non-negotiable support

Negotiation is a key factor in offenders' views of what constitutes a good, and more importantly, effective relationship with professionals (Barry 2007): being listened to, having their views taken into account, and even the increasing professional focus on self-assessment in risk of re-offending (Barry 2006b), are all crucial elements of negotiation that encourage engagement between worker and client. The Children's Hearings system in Scotland prides itself on taking the views of young offenders into account when deciding on a course of action, and indeed the UN Convention on the Rights of the Child does likewise. Thus the focus of the current Youth Crime Action Plan on 'non-negotiable support' appears to be grossly at odds with existing policy and practice initiatives relating to young people in the youth justice system.

As mentioned above, many of the respondents in the two studies explored here felt that part of the problem within residential and secure care settings was that staff did *not* negotiate with, or listen to, young people in their care. The sanctions imposed on looked after young people were often deemed unfair and disproportionate to the original incident that resulted in such sanctions. Equally, in terms of single separation and restraint, many young people suggested that they had to apologise before such sanctions were lifted, irrespective of whether or not they felt such an apology was justified: 'It's a power thing, I think. If you don't say "sorry" or accept what you have done, then you won't get out of your room' (13-year-old female); '[Restraint] just makes us more angry… They are backing you into a corner…it's a natural instinct to lash out' (15-year-old male).

Sanctions apart, the non-negotiable way in which visits are organised caused a similar reaction amongst respondents, with some suggesting that they were not consulted about who was on their 'visitor list' and why. Whilst it was implied that a young person could 'negotiate' with his/her social worker to have an additional name added to the list, it was the social worker's prerogative to refuse to allow certain people to visit: 'My best friends aren't allowed [on the list] because my social worker has decided that they are a bad influence' (15-year-old male).

Contact with the 'outside world' was an obvious source of comfort for many young people who were looked after and to be denied this contact only served to fuel their anger, resentment and frustration, not least if that contact was curtailed as a form of punishment.

Equally, school and programme work was also a non-negotiable aspect of being looked after and accommodated which many felt was inappropriate to their needs, and yet refusal to attend could result in sanctions being imposed:

> [The staff] just looked at you as their work, there was a pay cheque at the end of it. They weren't listening to what you were saying... In therapy, that psychotherapist asks you questions and doesn't give you any advice back. It's a waste of an hour. (14-year-old male)

Where young people felt that they were not listened to or supported whilst in care, they did have recourse to a complaints procedure. Approximately 50 per cent of respondents in secure care had made a complaint, but only a quarter felt confident that their complaint had been taken seriously. Complaints were often ignored or dismissed by staff as unjustifiable, and many young people were cynical about the value of complaining: 'You can't win with a complaint...nothing ever happens' (14-year-old male).

When asked what advice they would give to other young people being looked after, the comments implied that negotiation was not an option and that submission to authority was more likely to succeed. Advice to other young people such as to 'keep your head down', 'do what you are told' and 'get on with it' was common, albeit sadly defeatist.

Young people's attitudes to better/earlier intervention

'Better' intervention, for many young people in the youth justice system means non-coercive and negotiated engagement with workers within a caring rather than controlling environment. Whilst the majority of respondents spoke positively about certain members of staff in residential and secure care, there was felt to be a lack of consistency of approach within the staff group which left young people feeling discriminated against. There was also a concern that staff training and attitudes should be improved in order to ensure a more balanced response to the young people in their care. A lack of awareness by some staff of the care and exit plans for young people could also result in an inconsistent or inappropriate level of care.

In terms of earlier intervention, throughcare and aftercare arrangements were often seen as inadequate and 'too little too late' by young people who were looked after. The majority of respondents felt that the support they received was minimal or non-existent as a result of staff shortages and uncertainty about when a young person would be released from care. Greater opportunities on leaving care, such as education or employment, would greatly enhance these young people's chances of stopping offending and yet such opportunities were dependent on advance notice of a leaving date and the commitment and capacity of staff to negotiate constructive opportunities for young people in their communities.

Conclusions

Current UK policy relating to youth crime bears little resemblance either to the perceptions of young offenders about offending and desistance or to academic thinking on the subject. Government policy, notably in England and Wales but increasingly so in Scotland (Cavadino and Dignan 2006), very much reflects the emphasis on individual agency (both the deficit model and its concurrent responsibilisation strategies mentioned earlier) in the process of desistance. Structural factors are lost to agency factors, and agency factors themselves are manipulated to focus not on age and maturation but on the rational intentions of individual young people and the need to change their behaviour.

The research highlighted in this chapter suggests that the triple track approach adopted by the Youth Crime Action Plan will not work effectively because its doctrine runs counter to what young offenders themselves believe will most help both themselves and their communities. It would seem that whilst these young people's views and experiences of the desistance process fitted well with aspects of both the agency and structure debates in the academic literature on theories of desistance, their views and experiences were much less compatible with the policy directives aimed at reducing offending amongst this population of offenders.

The young offenders in these two studies felt that their offending was indeed a 'phase' that they were going through in youth and from which they would emerge as law-abiding adults – hence reflecting desistance at the level of personal agency. They also suggested that they would not resort to offending if they had constructive and meaningful alternative lifestyles, thus reflecting desistance at the structural level. The problem is, however, that theories of desistance can only reflect the reality if young people are allowed to grow up in a non-stigmatising and non-discriminatory environment where maturational development and structural supports are acknowledged as being essential ingredients in the desistance process. But this is not the case. Young people generally, and young offenders in particular, are subject to a myriad of rules, sanctions, labels and interventions which they often see as unjustified, disproportionate and liable to exacerbate rather than alleviate their youthful behaviour.

The political rhetoric is that the youth justice system will reduce, if not stop, offending amongst young people. The reality is that it will systematically fail in this regard if it does not take into account the views of young people themselves about what helps them in the process of desistance. Carrying out research on children and young people who are looked after and accommodated is difficult at the best of times (McCrystal 2008), but when such young people are also 'offenders' there is a tendency on the part of the system to protect them from scrutiny, ostensibly because of such young people's right to privacy and non-stigmatisation. However, if young offenders in state care cannot describe their circumstances and postulate on their predicament, a key stakeholder view is lost. McCrystal argues 'that children and young people are dependent upon adults' perceptions of whether participating in research is in their best interest' (ibid. p.93), and this indeed begs the question whether it is in *adults'* best interest to have the users of youth justice services voicing their concerns. Nevertheless, without those concerns being heard and being taken on board, youth justice will remain a battle of wills between policymakers and young people in trouble.

The process of desistance can only be understood as a dual process of agency and structure. Agency comes from meaningful and constructive engagement by young offenders in a non-authoritarian relationship with professionals. Structural opportunities equally need to be meaningful and constructive and negotiated with partners outwith the youth justice arena itself. Solomon and Garside (2008) question the extent to which the youth justice system in a vacuum can actually reduce youth crime, devoid of proactive and collaborative support and opportunities within other youth policy arenas, such as leisure, employment, education and housing.

The youth justice system can thus only be truly effective in helping young people stop offending – if indeed that *is* its main function – if it adopts a partnership approach not only between differing professional services, but also with young offenders themselves, so as to ensure that the support offered is truly negotiable, and that the interventions are appropriate and meaningful to young people rather than coercive and dogmatic.

References

Barry, M. (2000) 'The mentor/monitor debate in criminal justice: What works for offenders.' *British Journal of Social Work, 30,* 575–595.

Barry, M. (2006a) *Youth Offending in Transition: The Search for Social Recognition.* Abingdon: Routledge.

Barry, M. (2006b) *Effective Approaches to Risk Assessment in Social Work: An International Literature Review.* Edinburgh: Stationery Office.

Barry, M. (2007) 'Listening and learning: The reciprocal relationship between worker and client.' *Probation Journal 54,* 4, 407–422.

Barry, M. and Moodie, K. (2008) '*This Isn't the Road I Want to Go Down': Young People's Perceptions and Experiences of Secure Care.* Glasgow: Who Cares? Scotland.

Bennett, J. (2008) 'They hug hoodies, don't they? Responsibility, irresponsibility and responsibilisation in Conservative crime policy.' *Howard Journal 47,* 5, 451–469.

Cavadino, M. and Dignan, J. (2006) *Penal Systems: A Comparative Approach.* London: Sage.

Cornish, D. and Clarke, R.V. (1986) *The Reasoning Criminal.* New York, NY: Springer-Verlag.

Cruickshank, C-A. and Barry, M. (2008) '*Nothing Has Convinced Me to Stop': Young People's Perceptions and Experiences of Persistent Offending.* Glasgow: Who Cares? Scotland.

Edinburgh City Council (2007) *Breaking the Cycle, A Review of Persistent Offending in Edinburgh.* Edinburgh: Community Services Scrutiny Panel.

Farrall, S. and Bowing, B. (1999) 'Structuration, human development and resistance from crime.' *British Journal of Criminology 39,* 2, 253–268.

Gluck, S. and Gluck, E. (1940) *Unraveling Juvenile Delinquency.* New York, NY: Common Wealth Fund.

Goldson, B. (2005) 'Child imprisonment: A case for abolition.' *Youth Justice 5*, 2, 77–90.

Graham, J. and Bowling, B. (1995) *Young People and Crime.* London: Home Office.

Gray, P. (2005) 'The politics of risk and young offenders' experiences of social exclusion and restorative justice.' *British Journal of Criminology 45*, 6, 938–957.

HM Government (2008) *Youth Crime Action Plan.* London: Home Office.

Hill, M., Walker, M., Moodie, K., Wallace, B., Bannister, J., Khan, F., McIvor, G. and Kendrick, A. (2005) *Fast Track Children's Hearings Pilot, Final Report.* Edinburgh: Scottish Executive.

Hirschi, T. (1969) *Causes of Delinquency.* Berkeley: CA: University of California Press.

Home Office (2004) *Preventative Approaches Targeting Young People in Local Authority Residential Care, Development and Practice Report.* London: Home Office.

Kemshall, H. (2002) 'Effective practice in probation: An example of "advanced liberal" responsibilisation.' *Harvard Journal 41*, 41–58.

Leibrich, J. (1993) *Straight to The Point: Angles on Giving up Crime.* Dunedin, New Zeland: University of Otago Press.

McCrystal, P. (2008) 'Researching children and young people living in residential state care: Hurdles on the path to consent.' *Research Ethics Review 4*, 3, 89–94.

McNeill, F. (2006) 'A desistance paradigm for offender management.' *Criminology and Criminal Justice 6*, 1, 39–62.

Maruna, S. (2001) *Making Good: How Ex-convicts Reform and Rebuild their Lives.* Washington DC: American Psychological Association.

Moore, R., Gray, E., Roberts, C., Taylor, E. and Merrington, S. (2006) *Managing Persistent and Serious Offenders in the Community.* Cullompton: Willan.

Nacro (2005) *A Handbook on Reducing Offending by Looked After Children.* London: Nacro.

PA Consulting (2004) *Scottish Youth Justice Baseline.* London: PA Knowledge Ltd.

Rutherford, A. (1986) *Growing out of Crime: The New Era.* Winchester: Waterside Press.

Rutter, M. (1996) 'Transitions and turning points in developmental psychopatology: As applied to the age span between childhood and mid-adulthood.' *International Journal of Behavioural Development 19*, 603–626.

Sampson, R. J. and Laub, J.H. (1993) *Crime in the Making: Pathways and Turning Points Through Life.* Cambridge, MA: Harvard Univeristy Press.

Scotish Goverment (2008) *Preventing Offending by Young People: a Framework for Action.* Available at http://www.scotland.gov.uk/Publications/2008/06/17093513/7 (accessed 29 May 2009).

Shover, N. (1996) *Great Pretenders: Pursuits and Careers of Persistent Thieves.* Boulder, CO: Westview Press.

Solomon, E. and Garside, R. (2008) *Ten Years of Labour's Youth Justice Reforms: An Independent Audit.* London: Centre for Crime and Justice Studies.

CHAPTER 6

Youth, Crime and Punitive Public Opinion: Hopes and Fears for the Next Generation[1]

Shadd Maruna and Anna King

Introduction

With the age of criminal responsibility reduced to ten years of age in England and eight in Scotland, young people have become special targets in the so-called 'new punitivism' (Pratt *et al.* 2005). When the head of the Youth Justice Board resigned in 2007 in dismay, he pointed out that nearly three-quarters of the youth justice budget was spent on imprisonment with little left behind for more constructive work with young people (Morgan 2008). Indeed, the number of children in custody has more than doubled in the past 15 years. The Children's Commissioner for England, Sir Al Aynsley-Green, recently made the following denunciation of British youth justice policy:

> This demonization and lack of empathy for young people is a major issue for England. It causes anger and alienation… It is driving policy.

[1] Some parts of this article have previously appeared in Maruna, S. and King, A. (2008) 'Giving up on the young.' *Current Issues in Criminal Justice 20*, 129–135, Sydney: Sydney Institute of Criminology. Used with permission.

> At the moment we have a youth justice system dominated by a punitive
> approach. It doesn't focus on children's needs... Is there not an urgent
> need to review our youth justice programme to see why we are locking
> away so many kids? (quoted in Gaines 2007, p.1)

What is the psychology behind this punitiveness toward young people?
Certainly, 'moral panics' concerning the youth of the day are anything but
new (see Cohen 1972; Pearson 1983). Shakespeare, for instance, has a
character say, 'I would there were no age between sixteen and
three-and-twenty, or that youth would sleep out the rest; for there is nothing
in the between but getting wenches with child, wronging the ancientry,
stealing, fighting' (*Winter's Tale*, Act 3, Scene 3). What might be different
with contemporary punitiveness toward youth, then, is the combination of
these standard worries with a somewhat new fear: that the young may not
'grow out' of these behaviours upon reaching the age of 23 or even 33. That
is, even though conventional wisdom suggests that most young people will
eventually 'grow out of crime' (Rutherford 1992), conventional wisdom also
holds that 'once a criminal, always a criminal'. Conventional wisdom is not
known for its consistency. Even philosophers and social scientists struggle
with notions of free will and determinism, and criminologists endlessly
debate the nature and persistence of criminality as a construct. So it is no
wonder that members of the general public are not sure what they believe
about the stability or permanence of criminal behaviour.

Our research, however, suggests that this is a crucial issue in need of
further exploration. We label this construct 'belief in redeemability' (see
Maruna and King 2004). Our research suggests that some individuals feel
that criminality (or the origins of criminal behaviour) are largely set in stone
or 'fixed' (at least at a certain age) whereas others have a more malleable sense
of criminality and feel that 'even the worst' offender can change his or her
ways. The concept appears related to another, which we call 'generational
anxiety'. Whereas some of the people we interviewed in our research have
great hopes for the potential of the next generation of young people today,
others are far more pessimistic and worry that the young no longer have
respect for anything anymore.

We have found in our research that both of these beliefs are predictive of
numerous other attitudes and opinions regarding criminal justice matters, but

particularly determine one's level of 'punitiveness' or support for harsh penal sanctions for offenders. Those people who believe that criminality is a fundamentally stable construct also logically believe that offenders should be kept away from society for longer, even indefinite, periods of time. Likewise, those with the most concerns about young people's behaviour are most in favour of tighter, tougher sentencing practices. The combination of these two beliefs however – fears that the young are out of control and a lack of belief that they will 'grow out of it' – may be the key formula behind the punitive attitudes one sees today.

Stable attributions and moral behaviour

Fifty years ago George Vold (1958, p.258) argued: 'There is an obvious and logical interdependence between what is done about crime and what is assumed to be the reason for or explanation of criminality' (see also Fletcher 1966; Hogarth 1971; Nettler 1959). As such, criminologists seeking to understand why some members of the public are more punitive in their views than others have frequently turned to attribution theory in their explanation. Initially developed by Fritz Heider (1958), attribution theory involves a perceptual approach to attitude formation, exploring how individuals construct the meaning of an event, and the impact these implicit theories have for our social views.

In his original formulation, Heider (1958) was particularly interested in the pattern known as the 'fundamental attribution error', whereby individuals attribute their own mistakes to situational factors in the external world, but attribute the same behaviours in others to their core personality traits. When we see others behaving in negative ways, we tend to systematically underestimate the influence of environment and assume that it is the 'type' of people they are (Jones and Nisbett 1971). This bias, then, has implications for our social attitudes and behaviours. Indeed, an expansive body of research has found that these causal attributions are consistently implicated in a surprising array of behavioural dynamics (Weiner 1985).

For the most part, criminological research into punitive public attitudes begins and ends with Heider's (1958) initial dichotomy of 'dispositional' (originating from within the person's character) and 'situational' attributions (originating from the person's context). Cullen and colleagues (1985) describe these orientations as either 'classical' where crime is seen as a choice or 'positivist' where crime is seen as the product of social forces:

> Those who hold a classical understanding of crime causation and hence believe that crime flourishes because it is a rational, utilitarian enterprise will be more punitive than those positivists…who see crime as a manifestation of social constraint and social ills. (Cullen *et al.* 1985, p.310)

This correlation has been confirmed in both quantitative and qualitative studies of public opinion with diverse samples, including university students, probation officers, judges and nationally representative public samples (e.g. Carroll *et al.* 1987; Grasmick and McGill 1994; Sasson 1995; Sims 2003; Templeton and Hartnagel 2008, but see Viney, Waldman and Barchilon 1982). Scheingold argues that 'hard-line' conservatives view offenders as free individuals who choose to prey on others, whereas liberals are 'positivists' who argue that 'crime is associated with poverty…weakened family structures, inadequate slum schools, limited job opportunities, and the like' (1984, p.9). Additionally, a situational attributional style is also linked to political liberalism in general (see, for example, Jacobs and Carmichael 2002). Those who blame poverty on the actions of poor individuals themselves (e.g. laziness or poor work habits) tend to be less likely to support social anti-poverty programmes (Pellegrini *et al.* 1997).

Yet, the social psychological literature on attribution theory has advanced considerably since Heider's initial formulation on which these studies still rest. Rather than understanding attributions as merely 'dispositional' or 'situational', newer versions of attribution theory have broken down Heider's dichotomy into several different dimensions of attributions, such as stable/unstable, global/specific, controllable/uncontrollable, that appear to be better predictors of various attitudes than simple internality/externality (Peterson, Buchanan and Seligman 1993; Weiner and Graham 1999; Wilson and Linville 1985). According to Peterson (2000, p.48) measures of the internal–external dimension have 'more inconsistent correlates than do stability or globality, it is less reliably assessed and there are theoretical grounds for doubting that it has a direct impact on expectations per se'.

The stability of causes may be a particularly important dimension. For instance, making instable self-attributions for negative life events (e.g. it was a one-off 'fluke') is seen as highly adaptive; whereas, the feeling of hopelessness is 'a negative expectancy that follows directly from attributing failure to stable causes' (Weiner and Graham 1999, p.619). In other words, blaming a lost race on one's lack of effort or preparation (instable attributions) is likely to lead to better future performances than blaming the loss on stable attributions like one's lack of ability or potential (see Struthers and Perry 1996; Van Overwalle, Segebarth and Goldchstein 1989; Wilson and Linville 1985). When we believe that the causes of our failings are permanent, we logically tend to give up hope; whereas, if we tell ourselves that we can do better in the future, we leave open this possibility. In one experimental test of this theory, a group of college freshmen were told that it was normal that grades would improve from their first to second year in university. These students performed better in their second year than a control group of students who received no such attributional information (Wilson and Linville 1982).

Research by Dweck and colleagues suggests that both children and adults tend to hold one of two implicit theories of intelligence: entity theories or incremental theories of intelligence (Dweck and Leggett 1988; Dweck, Chiu and Hong 1995). Lay 'entity' theorists believe that intelligence is basically fixed and unmalleable. Some people are just smarter, and although others can learn new things or study very hard, they will never be as smart as those born/made that way. Whereas lay 'incremental' theorists believe intelligence is modifiable and believe that one can get smarter through study and exercising one's brain. The researchers found that these implicit theories have important implications for behaviour. For instance, children who ascribe to incremental theories of intelligence are more inclined toward and successful at challenging intellectual tasks. Although these theories are likely linked to the internal/external dimension of attribution theory, they are more reflective of the stable/unstable distinction. That is, entity theorists probably believe that intelligence is something that one inherits genetically. Yet someone could also believe that intelligence is a product of one's social environment as a child (external cause), but once it is fixed in stone at age four or five, it is unlikely to change.

A parallel dichotomy can be found in views about moral traits like honesty (see Dweck, Chiu and Hong 1995). Those who believe in a world where moral characteristics such as honesty are 'fixed' consistently interact differently in laboratory tests to those who ascribe to a more malleable or incremental view of morality (Chiu et al. 1997). In previous work (Maruna and King 2004) we developed this idea in our construct of 'belief in redeemability'. As with intelligence or morality, we argued that some individuals feel that criminality (or the origins of criminal behaviour) are largely set in stone or 'fixed', whereas others have a more malleable sense of criminality and feel that 'even the worst' offender can change his or her ways.

This dimension may or may not be related to beliefs about the origins of crime. For example, it is possible that those with a situational understanding of crime will be most likely to believe that criminality is malleable, but this is not necessarily the case. In fact, the core tenet of classical criminological theory, that 'crime is a choice', would seem to suggest that this is an unstable attribution. If one believes crime is freely chosen, presumably desistance from crime could also be a matter of free will. Likewise, some situational causes of crime (e.g. bad parenting) may be assumed to result in permanent or at least life course persistent criminality. Garland argues, 'Whether the offender's character is the result of bad genes or of being reared in an anti-social culture, the outcome is the same – a person who is beyond the pale, beyond reform, outside the civil community' (2001, p.185).

Cambridge University Public Opinion Project

In 2003 the authors undertook a mixed-method (qualitative/quantitative) examination of punitive public attitudes that we called the Cambridge University Public Opinion Project[2] or CU-POP (see Maruna and King 2004). The CU-POP involved three phases of data collection. The first phase of our research was the most traditional form of gauging public opinion, a postal survey of 940 adult householders living in the southeast of England. The survey contained a newly developed eight-item scale for measuring a general disposition toward the punitive treatment of offenders with items like 'With most offenders, we need to "condemn more and understand less"' and 'My general view towards offenders is that they should be treated harshly' (see King and Maruna 2008, for full scale). Based on these survey responses, we approached 30 of the respondents to take part in a face-to-face qualitative interview. Half of these were chosen because they had very high

---

2   The authors were formerly affiliated with the Institute of Criminology at the University of Cambridge. Both have since left.

scores on our measure of punitiveness toward offenders, and the other half had very low scores on our measure of punitiveness (i.e. were non-punitive), despite having near identical demographic profiles to the punitive group. The research also involved a third component – a small series of random assignment experiments involving attempts to manipulate or change punitive views – however, below, we focus on a few of the findings from the first two waves of data collection as they pertain to the question of 'redeemability'.

In addition to the punitiveness scale measure, respondents to the CU-POP postal survey were asked a series of questions related to variables that are thought to be predictive of punitiveness in the research literature. We included measures of victimisation, fear of crime, as well as numerous demographic factors thought to predict crime. We also included a number of scales tapping into some broader anxieties also thought to be related to punitiveness (see Tyler and Boeckmann 1997) including a two-item measure of 'generational anxiety' (alpha =.76):

1. The behaviour of adolescents today is worse than it was in the past.

2. Young people don't seem to have any respect for anything anymore.

In a series of regression analyses we found that 'generational anxiety' explained far more of the variance in punitiveness than any of the usual demographic or instrumental explanations for the construct. That is, when controlling for factors such as age, education, previous victimisation experiences and self-reported fear of crime, 'generational anxiety' appears to be one of the best predictors of punitiveness (see King and Maruna 2008).

The 'internal logic' in this relationship can be seen most clearly in the qualitative interviews with members of the 'high punitive' sample. One respondent aged 61, for instance, provided the following explanation for his response to the items about young people's behaviour:

> I mean, we was in [town] yesterday and the policemen spoke to a gang of children for firing pea-shooters, told them to simmer down. And he's on his wireless saying, 'Yeah, they've simmered down now.' And while he's saying that they're all firing the pea-shooters at the policeman. So you think to yourself, where do you go from here?

AK: *When you say that, where do you go from here, how do you mean exactly?*

Well, criminals have got to be punished. These children are – a good deal of them – are going to be criminals, aren't they, because they've got no respect now. So the penal system has got to reflect this… And has got to be, not these softer prisons, but they've got to be harder. They've got to know that they've been in prison. They've got to know that, 'Oh dear I don't want to go to prison again'. But unfortunately they say, 'Oh dear, I'm in prison again. Never mind, I'll soon be out. Get my lovely Christmas dinner and choice of menu, etcetera, etcetera.' I just feel that they're pampered. They shouldn't get a choice of menu. I'm not saying that you give them hard tack and water. But basic grub, give them that, that's it. Make them wash up their own things. Make them grow their own stuff. Everything grows out there, they should be self-sufficient. And as regards the question you've not asked: murderers should be hung.

Following previous research on punitive attitudes (e.g. Cullen *et al.* 1985; Grasmick and McGill 1994), we also included a measure of dispositional/situational attributions with items such as 'Crime is a choice – a person's social circumstances aren't to blame' and 'Crime is mostly the product of a person's circumstances and social context' (reverse item: R). In addition, however, we also included a four-item scale measuring individual beliefs in the redeemability of offenders (alpha=.64):

1. Most offenders can go on to lead productive lives with help and hard work.

2. Even the worst young offenders can grow out of criminal behaviour.

3. (R) Most offenders really have little hope of changing for the better.

4. (R) Some offenders are so damaged that they can never lead productive lives.

In a series of regression analyses, both measures (dispositional/situational and belief in redeemability) were strongly related to punitiveness, even controlling for a dozen other variables thought to be related to attitudes about crime (e.g. victimisation experiences, gender, age, education level). Of the two, however, belief in redeemability accounted for far more of the variance in explaining punitiveness (see Maruna and King 2009).

Essentially, we found that it was possible for individuals to hold either positivist and classical views about the nature of criminality and yet still be highly punitive in their beliefs, so long as they also believed that these circumstances leading to crime were non-malleable. In other words, positivists may only be non-punitive so long as individuals still believe that those pushed into criminality by whatever forces can change. Again, the logic of this belief is apparent from the qualitative interviews with members of the 'punitive' group. For instance, a 46-year-old female interviewee gave the following assessment of the ideal criminal penalty:

> What I would like to see is the old type prison where there was bread and water, I just think that [today's prison] is like a holiday camp to them. I don't see it as a deterrent even if they go to prison… I think these people really need to have everything taken away from them. Bring back boot camp.

When asked about her views on the aetiology of offending behaviour, however, the respondent clearly articulated a positivist position linking criminality to early childhood disadvantage:

> R: We've got so many young, unmarried mothers who have children and they swear and you see them walking down the streets…they don't have [children] for the right reasons. …[There are a group of children who live around here] known as the 'evil six'. They just like get into everything. Into every shop, they plague everyone; they're rude to everybody. They'll go straight through a shop and use a toilet or take a handbag or whatever. They constantly plague the town and you know they all come from broken homes or one parent families.

When asked to think of any young people she knows personally who were involved in crime she provided a perfect image of the irredeemability story:

> SM: *Can you think of any [young people in trouble] you know personally?*

> R: Yeah, he's a young boy who is in my son's class. He had a habit of stealing cars before he could drive with his friends and he nearly killed

his self in an accident... But, it don't seem to teach him anything. I don't know if he's out of hospital. His leg was broke, he was in no danger, but he comes from a broken home, he doesn't seem to learn by it.

SM: What would help in his particular situation?

R: When he was a little boy, I think he just wanted his parents to be there for him and they were doing their own thing. He didn't want it to be the way it was like he'd go on holiday with us and he'd end up banging all the food machines. He would from the age of four or five he would just cry and say he didn't want to be like that, but his brothers are like that and he's just fell into that.

SM: Is he trapped do you think? Does he have a chance?

R: I don't think he's got a chance, no. He don't know any different because he's the youngest one of, I think he's got two or three brothers all by different fathers like and I don't think he stands a chance now...I don't think there's any hope for him.

SM: What's the best the system can do in his case?

R: I don't know. I spoke to the ambulance driver that picked him up [after his car crash] and he just wanted to take him in a field and smack him because he's angry with him because we know him. But, I don't know what the system can do for him to be quite honest. I think he is beyond that. He hasn't done – as far as I know he hasn't stole from shops, he just has this fascination with cars. He just wants speed.

Like other interviewees, the respondent was genuinely concerned with the behaviour of the young people she knew, but felt she did not have any solutions for how to deal with them. Even though his criminality has deep social roots (in his early upbringing), at this point she feels that he may be lost to the world, and the only recourse the interviewee could imagine was a punitive one (taking him into a field and smacking him).

Conclusions

There is nothing new about generational anxiety. Indeed, worries about 'young people today' may be a timeless aspect of the ageing process.

Why this is so, is an interesting question. Theory and research on public opinion suggests that 'the young' can become a potent symbol for societies that are anxious about social change and the erosion of shared values and traditions (see esp. Girling, Loader and Sparks 2000; Tyler and Boeckmann 1997). Jock Young (2005), for instance, argues that the moral panics described in Cohen's seminal work *Folk Devils and Moral Panics* (1972) and Hall *et al.*'s *Policing the Crisis* (1978) both involved the viewing of 'major structural and value changes in industrial society as refracted through the *prism of youth*' (Young 2005, p.102, italics added). Young emphasises that in both cases the moral panics were not simply exaggerated fears or prejudices: 'You cannot have a moral panic unless there is something out there morally to panic about, although it may not be the actual object of fear but a displacement of another fear or, more frequently, a mystification of the true threat of the actual object of dismay (ibid.). With the benefit of hindsight, Young argues that the British public in the 1970s 'half sensed' the changes that would soon transform British culture: 'In ten years' time, the music being championed by the young [Mods and Rockers on Brighton Beach and elsewhere] would be mainstream, the austerity and self-discipline of the past regarded not with nostalgia but disdain' (ibid. p.103). Perhaps then, generational anxiety can also be viewed as a kind of barometer for approaching changes in the moral climate or perceptions of an impending unravelling of the fabric of the moral order.

Our research suggests that these concerns become particularly potent, however, when combined with a lack of 'belief in redeemability'. It is one thing to feel the young are out of control, but if one believes that little or nothing can be done to modify such criminality, once it sets in among the young, then this can lead to even more punitive responses. It makes perfect sense, for instance, to support incapacitative practices that would separate those young people from the rest of society (Stroessner and Green 1990). Rehabilitative interventions, of course, make little sense if criminality is a mostly permanent condition of individuals, and public anger about a 'do nothing' judiciary is also justified if the state is failing to contain a permanently deviant population. In short, if this loss of hope for the young is widespread, it may go some way to explaining public acquiescence (indeed, support in some cases) for the highly punitive policies directed at the young described in the introduction. Additionally, if these views about irredeemability are reflected back to young people themselves, they may give up hope that they can change their own lives, which may lead to self-fulfilling (and self-defeating) prophesies that serve to fuel public punitiveness (see Maruna 2001; Maruna *et al.* 2004).

The implications of these findings for those interested in influencing public opinion with regard to young people and the criminal justice system are therefore clear. Our research suggests that punitive attitudes may be driven by the perception that the younger generation is out of control and a lack of belief that they will mature or change for the better. Stories or empirical evidence that contradict these two beliefs, then, may have some impact on changes in such views.

Previous research has suggested that individuals become less punitive when they adopt a more 'positivist' belief system with regard to criminality. The implication of these findings was that individuals should be educated in the many causes of criminality that lie outside of a person's own control (the young person's family situation, upbringing, social circumstances and so forth). This research suggested that the best strategy for changing public views about youth justice was then to play on public sympathies with stories of young people as victims of circumstance who did not choose to grow up poor, be neglected and abused by their families and so forth. Our findings suggest that this strategy has some merit. Those respondents to our study who felt that crime was 'a choice' were indeed more punitive than those who viewed the person's circumstances as being more important. At the same time our findings temper the enthusiasm for the 'spread the positivism' implication. That is, we uncovered a group of lay 'positivists' who held strongly punitive views on the grounds that, even though delinquency may not be a choice, once it begins it is not likely to dissipate. This logically consistent version of positivism holds that we do not choose our fates, but that our fates are basically set in stone from our early origins. Our findings, therefore, would suggest the need to counter this deterministic version of positivism as well as a context-free version of classical criminology that fails to recognise the role of the social environment.

The 'message' is a somewhat complicated one, then: although young people should not necessarily be blamed for getting into crime in the first place (they may have been pushed into it by a variety of circumstances), they do still have the ability to change their lives (presumably with the support and help of the community). It is a message about the malleability of human nature and the ability for individuals to overcome adversity and change their lives. In short, it is a classic notion in redeemability.

Fortunately, the logic of such beliefs is also compelling and deeply rooted into most cultural world views. One of the respondents from the CU-POP research, a 42-year-old female interviewed because her scores placed her among the least punitive respondents to our survey, colourfully articulates this well-known story of the possibility of personal change and growth in the following quote:

> Well you do see kids that are a bit rude hanging around street corners and, you know, breaking in cars, and no respect, the whole, general, it's there. But, to an extent, that always has been. … It's just a bit of peer pressure, I'm assuming. I think, actually that they do grow out of it. I think of my brothers, as teenagers, just hideous, vile kids. … they grew out of it. I also had a nasty cousin…horrible, horrible little boy. Lovely now! So, in the last five years, he's suddenly got a job and he's fantastic. I really thought he was an absolute no-hoper.

These sorts of stories of individuals who may appear to be no-hopers at one point making good in later life may be a necessary counterweight to messages – positivist or classical – of individuals who are permanently 'bad' or fated to criminality.

References

Carroll, J.S., Perkowitz, W.T., Lurigo, A.J. and Weaver, F.M. (1987) 'Sentencing goals, causal attributions, ideology and personality.' *Journal of Personality and Social Psychology 52*, 107–118.

Chiu, C., Dweck, C.S., Tong, J.Y. and Fu, J.H. (1997) 'Implicit theories and conceptions of morality.' *Journal of Personality and Social Psychology 73*, 5, 923–940.

Cohen, S. (1972) *Folk Devils and Moral Panics: The Creation of the Mods and Rockers.* New York: St Martins Press.

Cullen, F., Clark, G., Cullen, J. and Mathers, R. (1985) 'Attribution, salience, and attitudes toward criminal sanctioning.' *Criminal Justice and Behavior 12*, 305–331.

Dweck, C.S. and Leggett, E.L. (1988) 'A social-cognitive approach to motivation and personality.' *Psychological Review 95*, 256–273.

Dweck, C.S., Chiu, C. and Hong, Y. (1995) 'Implicit theories and their role in judgments and reactions: A world from two perspectives.' *Psychological Inquiry 6,* 267–285.

Fletcher, J.F. (1966) *Situation Ethics: The New Morality.* Westminster: John Knox Publishers.

Gaines, S. (2007) 'Children's tsar attacks youth justice policy.' *Guardian,* 15 October. Available at www.guardian.co.uk/society/2007/oct/15/youthjustice.law, accessed 12 March 2009.

Garland, D. (2001) *The Culture of Control: Crime and Social Order in Contemporary Society.* Chicago: University of Chicago Press.

Girling, E., Loader, I. and Sparks, R. (2000) *Crime and Social Change in Middle England.* London: Routledge.

Grasmick, H. and McGill, A. (1994) 'Religion, attribution style, and punitiveness toward juvenile offenders.' *Criminology 32,* 23–46.

Hall, S., Critcher, C., Jefferson, T., Clarke, J. and Roberts, B. (1978) *Policing the Crisis: Mugging, the State, and Law and Order.* Basingstoke: Macmillan Education Ltd.

Heider, F. (1958) *The Psychology of Interpersonal Relations.* New York: Wiley.

Hogarth, J. (1971) *Sentencing as a Human Process.* Toronto: University of Toronto Press.

Jacobs, D. and Carmichael, J.T. (2002) 'The political sociology of the death penalty: A pooled time-series analysis.' *American Sociological Review 67,* 109–131.

Jones, E.E. and Nisbett, R.E. (1971) *The Actor and the Observer: Divergent Perceptions of the Causes of Behavior.* New York: General Learning Press.

King, A. and Maruna, S. (2009) 'Is a Conservative just a liberal who has been mugged?: Exploring the origins of punitive views.' *Punishment and Society 11 ,* 147–169.

Maruna, S. (2001) *Making Good: How Ex-convicts Reform and Rebuild their Lives.* Washington, DC: APA Books.

Maruna, S. and King, A. (2004) 'Public Opinion and Community Penalties.' In A. Bottoms, S. Rex and G. Robinson (eds) *Alternatives to Prison: Options for an Insecure Society.* Cullompton: Willan Publishing.

Maruna, S. and King, A. (2009) 'Once a criminal, always a criminal?: "Redeemability" and the psychology of punitive public attitudes.' *European Journal of Criminal Policy and Research 15,* 1. Avaialble at http://www.springerlink.com/connt/102886/?Content+Status=Accepted (accessed 29 May 2009).

Maruna, S., LeBel, T., Mitchel, N. and Naples, M. (2004) 'Pygmalion in the reintegration process: Desistance from crime through the looking glass.' *Psychology, Crime and Law 10,* 3, 271–281.

Morgan, R. (2008) 'New laws in the making won't keep children out of jail.' *Guardian,* 30 January, p.4 'Society'. Available at www.guardian.co.uk/society/2008/jan/30/youthjustice.rodmorgancomment, accessed 12 March 2009.

Nettler, G. (1959) 'Cruelty, dignity, and determinism.' *American Sociological Review 24,* 375–384.

Pearson, G. (1983) *Hooligan: A History of Respectable Fears.* London: Macmillan.

Pellegrini, R.J., Queirolo, S.S., Monarrez, V.E. and Valenzuela, D.M. (1997) 'Political identification and perceptions of homelessness: Attributed causality and attitudes on public policy.' *Psychological Reports 80*, 1139–1148.

Peterson, C. (2000) 'The future of optimism.' *American Psychologist 55*, 44–55.

Peterson, C., Buchanan, G.M. and Seligman, M.E.P. (1995) 'Explanatory Style: History and Evolution of the Field.' In G.M. Buchanan and M.E.P. Seligman (eds) *Explanatory Style.* Hillsdale, NJ: Erlbaum.

Pratt, J., Brown, D., Brown, M., Hallsworth, S. and Morrison, W. (2005) *The New Punitiveness: Trends, Theories, Perspectives.* Cullompton: Willan.

Rutherford, A. (1992) *Growing Out of Crime: The New Era.* Winchester: Waterside Press.

Sasson, T. (1995) *Crime Talk: How Citizens Construct a Social Problem.* New York: Aldine De Gruyter.

Scheingold, S.A. (1984) *The Politics of Law and Order: Street Crime and Public Policy.* New York: Longman.

Sims, B. (2003) 'The impact of causal attribution on correctional ideology: A national study.' *Criminal Justice Review 28*, 1–25.

Stroessner, S.J. and Green, C.W. (1990) 'Effects of belief in free will or determinism on attitudes toward punishment and locus of control.' *Journal of Social Psychology 130*, 789–799.

Struthers, C.W. and Perry, R.P. (1996) 'Attributional style, attributional retraining, and inoculation against motivational deficits.' *Social Psychology of Education 1*, 171–187.

Templeton, L.J. and Hartnagel, T.F. (2008) 'Causal attributions of crime and the public's punishment goals.' Unpublished paper.

Tyler, T.R. and Boeckmann, R.J. (1997) 'Three strikes and you are out, but why? The psychology of public support for punishing rule breakers.' *Law and Society Review 31*, 237–265.

Van Overwalle, F., Segebarth, K. and Goldchstein, M. (1989) 'Improving performance of freshmen through attributional testimonies from fellow students.' *British Journal of Educational Psychology 59*, 75–85.

Viney, W., Waldman, D. and Barchilon, J. (1982) 'Attitudes toward punishment in relation to belief in free will and determinism.' *Human Relations 35*, 939–949.

Vold, G. (1958) *Theoretical Criminology.* New York: Oxford University Press.

Weiner, B. (1985) 'An attributional theory of achievement motivation and emotion.' *Psychological Review 92*, 548–573.

Weiner, B. and Graham, S. (1999) 'Attribution in Personality Psychology.' In L.A. Pervin and O.P. John (eds) *Handbook of Personality: Theory and Research.* New York and London: The Guilford Press.

Wilson, T.D. and Linville, P.W. (1982) 'Improving the performance of college freshmen: Attributional theory revisited.' *Journal of Personality and Social Psychology 42*, 367–376.

Wilson, T.D. and Linville, P.W. (1985) 'Improving the performance of college freshmen with attributional techniques.' *Journal of Personality and Social Psychology* *49*, 287–293.

Young, J. (2005) 'Moral panics, Margate and Mary Poppins: Mysterious happenings in south coast seaside towns.' *Crime Media Culture 1*, 100–105.

PART TWO

Youth Offending and Youth Justice in Practice

CHAPTER 7

Beyond Risk Assessment: The Return of Repressive Welfarism?

Jo Phoenix

Introduction

This chapter explores some of the issues surrounding the risk assessment of young lawbreakers. The specific case study is one taken from youth justice professionals in England. Although the chapter focuses on assessment as part of a process of disposal, this is not a chapter on sentencing or disposal. Nor is it a chapter about assessment per se. It eschews an analysis of assessment processes, procedures, tools and techniques in favour of an analysis of the more subjective elements that accompany assessment, i.e. the various and multiple ways that youth justice workers come to make sense of the task of assessing young people, of the 'riskiness' that they present, of the disposals that they recommend to the courts and how they operationalise 'risk thinking' in their practice. It does this in order to offer some understanding about the conditions and constraints that shape the work of many youth justice workers and what the possible implications are for youth justice work of giving even greater emphasis to risk assessment in the future. In order to do so, this chapter starts by outlining some of the critical assumptions and arguments that have been made about the delivery of youth 'justice' in regard to young people since New Labour came to power in 1997. Using data collected for a larger project on decision making in youth justice in England, this chapter then argues first that youth justice workers are judicious in how they use governmental tools of risk assessment, often basing their assessment and recommendations on their own professional judgement and explanation of the young people's (past and potential future) lawbreaking. Second, there are 'official' and 'unofficial' risk assessments that shape quite different stories that justice workers can tell about their young charges both to other professionals and to the courts. One story is of young people being derelict in their citizenship duty to manage their own risks carefully; the other is of the state being negligent in its responsibilities to care for vulnerable, excluded and marginalised youth. Finally, when these stories are unpicked, it is clear that a contradiction between welfare and punishment still exists at the heart of risk assessments. However, in using the language of risk, this contradiction is expressed through recommendations for more youth justice interventions. The final section of this chapter argues that there is a potentially paradoxical effect of recognising the welfare needs of many young lawbreakers in a context shaped by risk thinking and managerialist strategies of governance – that is that highlighting the welfare needs of young lawbreakers can, and does, render them *more* not *less* punishable. With that, the future of risk assessment may well be that it ushers in a return to repressive welfarism.

Youth justice in England – the rise of risk and the punitive turn

There is growing consensus among critical writers that the changes to policy in regards to youth justice in England and Wales, subsequent to the Crime and Disorder Act 1998, have displaced contradictions between calls for care or demands to punish young lawbreakers in favour of a managerialist approach which seeks to do little more than 'manage' the problem (whatever that problem is defined as being). Part of this shift has been what several commentators have argued is the extension of punitive social controls over young, socially excluded and politically marginalised individuals (Goldson 1999, 2000, 2002, 2005) which reflect a generalised 'institutionalised intolerance' of young people (Muncie 1999). These changes mirror broader shifts towards punitiveness across criminal justice characteristic of many late modern capitalist societies (Pratt *et al.* 2005) across the globe. Weaving in and out of this consensus is a further assertion that increased levels of media and government demonisation of 'the young' have combined with changes in the governance of crime and of young people in ways that occlude official (or at the very least political) recognition of the wider social, political and material context of youth offending, i.e. poverty, vulnerability, abuse and neglect, educational exclusion and so on (Scraton 2004; Scraton and Haydon 2002). Specifically, it is claimed that a combination of different policy problematics exist which have had the effect of locating 'youth crime' as a major threat to the stability of communities and constructing young offenders *themselves* as being responsible for 'youth crime'. In this way, the general tenor, tone and direction of New Labour's policies initiatives vis-à-vis young lawbreakers in England and Wales has been to move interventions away from welfare provision and towards harsher and harsher punishments and tighter and tighter techniques of criminal justice control of troublesome youths.

However, this is not to say that the move can be described as a more or less simple push to punish young people more (although that may be an *effect*). Rather, these shifts have taken place through and by the rise of actuarial justice and managerialism and the dominance of risk thinking in crime control policies. Taking each in turn, the argument goes that criminal justice systems (including those designed to deal with young lawbreakers) in the UK, USA and other western countries have witnessed a shift away from higher goals – such as rehabilitation of the lawbreaker or retribution exacted – towards a drive to efficiency and effectiveness, defined in terms of managing the 'criminal population', 'the crime problem' and, more importantly, managing crime control agencies. Such management has underpinned changes to the very organisation of the system such that policies now revolve around standardisation of provision and delivery (with an accompanying set of targets for agencies, inter-agency agreements and new monitoring systems of those agencies). Central to the new forms of managerialism are strategies and technologies of risk assessment, risk management and risk reduction. Witness the publication of *The Scaled Approach* (Youth Justice Board 2008) which claims to be the first major overhaul of the 'new youth justice system' in England and Wales since its inception. This approach places risk 'work' at the very centre of youth justice and youth court practice. It claims that the aim of the 'overhaul' is to ensure that the intensity of interventions should match the assessment of risk of the young person in order that their risk of re-offending is reduced. In short, through a package of new targets, new guidelines for practice and a set of new sentences for the court, *A Scaled Approach* highlights the crucial role that should be played by risk assessment in the management and reduction of youthful crime.

The impact of actuarial justice, managerialism and risk thinking has been felt also in Scotland (see McAra 2006). Despite the pronounced differences between the Children's Hearings in Scotland and youth justice in England and Wales, risk and its assessment inflect practice north of the Border just as much as south (ibid.).

In relation to England, and a lesser extent Wales (see Field 2007), much has been made of the deeply contradictory and increasingly hybridised modes of governance of young lawbreakers that such changes have brought about. In particular, it is argued that the policy changes of the last ten years – regardless of their seemingly punitive effects – are not easily categorised, nor come from any necessarily coherent agenda or vision. Hence, Muncie (2006) draws attention to a range of rationalities and technologies of governance shaping youth justice policy in England and Wales today. He outlines the effect of neo-liberal modalities of governance which are achieved through the technologies of responsibilisation and risk management (see also Garland 2001). These modalities ensure that responsibility for youth crime and youth crime control is devolved to the local community, the family and the individual at the same time that central government retains its authority to make local authorities and communities accountable for any failure. They also create the conditions for the obsessive focus on risk, its assessment and its prevention that pervades current policy and provision. Muncie further highlights a set of rationalities for governance that cohere around neo-con-servative remoralisation of youth crime. Here in contrast, it is assumed that a *strong* central government has responsibility for targeting 'troublesome' communities, families and individuals for surveillance, monitoring and regulation in the name of protecting 'innocent' communities, families and individuals. Finally, Muncie details the various strategies by which the governance of wider (non-lawbreaking) populations is progressively achieved more and more through the governance of 'youth and disorder' (see also Simon 2007 and Rodger 2008). In the context of this chapter the importance of Muncie's analysis of the contemporary contours of youth justice governance in England and Wales is in showing the contested nature of youth justice policy and practice. More recently still, the move to bring youth justice into line with other childcare policy initiatives such as *Every Child Matters* (Department for Education and Skills 2003) means that now, more than any other time in history, 'it is increasingly difficult to prioritize any one of these modes of governance as ascendant or as above contestation, or indeed as acting in isolation from another' (Muncie 2006, p.788).

Other commentaries on wider criminal justice reforms also argue that criminal (and youth) justice practice is complex and inherently volatile. Kemshall (2003) notes many of the policy shifts are not always translated into practice in kind because practitioners *mediate* the policies in the process of implementing them. In this way, Kemshall recognises that however punitive the effects of the rise of risk thinking and the drive to make individuals, families and communities responsible for 'the crime problem' and 'crime', operational managers and practitioners nevertheless interpret and put into action the policies in the face of limited resources, pre-existing or well-established professional ideologies, local partnership arrangements and so on. To put it another way, managers and practitioners do not simply enact policy shifts, they make sense of them and adapt the policies in the process of implementation. The manner in which they do this is fundamentally shaped by the context that they inhabit (see also Kemshall 2008). In a similar vein Hughes (2007) and Hughes and Edwards (2002) argue that *any* attempt to govern through crime control is marked by profound instabilities which are 'caused' by both the limits or constraints experienced by those involved in doing criminal justice work and the very hybrid nature of contemporary crime governance. Hughes (2007) argues that analyses that assume that governmental rationalities are more or less 'coherent' over-simplify (if not occlude) the social processes of putting policy into practice. In the field of youth justice a host of recent empirical studies have confirmed what Kemshall (2003 and 2008), Hughes (2007) and Muncie (2006) have all indicated at the theoretical level: there are profound disjunctures between policy and practice. These studies attest to the way that the contradictions shaping youth (and criminal) justice also create spaces for practitioners to resist, subvert, challenge or accommodate changing policies (and governance). In short, at the empirical level, there is growing evidence that the subjective aims pursued by the key actors in youth justice practice are as complex, contradictory, contested, ambivalent and ambiguous as the policies themselves (Baker 2005; Eadie and Canton 2002; Field 2007; Kemshall 2008; Souhami 2007).

In a context where risk and responsibilisation are such key themes in youth crime governance, this chapter analyses how youth justice practitioners come to make sense of risk, its assessment and the utility of basing recommendations on it. In examining how these practitioners operationalised risk thinking in practice, the chapter raises some fundamental questions about, first, the assumption that there is a one-to-one referentiality between policy and guidelines and practice in regards to risk assessment and, second and more importantly, what it might mean to base recommendations for disposals on 'risk assessment'.

The data used here are a subset of data that comes from a larger study of decision making in regards to risk and need in youth justice. The aims of that study were to analyse and investigate the social, political and ideological conditions in which youth justice practitioners, including lay magistrates, Youth Offending Team (YOT) workers, police and solicitors assessed the risks and needs of and made decisions or recommendations about young lawbreakers and to describe and analyse the engagement (or not) of young people in those processes. The research project used a case study methodology conducted in a semi-rural English local authority (Haverset) which has one YOT and a youth court which sat one day per week. Eighty-seven open and semi-structured interviews were conducted with 36 young lawbreakers who at the time were being supervised by Haverset youth offending team and 51 people who made up those ordinarily responsible for the delivery of youth justice in Haverset. This included the entire YOT (excluding sessional workers), the full youth court panel of magistrates, a small sample of police officers tasked with operational or strategic responsibilities for youth crime in Haverset and a small sample of solicitors who all regularly appeared within the youth court. The interview data was supplemented with six months of ethnographic observation in Haverset youth court and the analysis of 40 current case files. The data used within this article is the data generated from interviews with the Youth Offending Team of Haverset.

Assessment – implementing and using standardised tools?

Part and parcel of the rise of risk thinking and of managerialism in the delivery of youth justice has been the development of tools of assessment (i.e. ASSET) which are supposedly there to guide and standardise the work of youth offending team workers throughout the jurisdictions that have adopted them. ASSET and other allied tools of assessment work through measuring individual young people against a set of personal and social factors which are seen as creating the conditions in which offending is more likely (or in the case of protective factors, less likely). In principle, when completed, these tools of assessment provide the practitioner with both an indication of how likely the individual is to re-offend and an evidential base that helps inform the professionals in their judgements. Although the Youth Justice Board and Scottish Government claim that the introduction of risk assessment tools are key in developing targeted, effective and efficient interventions with young people, critical commentators have located them as being intimately interconnected with neo-liberal modalities of governance that dematerialise youthful lawbreaking by individualising 'risk' (i.e. transforming social and collective 'risks' into individual ones) and responsibilising individual young people. So, for instance, Kemshall (2008) argues that what shapes tools like ASSET is not necessarily any 'evidence' about the links between risk factors and offending, but rather a blame laden discourse that presumes that 'right-minded' active citizens (regardless of their age) are prudential in managing their own risk behaviours. Fundamental to this discourse is the notion of entitlement to citizenship rights (including welfare and other social provisions) as based on *active* management of those risk behaviours. Importantly, when an individual is judged and found wanting in regards to how they manage their own risks, the state is thereby able to enforce its demand for citizenship responsibility (i.e. by making young people blameworthy and therefore suitable for punishment) whilst abrogating its own responsibility for ensuring basic standards of welfare provision. Here, Kemshall (2008) is pointing towards how something as seemingly benign as a standardised tool for risk assessment underpins asymmetrical citizenship in ways that permit greater and more biting use of punishments and other state interventions against the marginalised, excluded and poor (see also Carlen 1996).

What the preceding analysis establishes is the fundamental and crucial role that is played by the task of risk assessment – regardless of the specific tool that is used. It forms the basis of the shifts in youth governance that have been outlined in the beginning of this chapter and justifies the abrogation of the state's responsibilities towards its excluded and marginalised youth. Given that previous research also indicates that youth justice workers and others involved in the task of assessment are not 'policy dupes' or 'zombies' who mechanistically apply the tools, a question is begged about how practitioners (in this case YOT workers) make sense of the task of assessment and how this links with the explanations about youthful lawbreaking *and* the recommendations they make to agencies such as the court. In what follows I trace some of the ways that the YOT workers I interviewed talked about the structured tools of assessment, assessment more generally and the links between assessment and recommendations for intervention.

(Not) using ASSET

The small group of YOT workers that were interviewed discussed many of the problems that they encountered with ASSET in ways that indicated – contrary to policy assumptions – that ASSET was marginal to how professionals formed their view of the riskiness of young people. In general, these YOT workers discussed ASSET as being a 'meaningless', 'paperwork heavy' system of assessment that did not permit a 'truly professional assessment' of young people's risks and needs and offered little or no help when piecing together an explanation for youthful lawbreaking. Many of the YOT workers interviewed discussed basing their assessments on 'getting to know the young people and their families'. For these YOT workers completing or using ASSET was seen as an unnecessary use of YOT time:

> It's another piece of paperwork that you tend to put in your pile of paperwork to do when you've got the space to do the paperwork. In the meantime, you'll get on and you'll write your report and you'll do your ASSET when you're reminded by admin that ASSET has not been done yet. (YOT interview, no. 16)

In other cases the YOT interviewees talked about ASSET as an unhelpful and at times problematic tool in assessing young people:

> It's [i.e. ASSET] wrote by a computer, and formulated by a computer
> and, you know, it doesn't make sense, you know, you've got to read it
> and you think if I don't understand it how the hell can a young person
> understand what I'm saying. (YOT interview, no. 12)

Against this backdrop, there was a more specific feeling of scepticism about
ASSET. For some, the process of using ASSET was seen as distorting their
professional judgements about why young people offended or what they
needed (Pitts 2001):

> To be totally honest I would say it's a complete waste of time...if you're
> a good person you get nought, so obviously you wouldn't be a client,
> and if you are totally, you know, falling off, sitting on the edge of the
> cliff, you're a 4. (YOT interview, no. 15)

Subjective assessments and making sense of young people's lives

In the face of this scepticism about the structured tools of assessment, the
youth justice interviewees talked about the process of assessing risk as being
able to get to know and understand their young charges in order to explain
why they offended and what they needed. So more than half of the YOT
workers made comments about the incongruity between the supposedly
objective task of assessing using ASSET and the reality that 'everyone knows'
– that the task of assessment is subjective (see also Baker 2005):

> I think it needs to be subjective but also I think that because of that, you
> need to make allowances for that, and you can't, I think that you have to
> leave a bit of room for professional judgement, whatever the ASSET
> says. (YOT interview, no. 1)

When asked about how they made their assessments many of these same
YOT workers talked about 'get[ting] up close and personal', seeing 'where
the young person was at' and 'figur[ing] them out' in a holistic fashion: 'if
you've got to know them very well and you've seen everybody that's
interested or has any involvement with the family, then your assessment is a
breeze, you know' (YOT interview, no. 15); 'I spend my life going around,

building up a complete picture of a young person's life' (YOT interview, no. 4).

Having said that, although these YOT workers were judicious in their use of ASSET, they nevertheless also explained young people's lawbreaking using the same sort of logic that underpins the tools – i.e. notions of the actively risk-managing prudential citizen and, by extension, the reckless and therefore blameworthy citizen. For them, one of the major explanations for youthful lawbreaking was that such behaviours were the result of individual-istic pathological (or at the very least incorrect) responses to one's immediate environment. Put another way, the type and nature of young people's social circumstances *might* be considered as part of both the assessment of any young person's future riskiness and the explanation for their past offending only in as much as it formed the *context* for young people's 'faulty' reasoning. For many of these youth justice interviewees, young people's poverty of choices and other wider material conditions were not seen as that relevant. So, for instance, one YOT worker discussed the question of leisure pursuits and the boredom experienced by some of his charges:

> A lot of the kids say they're bored, they've got nothing to do, and I mean I appreciate that kids these days can't go out the same as when I was young [laughs]. We could go out for the whole day and wander and do whatever. I mean these days they can't, they have more restrictions put on them just because from a safety aspect as much as anything else… But as far as needs go, as far as what's been provided for them, I don't actually think that there is a lack of provision frankly…I think there's an awful lot of opportunities, more so than there ever was really, so I don't accept this being bored theory. (YOT interview, no. 18)

It is noteworthy that the majority of young lawbreakers coming under the supervision of this YOT came from areas of Haverset in which the local parks had disappeared (usually in the face of building new housing estates or shopping areas), where there were no local sports or leisure centres, where local youth centres had long since closed and where young people were banned from playing ball games in open areas. In this way, no matter how judicious their implementation and use of the standardised tools of assessment might be, these youth justice interviewees based their assessments of the riskiness of young people on the explanations that they created –

explanations which at least in part were shaped by notions of *individual* responsibility and/or pathology in regards to 'correct' personal risk management.

Young people's 'at riskiness' and the balancing act of YOT work

It has long been noted that there is a conceptual conflation between 'risk' and 'need' that resides at the heart of contemporary risk thinking, in relation to explanations of offending and the risk factor prevention paradigm, risk assessment, management and reduction. Specifically, it has been noted that social and material 'need' tend to be translated into or are fused onto the concept of 'criminogenic risk' (see Armstrong 2004; Goldson 2000, 2002, 2005; Hudson 2003; Smith 2003, 2006). In such a context one might expect to see youth justice workers using the categories of risk and need interchangeably. However, the YOT interviewees did not do this. Instead of assessing young people's 'risk', 'needs', 'criminogenic risks', 'vulnerability' or 'protective factors', they talked about assessing young people's 'at riskiness'. So although there was a widespread acceptance of the notion that welfare needs were also risk factors (i.e. being excluded from school or living in unsuitable accommodation were seen as both something for which a welfare-based response was required and a possible risk factor in future offending or an explanation of previous lawbreaking), the way in which these YOT workers constituted this risk/need nexus was *not* one where 'risk' necessarily meant risk of *offending*. Rather young people were just 'at risk' more generally and this generalised notion became the concept of risk that YOT workers used when making recommendations or when explaining young people's offending. In short, YOT workers used the notion of 'at riskiness' to justify (or 'evidence') a claim for greater YOT intervention, both to help young people 'address their offending behaviour' *and* support them through difficulties. Such conflation of risk and need into a more generalised notion of 'at riskiness' also meant that the YOT interviewees saw their own role as balancing the competing demands between dealing with offending and caring for young people or, to put it another way, between law enforcement and supporting the 'vulnerability' of young people:

> ...if you're talking from an intervention point of view, they do need to take responsibility because [YOT workers] can't work with [young

people] unless they don't [take responsibility]. But you have to balance that with, not excusing their behaviour but giving them a package of intervention and support that enables them to move away from the problems in their lives. (YOT interview, no. 8)

Whilst YOT *work* may have been discussed as a balancing act, individual YOT interviewees often talked about *themselves* as law enforcers. This was especially the case for those YOT workers who were newly qualified or had not been social work trained:

So I try to start really clearly from the beginning [with my young people], actually using words like we're a law enforcement agency, because we are. But we're here to nurture in a way, and it can be a real personal journey for some staff, I think, this over-identification with a vulnerable young person. (YOT interview, no. 13)

And, for many of these newly qualified YOT workers, the fundamental distinction between them and other social care workers was that 'we've always got the ace card of breaching them if they don't comply' (YOT interview, no. 14). For those other YOT interviewees who previously had been social workers or social work trained, there was a great deal of reticence expressed about vocalising their child welfare or child protection concerns over and above their explanations or assessments of young people as offenders:

Trickier is the conflict with my Social Services' responsibilities and understandings ... [It] makes it quite hard to maintain the balance of credibility that people [i.e. other YOT workers and the court] didn't feel, 'oh, so she's Social Services, she's taking that line'. You know, 'soft old social worker'. You know, 'dyed-in-the-wool do-gooder [laughter] who doesn't understand what mayhem these young people are creating for the ordinary people trying to live here.' (YOT interview, no. 17)

The implications are this: whilst individual youth justice workers may well use a generalised notion of at riskiness in their assessments and explanations of young people, they expressed some concern about how to translate those assessments into recommendations or decisions. For the accusation of being too closely allied to social work was understood as calling into question a

YOT worker's professionalism. Many individual YOT workers aligned themselves, at least rhetorically, with law enforcement whilst simultaneously recognising the difficulties experienced by many of the young people. In this respect, the 'balancing act' that they talked about was not just an effort to balance an understanding of the young person as *both* risky *and* needy, but also an effort to balance themselves, their professional reputations and their work between two competing, contradictory forces (i.e. the demand that they act as law enforcers and the acknowledgment of wider welfare and child protections concerns regarding any specific young person). When making recommendations, this often meant that the wider welfare concerns were either seen as not relevant or, as will be seen in the next section, became a reason for greater criminal justice interventions:

> A young man who's got an eating disorder, very vulnerable, very unloved, looked after for many years, back with mother, and would totally touch people's buttons. [*And by that you mean get them to be overprotective*] Totally. 'Oh it doesn't matter, don't bother reporting, I'll come to you', and we got to a point that I would constantly be saying to people in supervision or team meetings, in a constructive way initially, 'this can't happen'. And then having to be really quite, 'no'. The YOT manager had to get involved with one of them who I didn't supervise and actually say 'you cannot have contact with this young person'. (YOT interview, no. 13)

YOT work as 'plugging the gaps'

Yet there is another risk assessment that the youth justice interviewees talked explicitly about. It is an 'unofficial' assessment not based on the notion of a prudential risk-managing citizen or on the notion of a blameworthy, incorrect thinking one. Instead, it was based on the notion of the state's abrogation of its responsibilities towards young marginalised individuals. Here, YOT interviewees discussed at length the many and different ways that social provision for young people had systematically let them down and left them vulnerable to offending. Most of the YOT workers interviewed talked about the aggregate effect of gaps in wider social provisions which created a raft of unmet needs for the young people and which also operated to push young people into less than law-abiding behaviour. They spelt out the deleterious impact of a lack of educational services for young people unable to conform to the disciplines of traditional mainstream schooling, social services funding crises, a dearth of appropriate housing for those aged 16–18 years old who are not able to live at home, mental health services for young people stretched to the breaking point and inadequate services to help young people deal with drug or alcohol misuse issues. In this assessment, young people's offending is explained by reference to their unmet needs which are the result of a less than responsible state that does little or nothing about gaps in service provision. Of course, such explanations for young people's lawbreaking are not new. Professional recognition of the state's lack of care long predates the changes to youth justice witnessed in the last ten years (Taylor, Lacey and Bracken 1980). But, in the context of the rise of risk thinking and of managerialism, this recognition finds a particular type of expression in the way that youth justice workers make recommendations to the court and other professionals. For this alternative assessment of risk is one in which youth justice work is seen as 'plugging the gaps':

> It gets to a certain level where they [the young people] have got the capacity to start taking responsibility for their own actions, but whether their ability to make changes in their lives is virtually nil... So we're [the YOT] stuck really. Sometimes all they need is social pastoral help rather than being prosecuted. (YOT interview, no. 3)

The rest of this chapter focuses on what YOT workers had to say about the reports they wrote for the court and the recommendations contained therein. YOT assessments about the risks and/or needs of young people, as well as YOT workers' unofficial stories of the risks posed *to* young people, formed the basis of their recommendations to the court – or so it would seem. In the next section I trace the various ways that YOT workers discussed their court responsibilities.

Assessing risk: reports and recommendations for the court

All the YOT workers who were interviewed for this project agreed on one point – that pre-sentence and specific sentence reports (PSRs and SSRs) and any recommendations they made to the court had to be 'evidence-based', by which they mean that the recommendation had to contain a rational, seeming objective, explanatory justification for making the recommendation that was made. For these YOT workers, 'evidence' in a court report meant not introducing aspects of the young person's life for which there was no intervention, or recommending interventions which did not directly link to the elements of a young person's life which were highlighted as explaining their lawbreaking: 'We're not there to represent the defendant. We're not there to make mitigation for them because that's their solicitor's job. We're there to represent the situation, to represent the person, the crime in the context of this person's life' (YOT interview, no. 2).

Here, YOT interviewees talked about the usefulness of ASSET and other tools of assessment. ASSET (or its categories) became a means by which YOT workers could 'sell' the recommendation to the court:

> We need to constantly be looking at what the court needs. I mean the PSR is the document that is our business plan basically, so what we can offer to keep this person in the community. (YOT interview, no. 13)

Of course the perceived need to 'sell' the recommendation to the court occurs within a context in which the YOT workers knew that their court performance was judged by the degree of congruence between recommendation and eventual sentencing. In this way, most of the YOT interviewees talked about there being no space to include in the reports their own unofficial explanation of a young person that highlights systematic failures of responsibility by state agencies, if only because they saw that in a court context recommendations need to be 'useful' *to the court*, i.e. not raise issues over which the court could do little or nothing. The best that many of the YOT interviewees felt they could do was 'balance the picture' given to the bench of the young person:

> You're looking for, not reasons to get them off, but you're looking for things to balance out the picture. So, when somebody looks at the offence they don't just see 'oh, he started it', they see a picture... And you're looking for all these different things, and obviously in the offence analysis you look at the positive reasons, look at the reasons why this happened. You know that when he was sober he's fine. His offences occurred because of peer pressure. He's with a group of mates,

he's got this reputation for big hard man. … It's about evidence. It's not just, it is my professional opinion but it has to be backed with evidence…because if the Prosecutor went 'I don't agree with that', I need to be able to say 'well, he's low risk because he's never done it before, he's since got himself a full time job or he's moving out of the area, his dad takes him to work every day, blah blah blah blah blah'. (YOT interview, no. 1)

Repressive welfarism twenty-first century style

With an almost unanimous voice the YOT interviewees linked their unofficial assessment of risk to the recommendation for greater (not less) YOT involvement. An assessment of a young person as being at 'high risk' by the state's abrogation of its citizenship responsibilities towards young people created a justification for YOT workers to make a recommendation that the young person become fully engaged and work with the YOT. In this way, the 'risks' posed *to* young people by the dearth of welfare services could be offset. Put another way, punishment and increased criminalisation was seen as a form of welfarism:

> Now this is all additional work that we're taking on that Social Services haven't touched. We've got numerous cases where young people are really in crisis and actually shouldn't be where they are, you know. At least he got help from us! (YOT interview, no. 16)

There were two clear expressions of idea that welfare can be provided through youth (criminal) justice interventions. The first is the way that incarceration was seen by some of the YOT workers as providing young people with safety and security, or at the very least a means by which they can access a sense of community, companionship and respite:

> To some degree…they're actually safer in there than they actually are in their own road, or in their own house…safer from a lot of things… You know, serving a three month sentence for whatever and going to whatever prison, 'actually I'll be all right because [you'll] be in there too, and we can have chat about things'. (YOT interview, no. 15)

The second is how 'taking responsibility' for offending was located as liberating – even in a context where the social, material and political conditions of young people's lawbreaking is recognised and acknowledged:

> I think it's being able to take charge of their own lives. In my mind responsibility is a really good powerful thing. I think it's empowering... Whereas if you make it clear that, okay, we're not saying that your life's not shit, but what we are saying is you have choices, and we'll support you with those choices. ... Unfortunately we can't always give adequate support, that's the frustrating bit. (YOT interview, no. 16)

Conclusions

The preceding analysis raises some important general questions about policy reform and specific questions about what it means, in the current context, to create policies that place 'risk assessment' at the centre of recommendations (to the court) and interventions about and with young people. It raises a theoretical question about the role of the professional in implementing policy changes. As indicated in the opening sections of this chapter, this is a question that many others are also asking and one which takes on new importance given that the general direction of policy has had pronounced punitive effects in England and Wales witnessed by the high rates of child incarceration. Can practitioners 'resist' the direction and tenor of central governmental policy? The first conclusion to this chapter is that the preceding analysis indicates that there is a gap between official (i.e. state sanctioned) constructions of 'risk' as per the structured tools of assessment and professional (i.e. youth justice workers) assessments of risk. The above analysis further demonstrates that the process of identifying young people's 'riskiness' and making recommendations to the court has as much to do with the explanations that youth justice workers create about the young person's (past and potential future) lawbreaking as it always did. But, in the current context, the preceding analysis also shows that practitioners' efforts to introduce assessments of youthful lawbreaking which highlight service gaps may have unintended consequences. The language of risk and the assumptions contained within it prohibit youth justice workers from expressing their own (professional) assessments about the dearth of services for young people into any meaningful recommendation apart from criminal justice interventions. As a result, and perhaps a second conclusion that can be drawn, the language of risk and the tools at the disposal of youth justice workers in England and Wales have meant that many workers have not found ways to displace, transform or re-package young lawbreakers as anything other than suitable subjects of *criminal justice responses* albeit for non-criminal justice ends. In other words, what managerialism and risk thinking provides is the language, tools and strategies by which many 'needy' young people are rendered 'punishable' (often in the name of welfarism and usually because youth justice workers *do* recognise the state's abrogation of its responsibilities). At the risk of repetition, the paradoxical effect of current techniques, strategies and tools of risk assessment is that in the course of assessment, the very recognition of the lack of appropriate state responses to young people vis-à-vis welfare and childcare creates the conditions in which more punitive (and especially penal) responses become justified. With that, the final shift in dealing with young lawbreakers in jurisdictions that place supposedly objective 'risk assessments' at the centre of practice may well be a return to repressive welfarism, not in the name of the best interests of the child, but as a means to hold the state responsible for its obligations to vulnerable, marginalised and excluded young citizens.

References

Armstrong, D. (2004) 'A risky business? Research, policy and governmentality and youth offending.' *Youth Justice 4*, 2, 100–116.

Baker, K. (2005) 'Assessment in youth justice: Professional discretion and the use of ASSET.' *Youth Justice 2*, 5, 106–122.

Carlen, P. (1996) *Jigsaw: A Political Criminology of Youth Homelessness.* Buckingham: Open University Press.

Department for Education and Skills (2003) *Every Child Matters.* Green Paper, London: Stationery Office. Available at: www.dfes.gov.uk/everychildmatters, accessed 13 March 2009.

Eadie, T. and Canton, R. (2002) 'Practising in a context of ambivalence: The challenge for youth justice workers.' *Youth Justice 1*, 2, 14–26.

Field, S. (2007) 'Practice cultures and the "new" youth justice in (England and) Wales.' *British Journal of Criminology 47*, 2, 311–330.

Garland, D. (2001) *The Culture of Control.* Oxford: Oxford University Press.

Goldson, B. (1999) 'Youth (In)Justice: Contemporary Developments in Policy and Practice.' In B. Goldson (ed.) *Youth Justice: Contemporary Policy and Practice.* Aldershot: Ashgate.

Goldson, G. (2000) '"Children in need" or "young offenders"? Hardening ideology, organizational change and new challenges for social work with children in trouble.' *Child and Family Social Work 5*, 255–265.

Goldson, G. (2002) 'New Labour, social justice and children: Political calculation and the deserving–undeserving schism.' *British Journal of Social Work 32*, 683–695.

Goldson, G. (2005) 'Taking Liberties: Policy and the Punitive Turn.' In H. Hendrick (ed.) *Children and Social Policy: An Essential Reader*. Bristol: Policy Press.

Hudson, B. (2003) *Justice in the Risk Society*. London: Sage.

Hughes, G. (2007) *The Politics of Crime and Community*. Basingstoke: Palgrave Macmillan.

Hughes, G. and Edwards, A. (2002) *Crime Control and Community: The New Politics of Public Safety*. Cullompton: Willan Publishing.

Kemshall, H. (2003) *Understanding Risk in Criminal Justice*. Buckingham: Open University Press.

Kemshall, H. (2008) 'Risks, rights and justice: Understanding and responding to youth risk.' *Youth Justice 8*, 1, 21–37.

McAra, L. (2006) 'Welfare in Crisis: Key Developments in Scottish Youth Justice.' In J. Muncie and B. Goldson (eds) *Comparative Youth Justice*. London: Sage.

Muncie, J. (1999) 'Youth justice: Institutionalized intolerance: Youth justice and the 1998 Criminal Justice Act.' *Critical Social Policy 19*, 2, 147–175.

Muncie, J. (2006) 'Governing young people: Coherence and contradiction in contemporary youth justice.' *Critical Social Policy 26*, 4, 770–793.

Pitts, J. (2001) 'Korrectional karaoke: New Labour and the zombification of youth justice.' *Youth Justice 2*, 1, 3–16.

Pratt, J., Brown, D., Hallsworth, S., Brown, M. and Morrison, W. (eds) (2005) *The New Punitiveness: Trends, Theories, Perspectives*. Cullompton: Willan Publishing.

Rodger, J. (2008) *Criminalising Social Policy: Anti-social Behaviour and Welfare in a De-civilised Society*. Cullompton: Willan Publishing.

Scraton, P. (2004) 'Streets of terror: Marginalization and criminalization, and authoritarian renewal.' *Social Justice 31*, 1–2, 130–157.

Scraton, P. and Haydon, D. (2002) 'Challenging the Criminalization of Children and Young People: Securing a Rights Based Agenda.' In J. Muncie, G. Hughes and E. McLaughlin (eds) *Youth Justice: Critical Readings*. London: Sage.

Simon, J. (2007) *Governing through Crime*. Oxford: Oxford University Press.

Smith, R. (2003) *Youth Justice: Ideas, Policy and Practice*. Cullompton: Willan.

Smith, R. (2006) 'Actuarialism and Early Intervention in Contemporary Youth Justice.' In B. Goldson and J. Muncie (eds) *Youth Crime and Justice: Critical Issues*. London: Sage.

Souhami, A. (2007) *Transforming Youth Justice: Occupational Identity and Cultural Change*. Cullompton: Willan Publishing.

Taylor, L., Lacey, R. and Bracken, D. (1980) *In Whose Best Interests? The Unjust Treatment of Children in Courts and Institutions*. Nottingham: Russell Press Limited.

Youth Justice Board (2008) *Youth Justice: A Scaled Approach*. London: Youth Justice Board for England and Wales. Available at: www.yjb.gov.uk/scaledapproach, accessed 13 March 2009.

CHAPTER 8

Supervising Young Offenders: What Works and What's Right?

Fergus McNeill

Introduction

Recently, in connection with an ongoing research project exploring Scottish probation history,[1] I met a man in his mid-50s who had been on probation in the late 1960s when he was in his mid and late teens. We talked about how he got into trouble, in his case mostly street disorder and fighting at first, how he ended up on probation and what he made of the experience. Admittedly with the benefit of 40 years' hindsight, his analysis of his experience was as sharp as his memory of it. At first he had welcomed probation as an opportunity to talk to someone who might be able to help him make sense of a life that seemed to be spiralling out of control. He liked his probation officer – appreciating the interest that he showed, particularly in coming to see the young man play football – and valued the support that he provided. There was no sudden insight or miracle cure, however.

Though he stayed on probation for a few years, the prospects that it might turn his life around, prevent the ensuing escalation of his offending towards serious and violent crime, and spare him years in prison, were dealt a

---

1   This ongoing study – 'Oral Histories of Probation in Scotland' – is funded by the British Academy.

fatal blow, in his account, by one particular incident. As he recalled it, about 12 to 18 months into his probation order, he was arrested for a minor crime. His probation officer, perhaps somewhat exasperated at this setback (it being one of many), agreed with the magistrate that a short custodial remand might teach him a lesson. Although the probation officer subsequently provided a positive report and the young man avoided a custodial sentence, he regarded his probation officer's role in the remand as nothing less than a betrayal. Someone he had looked up to as a big brother who was trying to steer him right had, as he saw it, turned on him and fed him to the wolves. Their relationship never recovered and the distrust that the incident provoked soured all of his subsequent relationships with probation officers and social workers; and continues to affect his attitude to the 'helping professions' to this day. A couple of years later the probation officer visited him in prison, apparently to apologise; but his embittered former charge was in no mood for forgiveness.

What does this story have to say to debates about the effectiveness of community supervision and why do I tell it here in a chapter about interventions with young people? First, as a matter of historical record, probation in Scotland between the 1930s and the 1960s was mainly concerned with the supervision of juvenile offenders (McNeill 2005; McNeill and Whyte 2007), so this is a story about the practices which are my concern in this chapter. Second, though this may be an old story, its cadences echo through contemporary debates. Although we can characterise much of the recent debate about the effectiveness of community supervision as a debate about 'what works?', I want to argue here that both academic research and practice experience are pushing us towards the question of 'what's right?' – or at least towards the interfaces between debates about *technical* effectiveness and questions around the *moral* purposes and content of the supervision process and the complex relationships through which it is enacted. For this reason, in this chapter I plan to review some of the evidence about the effectiveness of community supervision before revisiting the by now familiar debates about 'what works' with a particular focus on exploring some of the affective and relational dimensions of supervision. In the final section I aim to open up the discussion by sketching out some links between these affective and relational aspects of supervision and the developing literature around legitimacy, compliance and criminal justice. Here we might find some of the keys that unlock the relationships between effect and affect in supervision. The fact that much of the literature to which I refer is principally concerned with community penalties for adults partly reflects my own interests and experience, but I will try to argue that debates emerging in that arena have relevance for youth justice too; indeed I will argue that it is both paradoxical and indefensible that the kinds of insights emerging around the supervision of adult offenders have not yet permeated debates about youth justice practice, where the rights claims of children and young people who have offended should command particular attention.

The effectiveness of community supervision

In this section I aim to explore the nature of community supervision and its effectiveness in general, before looking more specifically at some recent attempts to reform the legal processes and contexts of supervision and to alter its content and focus, specifically by linking supervision with surveillance.

Community supervision and its effectiveness in general

The supervision within the community of children and young people who have committed criminal offences necessarily takes different legal forms in different jurisdictions. In England and Wales, for example, youth courts can select action plan orders, reparation orders and drug treatment and testing orders, as well as the supervision order itself. Under sections 63–68 of the Powers of Criminal Courts (Sentencing) Act 2000, supervision orders of up to three years' duration can be imposed on children and young people at the point of conviction; the order can only be imposed where the offending is 'serious enough' to require such a measure – the restriction of liberty involved must be commensurate with the seriousness of the offence and the order must be the most suitable method available for the young person. The main effect of the order is to place the child or young person under supervision (provided by a local authority, a probation officer or a member of a multi-agency youth offending team) in respect of which the supervisor is obliged to 'advise, assist and befriend' the supervisee. In addition to the standard conditions of supervision orders (retaining contact with the supervising officer and complying with instructions), a wide range of additional conditions can also be imposed by the courts (see Morgan, Chapter 4, this volume; Nacro 2002).

In Scotland supervision orders may involve similar conditions and forms of intervention to England and Wales. The principal difference, however, is that they are located within a Children's Hearings system in which, in theory at least, the welfare of the child is paramount and no order should be imposed that is not beneficial *to the child* (Children (Scotland) Act 1995, section 16).[2] Crucially, the latter principle requires a parsimonious approach to intervention, but this is not a parsimony linked to proportionate punishment because the system is not concerned with the punishment of crime. Rather, the parsimony relates to the least intrusive intervention that can adequately meet the child's needs.[3] The arrangements in Northern Ireland are significantly different again (see www.youthjusticeagencyni.gov.uk/youth_justice _system).

It is of course notoriously difficult to assess the effectiveness of community supervision. In relation to adults undergoing community penalties, these difficulties have been effectively analysed by Farrall (2003a, 2003b) amongst others, and the methodological concerns that he raises are equally relevant to supervision within youth justice systems, at least to the extent that these systems are concerned with the reduction of reoffending. Farrall argues that evaluation methodologies have relied too much on official records of dubious veracity, often at the expense of collecting data from those subject to supervision, that they have neglected the complexity of the processes through which supervision *might* exercise some influence, and that they have neglected how supervision might interact with the social and personal contexts in which it is embedded.

Leaving these significant broader methodological issues aside for a moment, there are numerous technical problems with the common reliance

2   Children's Hearings are welfare tribunals headed by lay people from the local community. Children can be brought before a Hearing because they are beyond the control of parents, are being exposed to moral danger, are likely to suffer unnecessarily or suffer serious impairment to health or development through lack of parental care, are the victim of a sex or cruelty offence, are failing to attend school regularly, are misusing drugs, alcohol or solvents, or have committed an offence. If the Hearing thinks compulsory measures of supervision are appropriate, it will impose a supervision requirement, which may be renewed until the child becomes 18.

3   Section 16(5) of the Children (Scotland) Act 1995 does allow for 'derogation' from the paramountcy principle (i.e. that the child's best interests should be the paramount concern in decision making) 'for the purpose of protecting members of the public from serious harm (whether or not physical harm)'.

on reconviction data as a measure of the effectiveness of community supervision and of other sanctions. These problems include but are not limited to: the problem of 'pseudo-reconvictions' (that is, those convictions which follow the disposal in question but relate to offences committed *before* its imposition and therefore over which it could exercise no influence); questions of how to accommodate consideration of the nature, seriousness and frequency of any reconvictions; difficulties in determining the 'correct' timescales for analysing reconviction and, most fundamentally, the insuperable problem that re*conviction* data measure only the justice system's *response* to detected, reported and prosecuted offending and not to actual changes in the behaviour of offenders. The weight of criminological research suggests that this is, in fact, a very serious and double-edged problem. On the one hand, we know that relatively few offences lead to conviction. In Scotland in 2004–5 less than 13 per cent of recorded crimes and offences led to convictions and, of course, many other crimes and offences will never have come to the attention of the police (Scottish Executive 2006). On the other hand, we also know that the process of criminalisation of youthful offenders (through which some acts come to be sanctioned through the law and others do not) is a very uneven one and that, more particularly, 'known offenders' (and those from more socio-economically disadvantaged areas) are more heavily policed than the general population and therefore disproportionately vulnerable to further criminalisation and penalisation (McAra and McVie 2005). These are not minor methodological inconveniences; they call into question not just studies that seek to compare the efficacy of sanctions by comparing reconviction rates, but also much of the literature on 'what works' in which reconviction, despite its flaws, has tended to be the preferred measure of treatment effectiveness (McNeill 2009).

Notwithstanding these difficulties, a study of the effectiveness of community interventions with young people in England and Wales (Jennings 2003) concluded that such measures had delivered a fall in predicted reconvictions within 12 months of reprimand, warning or conviction of 22 per cent when measured against an 'adjusted predicted' reconviction rate. However, leaving aside the specific methodological limitations of this study noted by some commentators (Bateman and Pitts 2005; Bottoms and Dignan 2004), the largest improvements were associated with reprimands and final warnings. By contrast, orders (primarily supervision orders) aimed at young people involved in more persistent offending achieved at best marginal effects in terms of reduced reconviction; a finding that the Audit Commission (2004) underlined. A similar problem in tackling persistent offending was apparent in Feilzer *et al.*'s (2004) evaluation of 23 cognitive behavioural programmes in youth justice. Only 47 per cent of children and young people referred completed the programmes and 71 per cent of 'completers' re-offended within 12 months. Feilzer *et al.* (2004) concluded that 'methodological shortcomings' made it impossible to assess the independent effectiveness of the programmes in reducing offending.

Although the relative dearth of evaluative studies makes it difficult to reach reliable conclusions about the effectiveness of the Children's Hearings System in tackling youth offending, some studies undertaken in the late 1990s exposed certain problems including: a lack of clarity about decision making, substantial 'drift', and a failure to prevent escalation in the offending of a small group of typically older boys and young men at high risk of progression to the adult courts and thence to custody (often at the age of 16 in Scotland) (Hallett *et al.* 1998; Waterhouse *et al.* 2000). Despite such problems, however, there is some emerging evidence that interventions within the Hearings system can, in some circumstances at least, deliver encouraging reductions in youth offending. For example, the positive evaluation of the Freagarrach Project (which provides intensive supervision for young people involved in persistent offending) implies that such success could be achieved within the Hearings system, at least where the right kind of services were provided for children and young people (Lobley, Smith and Stern 2001; Lobley and Smith 2007).

Reforming supervision's contexts and processes[4]

It was partly to explore the capacity of the Hearings system to adequately respond to persistent offending that a Fast-Track Hearings pilot was introduced in a number of sites in early 2003, specifically targeting persistent offenders under 16. Fast Track Hearings were distinguished from any other type of Children's Hearing by the speed with which referrals were processed

---

4   A more detailed account of the developments discussed in this section of the chapter is
       provided in McNeill (forthcoming).

as well as by their focus on more comprehensive assessments including risk assessment, on provision of appropriate programmes and on reduced re-offending rates. An evaluation of the pilot showed that, in most respects, Fast Track was largely meeting its objectives, in that the findings were positive with regard to reduced timescales and other aspects such as assessment and action plans (Hill *et al.* 2005, p.25). However, the evidence about the impact of the initiative on offending was mixed. For the 228 Fast Track referrals processed during the first 12 months of the pilot, the number of offences committed in the first 6 months following referral dropped by over 500 (23 per cent). However, data from comparison sites where the specific procedures and resources associated with the Fast Track pilot did not apply, revealed even better apparent performance. Thus, whereas for young people in the Fast Track sites the mean number of offences committed fell from 9.1 to 7.5 (N=167), in the comparator sites the mean number of offences dropped from 10.7 to 5 (N=56). Put another way, the percentage of young people reducing offending ranged from 50 to 82 per cent in the pilot sites, but from 70 to 91 per cent in the comparison sites.

In discussing these apparently perplexing findings, Hill *et al.* (2007) are quick to note the limitations of the data, in particular rueing the fact that the Scottish Executive did not fund a self-report study of re-offending. They also note that the level of business changed significantly in the pilot and comparison sites during the study; thus, although pilot and comparison sites had similar levels of offence referrals prior to the initiative, offence referrals subsequently rose in the pilot sites by 42 per cent, but by only 8 per cent in the comparison sites. As a result, despite the additional resources provided for the initiative, *less* money was spent per case in the Fast Track sites than in the comparison sites. Hill *et al.* (2007, p.134) speculate that the success of the comparison areas might be explained partly by 'an emphasis on early intervention, the cumulative benefits of falling numbers of "difficult" cases allowing more to be spent per case and perhaps a better balance of direct work as opposed to assessment and report writing' (the latter being prioritised in Fast Track procedures).

Despite their own hesitancy about the real import of their study, Hill *et al.* also note that:

the Scottish Executive regarded the data on offending, despite its limitations, as conclusive. This suggested that the additional resources had not produced the desired reductions compared with elsewhere in Scotland, so 'Fast Track' was not rolled out nationally as had been intended. Instead the Executive decided to concentrate on seeking improvements in decision making and services by means of imposing National Standards. Interestingly, at about the same time, the review of the Children's Hearings that had been prompted by critical comments produced a largely positive report committed to the centrality of the child's welfare, while also recognizing the need for changes. (2007, p.135)

It is interesting and instructive, perhaps even salutary, to compare the response to the largely positive but inconclusive Fast Track evaluation with the response to the evaluation of the pilot Youth Courts. Despite overall falling youth crime rates, and despite the opportunity of sending 16 and 17-years-olds through the Hearing System, the Scottish Executive opted to pilot a court-based approach and (re)introduced a designated Youth Court for 16 and 17-year-old persistent offenders in June 2003. This initiative was proposed as a means of 'easing the transition between the youth justice and adult justice system', and for increasing public confidence in Scotland's system of youth justice. Initially established as a two-year pilot in one Sheriff Court, a second pilot Youth Court was incepted, even though the level of referrals to the Youth Court were far less than anticipated and despite the fact that the final evaluation of the first site was yet to be published (McIvor *et al.* 2006; Piacentini and Walters 2006).[5]

This development met with much criticism, not least because the processing in adult courts of persistent 16 and 17-year-olds represented a stark deviation from a 'child centred' and needs-oriented state apparatus for dealing with young offenders to one based on deeds and individual responsibility (Piacentini and Walters 2006). The objectives of the Youth Court centred on reducing the frequency and seriousness of re-offending by 16 and 17-year-old offenders, particularly persistent offenders (and some 15-year-olds); promoting the social inclusion, citizenship and personal

---

5   The feasibility study estimated that around 600 cases would be referred in a year; there were 147 referrals involving 120 young people in the first six months of the pilot.

responsibility of these young offenders whilst maximising their potential; establishing fast track procedures for those young persons appearing before the Youth Court; enhancing community safety by reducing the harm caused to individual victims of crime and providing respite to those communities which experience high levels of crime; and testing the viability and usefulness of the Youth Court model (Youth Court Feasibility Project Group 2002).

The Youth Court possesses the same powers of sentencing as the adult summary court and deals with cases referred on a persistence criterion (defined as 'at least three separate incidents of alleged offending in the previous six months' (including the current charge) – notably a lesser standard than that used in the Fast Track Hearings) or on 'contextual criteria', used as an indication of risk, and which lead the police and/or the Procurator Fiscal to believe that the offender is vulnerable to progress to more serious offending which would diminish community safety. The evaluations by McIvor *et al.* (2004, 2006) showed that, in reality, almost twice as many offenders were referred to the Youth Court on 'contextual' grounds than on the grounds that they were persistent offenders.

Somewhat like the Fast Track Hearings, Youth Court processes and practices focused on meeting targets that were set to try to ensure that cases are processed more quickly; in the majority of cases, alleged offenders made their first appearance in court within ten days of the date that the crime was committed. 'Rolling-up' of pre-existing charges allowed offenders to be dealt with simultaneously for all alleged crimes committed in the same period. Designated sheriffs shared the work in the Youth Courts and oversaw the offender's performance during supervision, allowing for sentences to be amended as necessary. There was a wide range of services and 'dedicated programmes' for offenders available including offending reduction programmes, addictions services, alcohol and drug awareness family group conferences and restorative justice services; these services are provided by a range of service providers through local authority social work departments.

Piacentini and Walters (2006), who were members of the team that conducted the evaluation, in a highly critical article that draws primarily on the views of sentencers and young people, reach the conclusion that the Youth Court embodies 'double bind' justice (taken from Muncie 2004, p.214) where young people in need of support become subject to fast-track punishment, supervision and increased regulation. They argue that the range of interventions and programmes at the disposal of the Youth Court are testimony to how the parameters of correction become entwined with inclusion norms that are delivered by authorities of expertise (p.49). They raise a series of concerns about 'violations of children's rights, due process, increased use of detention and net widening...[and] a seriously flawed process premised on actuarial justice' (p.55).

Though the Youth Courts made extensive use of community sanctions, if these sanctions did indeed, as Piacentini and Walters (2006) feared, represent 'up-tariffing', this raises possible concerns about consistency, proportionality in sentencing and increased risks of default. Unfortunately, the key questions about net-widening and up-tariffing were not questions that the evaluation could answer directly. Precisely because the Youth Courts deal with higher-tariff *persistent* offenders, one would expect the patterns of disposals imposed to differ from those imposed on *all* young offenders in adult courts. Moreover, one would expect the patterns of disposal to differ in precisely the manner that they do – higher tariff offenders would be expected to attract more sentences involving supervision and greater use of custody. Popham *et al.* (2005) note that, in the Hamilton Sheriff Court, comparing the overall sentencing patterns in relation to 16 and 17-year-olds dealt with on summary procedures in 2002 (prior to the Youth Court) and in 2004 reveals no significant differences in sentencing patterns. So, although the Hamilton Youth Court may be more interventionist (perhaps even more correctionalist) than the adult courts, this may be an artefact of differences in the nature of its business caused by the referral criteria.[6]

In political terms, one of the lessons of the Fast Track Hearings evaluation was that the Executive was principally concerned with reconviction data. In this regard, the Youth Court pilot fared comparatively well; despite the fact that the target group was persistent offenders and that fast-tracking would increase the likelihood of their speedy reconviction, rates of reconviction within six months for young offenders appearing at the Youth Court were (at 16 per cent) lower than those at comparison adult summary

6   Notably, the early evidence from the Airdrie Youth Court pilot (where the persistence criteria were not used) (Barnsdale *et al.* 2005) was that it used custody significantly less than the adult summary court in relation to 15–17-year-olds, though this was probably because, in that site, the Youth Court processed a higher proportion of young first offenders than the adult court.

courts (at 21–26 per cent). In the Executive's rush to laud the success of their flagship initiative, the research team's caution about the limitations of this data (in terms of short follow-up and relatively low numbers) were ignored – just as in the case of the negative findings from the Fast Track evaluation.

Supervision and surveillance

Though Fast Track Hearings and Youth Courts represent systemic efforts to enhance the effectiveness of youth justice, it is a moot point whether or not they represent innovation in terms of the *form and content* as opposed to the *context and process* of supervision. With regard to supervision's form and content, one of the most significant recent developments in the community-based supervision of young people in the UK jurisdictions has been the provision of more intensive forms of supervision, sometimes involving electronic monitoring (see Morgan, Chapter 4, this volume). Thus, in England and Wales, Intensive Supervision and Surveillance Programmes (ISSPs) can now be deployed as part of a supervision order where a young person meets certain (non-statutory) eligibility criteria relating to persistence; these include having been charged, warned or convicted of offences committed on four or more separate occasions in the preceding 12 months and having received at least one previous community sentence or custodial penalty, or being at risk of custody because the current charge is so serious that an adult could be sentenced to 14 years imprisonment or more. As the name suggests, such programmes combine intensive supervision and *surveillance* either by tracking, tagging, voice verification or intelligence led policing (Moore 2005; Nellis 2004). In Scotland, Intensive Support and Monitoring Services (ISMSs) were introduced under the Anti-Social Behaviour (Scotland) Act 2004 and have been piloted in seven areas. ISMS combine Movement Restriction Conditions (MRCs) with intensive support and are intended to provide an alternative to secure care, to be part of a reintegration plan following secure care, or to be a measure for dealing with breach of an anti-social behaviour order.

Based on his experience of evaluating ISSPs in England and Wales (Moore *et al.* 2004, 2006), Moore (2008) concludes that intensive community programmes have experienced varying degrees of success. While well-targeted programmes with a strong rehabilitative component can have a positive impact on re-offending, a range of difficulties remain. These include problems in defining persistence and identifying 'high risk' offenders; associated issues in relation to labelling of young people; exposing young people to ever more demanding and controlling forms of intervention, and political enthusiasm for the surveillant aspects of ISSPs that run ahead of the evidence of their effectiveness. On this last point, it is interesting to note that a recently published evaluation of the Scottish ISMS (Boyle 2008), admittedly affected by a range of methodological limitations, reaches the conclusion that ISMS represent a qualified success, but stresses that most stakeholders (including those young people subject to them) attributed their effectiveness to the intensive *support* provided, and were much more equivocal about the value of the monitoring element.

Intensive supervision programmes are particularly relevant to this discussion because their blending of rehabilitative approaches focused on *supporting change* with more direct measures of *external control or constraint* renders more explicit the familiar care and control tension that is present in any form of community supervision whether in youth justice or adult criminal justice. In the next section, through a brief analysis of some of the emerging themes within the literature about promoting change in and with offenders (so as to reduce their offending *and* improve the quality of their lives), I aim to suggest how this tension might impact – for better and worse – on the effectiveness of community supervision.

The affective dimensions of community supervision

The question of the effectiveness of community supervision in general (or of the effectiveness of particular sanctions) is somewhat different from the question of the effectiveness of particular practice methods and approaches. Until very recently, most discussions of what kinds of methods and approaches to intervention work best in reducing reconviction have had little to say about the affective, emotional and relational aspects of intervention. Rather 'what works?' is presented as a technical question, the empirical resolution of which directs us to a set of practical principles that, it is argued, should underpin interventions. In very brief summary, these principles suggest that the intensity of the intervention should match the level of assessed risk of re-offending (the risk principle); that the focus of intervention should be on those 'criminogenic needs' that are directly correlated with offending (the criminogenic needs principle) and that the methods used should be responsive to the learning styles of offenders (the responsivity principle) (Andrews and Bonta 2003).

I do not intend to rehearse here the by now familiar debates about whether the application of these principles is a *necessary* component of offender rehabilitation (for useful reviews see McNeill 2009; Ward and Maruna 2007), nor to engage with the considerable literature on the problems that have emerged in the UK in translating them into practice (see Raynor 2004, 2008). For present purposes, it is more important to ask, even if these principles are necessary, whether they represent *sufficient* conditions for the effective and ethical supervision of offenders – whether of young people or adults.

The answer to this question is an increasingly clear and unequivocal 'no', even from the advocates of 'what works?', or more specifically, the Risk-Needs-Responsivity (RNR) model. It is possible to identify at least four key limitations of the 'what works?' approach,[7] at least in so far as it has been implemented in and through accredited programmes in the UK – and to some extent in other jurisdictions (see McNeill 2009). First, it has become clear that the success of such programmes depends to a significant extent on their success in securing widespread organisational support; there are myriad ways in which a hostile organisational or professional environment can undermine or diminish the impact of programmes (Raynor 2004). These problems are not limited to what some might see as problems of professional resistance – arguably greater problems are created by managerialised implementation of programmes that place performance targets ahead of professional delibera-tions about the appropriate targeting and sensitive delivery of such interven-tions (Raynor 2008). Second, the professional skills and personal qualities of those delivering the programmes (and providing the wider support and supervision within which they are or should be embedded) turn out to be critical factors in their success (Dowden and Andrews 2004; McNeill *et al.*

---

7   I am conscious in writing this that to speak on 'the "what works?" approach' is to over-simplify and homogenise the range of programmes, strategies and approaches that have been or could be associated with 'what works?' generally and with the RNR model more specifically, Necessarily, I am painting with a broad brush here.

2005). Third, just as programmes need to be embedded in supportive organi-sational and professional contexts, so it transpires that for those undergoing such interventions, the wider familial and social contexts within which their learning is situated matter a great deal to the success of the enterprise (Farrall 2002; McNeill *et al.* 2005). It is not a simple thing to transfer programme learning into the 'lived realities' of offenders' lives and communities. Fourth, the extent to which offenders are or can be motivated to change is highly significant to the likely success of programmes – yet programmes in the UK have been least good at retaining those offenders who seem to need them most (Burnett and Roberts 2004).

Developing recognition of these deficits in prevailing approaches to in-tervention owes much, in the UK at least, to the emergence and impact of recent research on desistance from crime (Farrall 2002; Maruna 2001; Rex 1999) – though some similar lessons have been emerging from within the 'what works' movement itself and from the broader literature on the effective-ness of psycho-social interventions in many settings (see McNeill *et al.* 2005). Reviewing the relevance of desistance research – which is concerned not with 'what works?' but with how and why people stop offending – and specifically with its implications for supervision in the community is beyond the scope of this chapter (see McNeill 2006a, 2006b, 2009), but there are some central arguments which shed significant light on the limited successes of 'what works?' approaches to date.

First, desistance is an inherently individualised and subjective process, so intervention approaches need to be able to accommodate and exploit issues of identity and diversity. The types of one-size-fits-all interventions too often associated with misinterpretations and over-simplified applications of 'what works?' will not work where they fail to recognise the heterogeneity and complexity of desistance processes. Second, the development and maintenance not just of motivation but also of hope emerge as key tasks for supervisors, partly because desistance turns out to be characterised by ambivalence and vacillation but also to be encouraged by hopefulness. Third, desistance can only be understood and supported within the context of human relationships; not just relationships between supervisors and offenders (though these matter a great deal) but also between offenders and those who matter to them. Young people often conceptualise relationships as a primary source of the distress they experience (Armstrong, Hill and Secker

1998) *and* as a key resource in the alleviation of their difficulties (Hill 1999). More specifically, we know that the relational experiences of most young people involved in offending are characterised by disconnection and violation (Liddle and Solanki 2002; McNeill and Batchelor 2002). So approaches that are insensitive to the relational contexts of change unavoidably limit their potential impact. Fourth, although 'what works?' approaches require and commend a focus on offenders' risk and needs, they tend to neglect offenders' strengths and the personal and social resources that they can use to overcome obstacles to desistance. There is some evidence that young people's own resources and social networks are often better at resolving their difficulties than social services' personnel (Hill 1999). More broadly, 'resilience perspectives' underline the part that protective factors and processes play in positive development, even in spite of adversity. In terms of practice with young people, such perspectives entail an emphasis on the recognition, exploitation and development of their competences, resources, skills and assets (Schoon and Bynner 2003). Interventions need to support and develop these capacities. Fifth, desistance seems to be about discovering agency or the capacity to govern and direct one's own life, so interventions need to encourage and respect self-determination; this implies working *with* offenders not *on* them. Finally, interventions based only on human capital (meaning the resources that reside *within* individuals) will not be enough. Supervision needs to involve work on offenders' and communities' social capital (meaning the resources that reside in relationships and social networks) (see McNeill and Whyte 2007).

I hope that it is by now becoming clear that how people *feel* about their situations, relationships, behaviours, supervisors and experiences of supervision are bound to be highly significant influences on the outcomes of supervision. As long ago as 1964 (three years before the supervision experiences of the former probationer whose story opened this chapter), casework theorists were articulating the crucial links between capacity, opportunity and motivation in our experiences of change (Ripple, Alexander and Polemis 1964). They argued that in order for change to occur, all three features need to be present: people need to have or to acquire the capacity to be different or to act differently; they also need to have or to acquire access to opportunities, and they need to be motivated or to get motivated to change. In terms of the practice of supervision, these three preconditions entail three roles or tasks for supervisors: they need to be educators who can develop and deploy human capital; they need to be advocates who develop and deploy social capital, and they need to be counsellors who can develop and deploy motivation. Crucially, in relation to motivation, it has been argued that 'what works?' approaches that focus too narrowly on tackling risk factors and correcting capacity 'deficits' within offenders, while neglecting the relationships that matter to them and the realities of their lives, run the risk of failing to motivate offenders, and even of playing an unwitting part in producing defiance and dangerousness (see Barry, Chapter 5, this volume; Ward and Maruna 2007).

Conclusions: legitimacy, justice and injustice

In the preceding discussion I have tried to problematise and explore the evidence about the effectiveness of community supervision, and to critically engage with debates about 'what works?' in interventions with young and adult offenders. My arguments suggest that misreading the evidence both about supervision and about 'what works?' can produce too managerialised, reductionist and de-contextualised a version of supervision, but in this concluding discussion I want to briefly link these arguments to normative rather than technical questions about youth justice policy and practice.

Several commentators have suggested that 'what works?' approaches have been at worst complicit with correctionalism and at best vulnerable to cooptation to it (Goldson 2001; McNeill 2006b; Muncie 2002; Robinson 2001). By correctionalism, I mean an approach to youth justice policy and practice that narrowly emphasises constructions of individual responsibility and parental accountability for the behaviour of children and young people, entailing a concomitant policy and practice focus on correcting personal and/or parental 'deficits' (Goldson and Jamieson 2002; see also Barry in Chapter 5, Morgan in Chapter 4 and Phoenix in Chapter 7, this volume). This is problematic not just because it is myopic and muddle-headed about how and why youthful offending comes about, but because of the way that it constructs young offenders (and sometimes their parent or parents) as objects on which supervision operates in the interests of crime reduction, rather than as subjects with whom youth justice workers should engage in their interests *and* in the interests of their communities. This objectification of offenders as the raw material on which so-called 'justice' processes operate in the interests of others (usually cast as 'the law-abiding majority') is arguably much more pronounced in the adult system, at least in some jurisdictions (see Garland 2001; McCulloch and McNeill 2007). Nonetheless, it is at least a potential threat (and some contributors to this volume would suggest already a reality) in systems defined by crime-reducing objectives as opposed to concerns of welfare and/or justice for children and young people.

Yet as we have seen in this chapter, the evidence suggests that, ironically perhaps, in order to promote desistance (and thus reduce crime) it seems that it is necessary to treat people and engage with people in particular ways; ways that turn out to be characterised by certain fundamentally moral virtues or values. Thus I have argued elsewhere, in connection with adult probation, that supporting desistance requires supervisors to demonstrate optimism, hopefulness, patience, persistence, fairness, respectfulness, trustworthiness, loyalty, wisdom, compassion, flexibility and sensitivity (to difference), for example (McNeill 2006a). More specifically, as Tyler's (1990) increasingly influential work on procedural justice suggests, it requires the authority of the supervisor to be exercised in ways that are perceived to be legitimate by the person being supervised – at least if offenders are to be *persuaded* to comply with supervision and with the law (see Bottoms 2001; Robinson and McNeill 2008).

But of course, getting people to sign up to and abide by the 'social contract' – of living by society's rules in return for receiving the many benefits of social life – depends on the credibility of that contract in both prudential and moral terms. In other words, signing up is likely only where people anticipate benefits for themselves and where they are convinced that the deal will be administered fairly and without favour. Yet the experiences of personal and social violation and injustice that too often characterise the lives of young offenders fundamentally damage that credibility – and to then proceed to make demands that they accept their 'responsibilities' when their rights have rarely been respected is to invite resentment and disengagement. In the context of social injustice, the demand that offenders comply with their own responsibilisation, so common in contemporary policy and practice discourse, simply lacks legitimacy. But any acknowledgement of this legitimacy deficit is cursorily dismissed as making excuses for offenders.

Nonetheless, as many penal philosophers have recognised, the existence of social injustice and, in consequence, the denial of the rights of citizenship to some, creates serious moral problems for the punishing polity – problems that are particularly acute in youth justice contexts because of the peculiar rights and protections that children must be afforded. In order for criminal or youth justice to make sense and retain moral credibility, the response to injustice therefore must be 'a genuine and visible attempt to remedy the injustices and exclusion that they [that is, some offenders] have suffered' (Duff 2003, p.194). Duff (p.194) suggests that this implies that:

> [T]he probation officer…will now have to help the offender negotiate his relationship with the polity against which he has offended, but by whom he has been treated unjustly and disrespectfully: she must speak for the polity to the offender in terms that are censorious but also apologetic – terms that seek both to bring him to recognize the wrong he has done and to express an apologetic recognition of the injustice he has suffered: *and she must speak to the polity for the offender,* explaining what is due to him as well as what is due for him (emphasis added). (ibid.)

To put it in simple terms, if it is *the* objective – or even *an* objective – of the youth justice system to reduce re-offending, then for both moral reasons and practical purposes it transpires that the system must also be about remedying injustice and doing right by those whom society has so often failed. In some respects it seems deeply regrettable that it is necessary to develop these empirical arguments about the wider social benefits of doing right by young people in trouble. No doubt it would be better if such obligations were recognised as arising from children's and young people's rights. But, sadly, in the contemporary context of demonisation of young people and insecurity about youth crime and disorder, it is equally necessary to make explicit how technical arguments about effectiveness connect with moral questions about legitimacy and social justice. That 'what works?' and 'what's right?' turn out to be so irretrievably intertwined perhaps offers us some potential protection from the worst excesses of punitiveness.

By way of illustration it seems fitting to end by returning to the story of the probationer with which this chapter began. In 1967 he was a young person who had experienced significant social and familial adversity and who wanted help to understand what was going wrong in his life. An opportunity for change at that stage was lost at least in part because the probation officer resorted to a 'short sharp shock' strategy that the young man construed as an injustice and a betrayal – another violation, another abandonment – and from a source that he was learning to trust. The probation officer's moral legitimacy was lost and with it his prospect of exercising positive influence. But the damage was both deeper and broader than that. More than 40 years later, the ex-probationer summed up the enduring effect on his attitude to social work agencies and the like:

> Now I am still very bitter towards them… That prevents me from encouraging anybody to get involved with them… Because I always thought people like that could help me. And I feel as if they let me down.

References

Andrews, D. and Bonta, J. (2003) *The Psychology of Criminal Conduct,* 3rd edn. Cincinnati, Ohio: Anderson Publishing.

Armstrong, C., Hill, M. and Secker, J. (1998) *Listening to Children.* London: Mental Health Foundation.

Audit Commission (2004) *Youth Justice 2004: A Review of the Reformed Youth Justice System.* London: Audit Commission.

Barnsdale, L., MacRae, R., McIvor, G., Brown, A., Eley, S, Malloch, M., Murray, C., Popham, F., Piacentini, L. and Walters, R. (2005) *Evaluation of the Airdrie Sheriff Youth Court Pilot.* Edinburgh: Scottish Government.

Bateman, T. and Pitts, J. (2005) 'Conclusion: What the Evidence Tells Us.' In T. Bateman and J. Pitts (eds) *The RHP Companion to Youth Justice.* Lyme Regis: Russell House Publishing.

Bottoms, A. (2001) 'Compliance and Community Penalties.' In A.E. Bottoms, L. Gelsthorpe and S. Rex (eds) *Community Penalties: Change and Challenges.* Cullompton: Willan Publishing.

Bottoms, A. and Dignan, J. (2004) *Youth Crime and Youth Justice: Comparative and Cross-national Perspectives.* Chicago, University of Chicago Press.

Boyle, J. (2008) *Evaluation of Intensive Support and Monitoring Services (ISMS) within the Children's Hearings System.* Edinburgh: Scottish Government.

Burnett, R. and Roberts, C. (eds) (2004) *What Works in Probation and Youth Justice: Developing evidence-based practice.* Cullompton: Willan Publishing.

Dowden, C. and Andrews, D. (2004) 'The importance of staff practice in delivering effective correctional treatment: A meta-analytic review of core correctional practice.' *International Journal of Offender Therapy and Comparative Criminology 48,* 2, 203–214.

Duff, A. (2003) 'Probation, punishment and restorative justice: Should al truism be engaged in punishment?' *Howard Journal 42*, 1, 181–197.

Farrall, S. (2002) *Rethinking What Works with Offenders: Probation, Social Context and Desistance from Crime*. Cullompton: Willan Publishing.

Farrall (2003a) 'J'accuse: Probation evaluation research epistemologies. Part one: The critique.' *Criminology and Criminal Justice 3*, 2, 161–179.

Farrall (2003b) 'J'accuse: Probation evaluation research epistemologies. Part two: This time its personal and social factors.' *Criminology and Criminal Justice 3*, 3, 249–268.

Feilzer, M. with Appleton, C., Roberts, C. and Hoyle, C. (2004) *The National Evaluation of the Youth Justice Board's Cognitive Behaviour Projects*. London: Youth Justice Board for England and Wales.

Garland, D. (2001) *The Culture of Control: Crime and Social Order in Contemporary Society*. Oxford: Oxford University Press.

Goldson, B. (2001) 'A rational youth justice? Some critical reflections on the research, policy and practice relation.' *Probation Journal 48*, 2, 76–85.

Goldson, B. and Jamieson, J. (2002) 'Youth crime, the "parenting deficit" and state intervention: A contextual critique.' *Youth Justice 2*, 2, 82–99.

Hallett, C. and Murray, C. with Jamieson, J. and Veitch, B. (1998) *The Evaluation of Children's Hearings in Scotland. Volume 1: Deciding in Children's Interests*. Edinburgh: Scottish Office Central Research Unit.

Hill, M. (1999) 'What's the problem? Who can help? The perspectives of children and young people on their well-being and on helping professionals.' *Journal of Social Work Practice 13*, 2, 135–145.

Hill, M., Walker, M., Moodie, K., Wallace, B., Bannister, J., Khan, F., McIvor, G. and Kendrick, A. (2005) *Fast Track Children's Hearings Pilot*. Edinburgh: Scottish Executive.

Hill, M., Walker, M., Moodie, K., Wallace, B., Bannister, J., Khan, F., McIvor, G. and Kendrick, A. (2007) 'More haste, less speed? An evaluation of Fast Track policies to tackle persistent youth offending in Scotland.' *Youth Justice 7*, 2, 121–138.

Jennings, D. (2003) *One Year Juvenile Reconviction Rates: First Quarter of 2001 Cohort. On Line Report 18/3*. London: Home Office.

Liddle, M. and Solanki, A. (2002) *Persistent Young Offenders*. London: Nacro.

Lobley, D. and Smith, D. (2007) *Persistent Young Offenders: An Evaluation of Two Projects*. Aldershot: Ashgate.

Lobley, D., Smith, D. and Stern, C. (2001) *Freagarrach: an Evaluation of a Project for Persistent Juvenile Offenders*. Edinburgh: Scottish Executive.

McAra, L. and McVie, S. (2005) 'The usual suspects? Street life, young people and the police.' *Criminology and Criminal Justice 5*, 1, 5–36.

McCulloch, T. and McNeill, F. (2007) 'Consumer society, commodification and offender management.' *Criminology and Criminal Justice 7*, 3, 223–242.

McIvor, G., Malloch, M., Brown, A., Murray, C., Eley, S., Piacentini, L. and Walters, R. (2004) *The Hamilton Sheriff Youth Court Pilot: The First Six Months*. Edinburgh: Scottish Executive Social Research.

McIvor, G., Barnsdale, L., MacRae, R., Dunlop, S., Brown, A., Eley, S., Malloch, M., Murray, C., Murray, L., Piacentini, L., Popham, F. and Walters, R. (2006) *Evaluation of the Airdrie and Hamilton Youth Court Pilots.* Edinburgh: Scottish Executive Social Research.

McNeill, F. (2005) 'Remembering probation in Scotland.' *Probation Journal 52*, 1, 25–40.

McNeill, F. (2006a) 'A desistance paradigm for offender management.' *Criminology and Criminal Justice 6*, 1, 39–62.

McNeill, F. (2006b) 'Community Supervision: Context and Relationships Matter.' In B. Goldson and J. Muncie (eds) *Youth Crime and Justice.* London: Sage.

McNeill, F. (2009) *Towards Effective Practice in Offender Supervision.* Glasgow: Scottish Centre for Crime and Justice Research. Available at www.sccjr.ac.uk/pubs/Towards-Effective-Practice-in-Offender-Supervision/79, accessed 13 March 2009.

McNeill, F. (forthcoming) 'Youth Justice: Policy, Research and Evidence.' In J. Johnstone and M. Burman (eds) (forthcoming) *Youth Justice in Scotland.* Edinburgh: Dunedin Academic Press.

McNeill, F. and Batchelor, S. (2002) 'Chaos, containment and change: Responding to persistent offending by young people.' *Youth Justice 2*, 1, 27–43.

McNeill, F., Batchelor, S., Burnett, R. and Knox, J. (2005) *21st Century Social Work. Reducing Re-offending: Key Practice Skills.* Edinburgh: Scottish Executive.

McNeill, F. and Whyte, B. (2007) *Reducing Reoffending: Social Work and Community Justice in Scotland.* Cullompton: Willan Publishing.

Maruna, S. (2001) *Making Good.* Washington, DC: American Psychological Association.

Moore, R. (2005) 'The use of electronic and human surveillance in a multi-modal programme.' *Youth Justice 5*, 1, 17–32.

Moore, R. (2008) 'Intensive Supervision and Surveillance Programme (ISSP).' In B. Goldson (2008) *Dictionary of Youth Justice.* Cullompton: Willan Publishing.

Moore, R., Gray, E., Roberts, C., Merrington, S., Waters, I., Fernandez, R., Hayward, G. and Rogers, R.D. (2004) *National Evaluation of the Intensive Supervision and Surveillance Programme: Interim Report to the Youth Justice Board.* London: Youth Justice Board for England and Wales.

Moore, R., Gray, E., Roberts, C., Taylor, E. and Merrington, S. (2006) *Managing Persistent and Serious Offenders in the Community: Intensive Community Programmes in Theory and Practice.* Cullompton: Willan Publishing.

Muncie, J. (2002) 'Policy transfers and "what works": Some reflections on comparative youth justice.' *Youth Justice 1*, 3, 27–35.

Muncie, J. (2004) *Youth and Crime*, 2nd edn. London: Sage.

Nacro (2002) *Youth Crime Briefing: Supervision Orders – An Overview.* London: Nacro.

Nellis, M. (2004) 'The "tracking" controversy: The roots of mentoring and electronic monitoring.' *Youth Justice 4*, 2, 77–99.

Piacentini, L. and Walters, R. (2006) 'The politicization of youth crime in Scotland and the rise of the "Burberry Court".' *Youth Justice 6*, 1, 43–59.

Popham, F., McIvor, G., Brown, A., Eley, S., Malloch, M., Murray, C., Piacentini, L. and Walters, R. (2005) *Evaluation of the Hamilton Sheriff Youth Court Pilot 2003–2005*. Edinburgh: Scottish Executive.

Raynor, P. (2004) 'Rehabilitative and Reintegrative Approaches.' In A. Bottoms, S. Rex and G. Robinson (eds) *Alternatives to Prison: Options for an Insecure Society*. Cullompton: Willan Publishing.

Raynor, P. (2008) 'Community penalties and Home Office research: On the way back to "nothing works"?' *Criminology and Criminal Justice 8*, 73–87.

Rex, S. (1999) 'Desistance from offending: Experiences of probation.' *Howard Journal of Criminal Justice 36*, 4, 366–383.

Ripple, L., Alexander, E. and Polemis, B.W. (1964) *Motivation, Capacity and Opportunity: Studies in Casework Theory and Practice*. Chicago: School of Social Service Administration, University of Chicago.

Robinson, G. (2001) 'Power, knowledge and "what works" in Probation.' *Howard Journal of Criminal Justice 40*, 3, 235–254.

Robinson, G. and McNeill, F. (2008) 'Exploring the dynamics of compliance with community penalties.' *Theoretical Criminology 12*, 431–449.

Schoon, I.J. and Bynner, H. (2003) 'Risk and resilience in the life course: Implications for interventions and social policies.' *Journal of Youth Studies 6*, 1, 21–31.

Scottish Executive (2006) *Statistical Bulletin CrJ/2006/0: Criminal Proceedings in Scottish Courts, 2004/05*. Edinburgh: Scottish Executive.

Tyler, T. (1990) *Why People Obey the Law*. Princeton, NJ: Princeton University Press.

Ward, T. and Maruna, S. (2007) *Rehabilitation: Beyond the Risk Paradigm*. London: Routledge.

Waterhouse, L., McGhee, J., Whyte, B., Loucks, N., Kay, H. and Stewart, R. (2000) *The Evaluation of Children's Hearings in Scotland. Volume 3 – Children in Focus*. Edinburgh: Scottish Office Central Research Unit.

Youth Court Feasibility Group (2002) *Youth Court Feasibility Group Report*. Justice Department, Edinburgh: Scottish Executive.

CHAPTER 9

Incarcerating Young People: The Impact of Custodial 'Care'

Mark Halsey and James Armitage

Introduction

Incarceration means more than spatial confinement. Countless studies attest to this fact by highlighting the psychological (Harvey 2007; Toch 2002), social (Irwin 1970; Maruna and Immarigeon 2004; Sykes 1999), emotional (Ashkar and Kenny 2008, Van der Laan *et al.* 2008) and physical violence (Edgar, O'Donnell and Martin 2002) which frequently accompany periods of detention or imprisonment. The primary aim of this chapter is to further contribute to the literature on the 'effects of imprisonment' (Liebling and Maruna 2005) by focusing on what lock-up *does* to young people, specifically juveniles (Lyon, Dennison and Wilson 2000). We take as our starting point the idea that juvenile detention facilities (and less so prisons) are at least in the formal sense of the term designed to 'care' for those who reside within them (whether for days, weeks, months or several years). We also take seriously the notion that the deprivation of liberty (that is, the right and capacity to associate and move freely in the world) (see Sykes 1999) is or should be the defining punitive aspect of a fully custodial sentence.

The chapter is divided into two sections. The first section offers a brief empirical overview of juvenile detention in Australia with particular attention paid to Indigenous status, and to the South Australian context. As a precursor to such discussion it is important to know that although the numbers of young people in detention have reduced markedly over time (from 1352 individuals as at 30 June 1981 to 545 individuals as at 30 June 2002), this 'historical low' has increased by almost one-fifth in recent years (2003 to 2006) (Taylor 2007, p.11). As shall be seen, there are numerous problems faced by those sentenced and/or remanded to secure care facilities. Such problems are the primary focus of the second section of the chapter. Here, the authors draw, respectively, on interviews with young people in detention[1] (Halsey) and on workplace experiences (Armitage) concerning the South Australian juvenile detention system. Our aim, therefore, is to shed light on *both* what it means to be the *recipient of care* as well as what it is to be the custodial *caregiver* in the context of juvenile detention.

Overview of detention in Australia

With the exception of Queensland,[2] all state and territories in Australia define a juvenile as aged 10 up to, and including, 17 years. In reality, and given a proportion of young people in detention offend whilst a juvenile but are not sentenced until they are an adult (18 years), secure care is often constituted by a cohort of persons aged above 17 years. This group – like the general age cohort – divides into those on remand and those who have been sentenced as a juvenile and therefore permitted to serve their time in a juvenile facility.[3] As of 30 June 2006 there were 190 young people aged 18 or above residing in such facilities (Taylor 2007). When 'added' to the 10 to 17-year-old cohort, those aged 18 and above accounted for nearly one quarter (n=23%) of the national secure resident population (n=841) as at 30 June 2006 (Taylor 2007). Such persons are therefore included in our qualitative analysis and

---

1   All narrated excerpts are drawn from in-depth interviews (n=122) conducted by Halsey since September 2003 with young men sentenced to detention in South Australia. The lead author expresses his sincere thanks to all participants in this research and to Flinders University and the Australian Research Council for funding the project.

2   Queensland stipulates an age range of 10 to 16 years.

3   Generally speaking, persons committing offences prior to their eighteenth (or, in Queensland, seventeenth) birthday, who are subsequently sentenced to a period of incarceration, serve their time in juvenile facilities. Exceptions here would be those forcibly transferred to prison due to escaping or to repeatedly bad behaviour within a juvenile facility, as well as those who turn 18 'mid-sentence' who make an application to the appropriate authority to serve the remainder of their time in an adult custodial institution. It is not so uncommon to find persons aged 18 to 20 years on remand or serving (the final stages of) a detention order in juvenile facilities. There are rarer occasions where adults aged well into their 20s are required, due to the time differential between age at offence and date of arrest, charge, conviction and sentence, to serve their time in such locations.

commentary, not just because of their prevalence but also due to the impact which this older or more 'mature' cohort has on the day to day climate and operation of juvenile facilities.[4] The overview immediately below is given primarily in relation to those aged 10 to 17 years.

As at 30 June 2006, there were 651 juveniles aged 10 to 17 detained across 23 facilities throughout Australia (Taylor 2007). This amounted to a detention rate of 29.1 persons per 100,000 relevant population.[5] The overwhelming majority (92%) were male and just over 8 in 10 (83%) of the total detained population were aged 15 to 17 years (see Taylor 2007). Since 1981 the rate at which juveniles are detained in secure care has dropped from 64.9 to 29.1 per 100,000 relevant population, with the female rate reducing from 22.9 to 4.6, and the male rate from 105.2 to 52.4 (Taylor 2007). A quite different picture of juvenile detention emerges according to whether the primary reference point is taken to be a census date (n=651 for 30 June 2006) or yearly flow data (n=4576 for the period 2005/06) (Australian Institute of Health and Welfare (AIHW) 2008, p.28).[6] By this count, the number of persons subject to at least one episode of detention (sentenced or remanded) during an annual cycle in Australia is roughly ten times greater than the detention population on discrete days in that cycle. Many of these persons are in fact one and the same individual released from and returned to juvenile detention in the same year. A recent major review of recidivism research in Australia noted that:

- approximately half of all juveniles in detention across Australia have spent time in [detention] on at least one prior occasion

- more than half of those released from detention will be reconvicted within at least six months

4   In South Australia – the main focal point of our analysis – persons aged 18 and above have recently accounted for one fifth of the secure care resident population (Taylor 2007, p.38). Assuming each of the 10 individuals known to be 18 and above as at 30 June 2006 were male, this would mean that just under a third of the 36 beds available at Cavan Training Centre were occupied by such persons (derived from Taylor 2007, p.4).

5   As at 30 June 2006, 58.4 per cent of the 651 juveniles in detention were on remand – a figure that has remained relatively stable for some years (Taylor 2007, p.36).

6   The 2008 AIHW report is the fourth in the series. It is based on the Juvenile Justice National Minimum Data Set first established to record juvenile community based supervision and detention data in the 2000–01 reporting period. A degree of interpretive caution is called for as the AIHW report invokes a slightly higher number of 10 to 17-year-olds in detention than the data set previously mentioned (see AIHW 2008, p.14).

- nearly [8] in every 10 juveniles released from detention will be subject to supervision (community or custodial) by a corrective services agency within seven years and almost half will be imprisoned as an adult

- juvenile detainees are likely to be reconvicted of new offences much sooner than adult prisoners. (Payne 2007, p.xii)

The relationship between the annual number of juveniles subject to detention as against community supervision is also important (as a proportion are often subject to both within very short time-frames). In 2006/7 there were '12,765 young people' subject to either community supervision or detention (AIHW 2008, p.xi). Of the '8,808 young people [who commenced and] completed at least one supervision *period*[7] in 2006–07', three-quarters of the supervised time amassed by this group was spent in some form of 'community based supervision' (chiefly probation) (ibid., p.xi). By comparison, 'Only 4% of person days were spent in sentenced detention, while around 12% was spent in other forms of sentenced supervision such as suspended detention and parole' (ibid., p.xi). The fact that the majority of juveniles (80%) experienced only one supervision period during 2006/7 indicates that each of these were likely to be of a longer duration. The national median length of time for which persons were sentenced to detention was three months.[8]

Indigenous incarceration

Current and historical rates of incarceration for Indigenous juveniles tell a very different story to aggregated national figures. As of 30 June 1994 – the date from which reliable comparable data exists – the rate of incarceration for this cohort was 413.9 per 100,000 relevant population. After 'spiking' in the March quarter of 1997 at 467.9, the national rate of juvenile Indigenous incarceration as at 30 June 2006 had only fallen to 315.1[9] per 100,000

7   To be counted as a 2006/07 supervision period, it must occur between 1 July and 30 June. A 'new' supervision period needs to be separated by at least one day on which no supervision was prescribed.

8   Only two per cent of the total supervision time in 2006/07 related to remand in custody. The median time for those remanded was two days (AIHW 2008, p.xii).

9   The March 2006 census figure was 352.4 per 100,000 – only marginally lower than the first year for which figures are reliably available – 1994.

relevant population (Taylor 2007). From 30 June 1994 to 30 June 2006 the non-Indigenous rate of juvenile incarceration fell from 24.3 to 15.1 (Taylor 2007, p.21). Taken together, in this 12-year period the national Indigenous rate reduced by less than a quarter whilst the rate for non-Indigenous juvenile incarceration fell by more than a third (with the latter working off a remarkably lower base). Put bluntly, *as of 30 June 2006 Indigenous juveniles were over-represented in juvenile facilities to a factor of 20.9* – 'meaning that Indigenous young people were 21 times more likely to be detained per population than non-Indigenous young people' (Taylor 2007, p.18). It is hardly surprising, then, that 330 (51%) of the 651 juveniles incarcerated as at 30 June 2006 aged 10 to 17 years identified as Indigenous.[10] This figure is placed into further perspective by considering that Indigenous persons constitute less than 5 per cent (n=106,056) of all persons aged 10 to 17 nationally (n=2,265,533) (AIHW 2008, pp.18–19). The proportion of Indigenous detainees drops only slightly (to 44%) when calculated against the 10 to 18 years and above total secure care population.

The number of Indigenous persons in juvenile facilities varies markedly across Australian states and territories. The most vivid example of this is the Northern Territory. There, at 30 June 2006, 96 per cent of the secure care resident population (n=25) identified as Indigenous. This figure of course needs to be viewed in the larger demographic context. The Northern Territory is home to nearly 44 per cent of the national (non-custodial) Indigenous juvenile population whereas states such as Victoria and South Australia evince, respectively, just 1.3 per cent and 3.5 per cent of such persons (Taylor 2007, p.16). Having said this, the Northern Territory incarceration rate for Indigenous juveniles has quadrupled since 1994 (from 87.8 to 214.7) (Taylor 2007). As recently as March 2005, Western Australia incarcerated 766.2 Indigenous juveniles per 100,000 (only marginally below the 1994 incarceration rate of 798.3 per 100,000 Indigenous juveniles aged 10 to 17 (Taylor 2007, p.19). Indeed, when examining the longer term trends, Western Australia marginally outstrips the Northern Territory in its incarceration of Indigenous juveniles. In the former location, an Indigenous person aged 10 to 17 years is '32 times more likely to be detained per population'

---

10   There were 68 Indigenous persons aged 10 to 14 years, and 262 aged 15 to 17 years in detention as of 30 June 2006 (Taylor 2007, pp.13–14).

than their non-Indigenous compatriots (Taylor 2007, p.24). It is manifestly clear that Indigenous over-representation in the juvenile detention system is worse now than over a decade ago. More problematically, this worsening of conditions has continued to evolve even in light of the Royal Commission into Aboriginal Deaths in Custody (Johnston 1991) which specifically called for measures to dramatically reduce the numbers and proportions of Indigenous people in secure care/prison.

South Australia

As at 30 June 2006, and for juveniles aged 10 to 17, South Australia recorded an incarceration rate of 25.2 per 100,000 (marginally lower than the national rate of 29.1). The South Australian rate for males was 46.6 per 100,000 (again marginally lower than the national rate of 52.4) (Taylor 2007). South Australian Indigenous juveniles are over-represented in detention by a ratio of 13 to 1 (ibid.). Since 1994, the rate of incarceration of non-Indigenous persons has remained, with few exceptions, close to or higher than the national average (ibid.). In 2005 – the most recent year for which comprehensive sentencing and custodial data is available – there were 78 secure detention orders made by the Youth Court. The minimum total effective sentence was 1 week, with the maximum being 91 weeks (22 months) and the average detention period amounting to 23 weeks (6 months). Twenty-five orders (32% of all secure detention orders for the 2005 calendar year) spanned 6 to 12 months, whilst 7 orders were imposed for durations ranging from 12 to 24 months. Around 90 per cent of detention orders were stipulated at less than 12 months. One-third of such orders (n=28) were stipulated with regard to the major charge 'criminal trespass', whilst 1 in 6 (n=12) were made for the offence of 'larceny / illegal use of vehicle'. Fewer than 1 in 5 (n=14) orders related to 'offences against the person' (Office of Crime Statistics and Research (OCSAR) 2006). A brief profile of those admitted into custody (n=967) during 2005 can be given as follows: 76 per cent (n=739) were male; 40 per cent (n=389) were identified as Indigenous; and 91 per cent (n=879) were either unemployed, a student or assigned some other status. Of the 67 persons in custody on 30 June 2005, over half (n=36) were in sentenced detention, just under half (n=30) were on remand, and one person was in police custody. Forty per cent of these juveniles were identified by social workers as Indigenous. Of the 66 juveniles on remand or serving a detention order at 30 June 2005, 50 (76%) were aged 15 to 17 years – the age cohort from which the interview excerpts below are drawn (see OCSAR 2006, Tables 5.1 to 5.5). The focus on South Australia should permit a good degree of generalisability to the national scene where the vast majority of juvenile detainees are male (n=92%), where those aged 15 to 17 account for two-thirds of the total detained juvenile population (AIHW 2008, pp.51–52) and where Indigenous young men constitute, by daily average, 49 per cent of this age cohort (AIHW 2008).

Detention from a recipient of care perspective

In previous publications (Halsey 2006, 2007a, 2007b, 2008a, 2008b) the lead author has brought to light a diverse range of views narrated by young men in secure care (as juveniles) and prison (as adults). These views are generally not repeated here. Instead, we focus on five themes which seem to directly speak to the concept of 'care', namely: cultural awareness; power and humiliation; hyper-retribution (punishing the punished); tendency toward infantilisation and emotional detachment.

Cultural awareness

It is manifestly clear that detention – in spite of sporadic efforts by youth workers to support some cultural-based activities – substantially entrenches the cultural dislocation imported into custody by Indigenous young men. Care, in this context, means a predominantly Anglo-Saxonised conception of need and rehabilitation translating into tokenistic attempts to provide culturally appropriate initiatives. In a sense, incarceration is the great (if violent) leveller of cultural difference. Young men in detention are residents first and foremost and subsequently, and somewhat inconveniently, persons of a particular age, cultural heritage, pedagogical competence and so forth. The following excerpt speaks to this theme:

I: Are there any good things about being in here?

P: No, not really.

I: Not really? Do you feel as though it's time wasted or do you feel as though you're using the time to, I don't know, increase the chances of you never coming back?

P: No, it's time wasted…

I: Is there anything specific you'd like to see happen? …

P: More – more indigenous programs and stuff like that… But they just want us to do like work on computers and shit like that… Most stuff what is in here, it's like – it's sort of stuff – like, not being racist or anything, but it's like more stuff what white people would use, you know…and there's nothing in here what any black person would use if they're traditional mob and stuff like that here… If, yeah, they're full blood, you know… They don't do dot paints that often. They don't make didgeridoos, anything like that… It's like making tables and doing welding…and making frames for mirrors and stuff. It's just shit like that. And learning how to cook all just stupid stuff, you know – just like mince and shit like that.

I: Would you like to learn something about, like, traditional Aboriginal cooking and recipes and bush tucker – that kind of stuff? …

P: Yeah. Like cooking on the fire or, you know, like kangaroo tail and stuff… Like being able to cook that kind of stuff… But in here it's all like pots and pans and stove…

I: Do you think a lot of other indigenous lads would like to learn how to do that?

P: Yeah… We ask all the time to have like fires in the outer rec[recreation area] and that to cook up and that… But no, they don't let us.

I: What about when you ask about…traditional painting, like dot painting? What goes on there? [What] do they say? …

P: 'Oh, yeah, we'll do it this Thursday – we'll do it this Thursday,' or something…and it comes up to the Thursday and you don't even end up doing it… I've got a real big painting hanging in my room…and it's not even finished yet… There's only a couple of stuff I need to do on it…

And I keep on asking them if I can finish it and they reckon, 'Yeah, this Thursday,' and, yeah, it never comes to that Thursday. (A, 54: 8).[11]

Power and humiliation

A second theme, which is experienced at one point or another by all residents (whether on remand or sentenced), has to do with the overt power imbalance which characterises the staff/resident relationship. Often, this power – in the direct sense of the term denoting the capacity and right to get things done by recourse to physical force – is used with restraint and exercised responsibly. We make no pretence toward the notion that it is (ever) easy to manage the many and varied scenarios that arise in secure care environments. But we do argue that power can be wielded in insidious ways – ways whose effects are interpreted very differently depending on one's status as a resident or worker.

> P: One time I was in a situation where, cos my nephew's in here, I had to calm him down. And he was smashing [stuff], he broke his TV, fucking smashed his toilet seat, fucking cupboard, this, that, chair. He's... swinging TV cords around, holding big pieces of glass, yeah... So, yeah, I calmed him down and he was sitting at his door, calmed him down and got him in the room, talking to him and, yeah, went in the cabin [cell for solitary confinement], sat with him and he was like, 'They're [the staff] fucking laughing', yeah. They were serious [when they asked for my help to calm him down] and then...they all laughed about [it], [like it was] a big joke... Just fucking – why look and laugh? They tell us fucking, 'Don't take it personal.'
>
> I: Sure, but...isn't that the ultimate form of disrespect to be laughed at? That's what you're getting at, isn't it?
>
> P: Yeah. (B, 23: 32)

Things which would not be given a second thought beyond custodial walls are often matters of great and nuanced consequence when incarcerated. In the previous excerpt, humiliation (an internal dressing down with no hope of an easy return to a dignified place) results from an abuse of power. At the very least, a bungled effort to bring levity to what appears patently to be a quite

11   With regard to excerpts displayed in this chapter, I=Interviewer, P=Participant.

traumatic event for the residents has transpired. These 'small' incidents occur frequently to the point where they border on being normalised by both staff and those in their care. What is particularly noteworthy in the current scenario is that staff temporarily ceded their power to a resident in order to permit him to assist in restoring order to a situation which threatened to spiral further out of control. With the trust in the resident proving to be well placed, the traditional and abiding power imbalance was re-established in an instant through the gesture of laughter and an off-handed comment ('Don't take it personal').

Hyper-retribution (punishing the punished)

To those unfamiliar with the role of secure and prisons, it is easy to forget that their primary purpose is to deprive people of their liberty – not to further punish those who reside within. Although secure care facilities have a legislated responsibility to protect and care for those in detention (and indeed sometimes because of this safety and protection obligation), punitive measures over and above the established pains of confinement are deployed. In such contexts it is necessary to consider the ways in which 'care' and 'protection' of residents (and staff) is achieved. From talking with young men in secure care, it is clear that 'consequences' are part and parcel of life in detention. Examples of the more common kinds of consequences are individual or unit lock down, suspension of visits or phone calls, being sent to the 'cabin',[12] and, in cases of repeatedly problematic behaviour, refusal of conditional release. But amongst the sometimes effectual but often inflammatory nature of the ebb and flow of consequences, there are forms of control (retribution) which stand out as overtly and pointlessly punitive if not damaging to the recipient of such treatment. This was arguably the case in the following scenario concerning the consequence dealt to a 17-year-old young man for causing, in company, a major disturbance in the custodial facility (which resulted primarily in damage to property but carried charges of attempted escape).

---

12   One participant (see D further below) described the cabin simply as a 'concrete room'. More particularly, it is a cell located in a separate place to the main units.

P: The stress in my mind was so full on...I started losing it... I stopped eating... They put me on anti-depressants...[which] helped out a bit... I'd get let out for an hour a day and that [went] on for about three or four months... I was just in total lock down...

I: What was that doing to you? ...

P: It broke me... I cried in there heaps of times, you know... Just the silence, so long sometimes, can get to you. You know, being on your own, in a room with no TV, no radio, you got one sheet, a bar of soap and a cup. That's all you got in your room. And a pillow... Nothing. Absolutely nothing apart from that... It was hard, you know... I'd never wish it on anybody... Solitary confinement... Turned the power off, turned the water off... No lights... The most [frequent] thing going through my mind...was my parents... I was allowed a two-minute phone call. That was enough to say, 'Hi, bye, I love you'... Twice a week...

I: What did you take away from [all this]?

P: Not to do it again... [I learned] how to deal with myself, how to take that loneliness and use it. It's hard to say what I learnt from it, you know, because I'm locked up again... (C, 2m30s, I3)

Tendency toward infantilisation

An important aspect of caring for children in custody is education – what to teach, and possibly more importantly, *how* to teach or impart the information in ways which generate good learning outcomes appropriately matched to the capabilities of each student. Among those unique young men interviewed to date (n=56), none had completed schooling beyond year 10 and many left or were expelled from school prior to completing six or seven years of basic education. To be a teacher in the context of secure care is, to say the least, a complex task. Effective teaching requires there to be a sense of order and discipline amongst the class and a durable respect for the teacher(s). The techniques which students in 'free' society use to undermine or control the efforts of educators and fellow classmates, are engaged in especially pointed ways in custody. For example, the combination of masculine bravado (spurning of all things 'intellectual') and street credibility or kudos makes for a 'built in' or subcultural resistance to formalised educational rituals. Added to such resistance is the idea that custodial based teachers should or need to be hyper-attentive to those students who 'try it on' in class. Here, the undermining of the teacher's authority comes to be managed as potentially a challenge to the order of the facility writ large. Again, the smallest 'transgressions' can quickly develop into a conflict of greater magnitude requiring an inevitably punitive response. In these situations teachers are viewed as extensions of the (largely despised) authority of those who work in the units. Care becomes synonymous not with the attention paid to the quality, content and style of learning occurring in class but with the swiftness with which disciplined action is dealt those who show disrespect or who would interrupt proceedings.

> I: What do you think staff should do more of? What could they do better?
>
> P: I don't know. Try to be a bit more normal instead of trying to act like an authority figure or something. They should try to be more – just act like they would on the outside. Do you know what I mean? Not be – not think they're so great just cause they've got a walkie-talkie and a response button... They think they're all fucking, rah-rah, 'I'll get you sent out of here', whatever... Especially in [the] school [within lock up]. The teachers, like if you do one wrong thing, like a lot of the time something starts and you just get sent to the cabin, and that'd be it... [One] time I...was laying on my chair. The staff there took the chair off me eventually and made [me] sit on the floor and I said, 'I'm not a fucking dog, I don't want to sit on the floor,' and she said, 'Well, stiff shit, off to the cabin.' I was sent to the cabin cause I wouldn't sit on the floor.
>
> I: To the cabin?
>
> P: Yeah. It's a concrete room... You know, just cause I wouldn't sit on the floor... That was just bullshit. (D, 28: 50)

Emotional detachment

The final theme we wish to mention here – that of emotional detachment – is one discussed briefly by Halsey (2006, 2007a, 2008b) in previous work. However, we feel it is of such importance that it is necessary to revisit the issue here. One of the key precursors to behavioural problems is that of sustained emotional and social detachment from the world of significant others (parents, friends, guardians, and the like). Just as tobacco companies are in 'the nicotine delivery business',[13] secure care facilities and prisons are primed to deliver sustained socio-emotional detachment to their clients. We realise that efforts are made to cater for specific circumstances (day leave to attend funerals) and that techniques for contact with the 'outside' world do exist for residents (phone calls, letters, contact with occasional sports people entering the facility to run a particular programme, and so forth). But, in the main, social skills and emotional development are largely put on hold. This, we argue, has been made all the worse through a lengthy prohibition on contact visits with family and friends.[14]

> P: One thing I'd definitely change [is] contact visits, meaning, like, you go to Yatala [Labour Prison], you go to the notorious San Quentin…[there's] contact visits, you know what I mean… Yeah, definitely, it's ridiculous, man [that this place does not allow contact visits]. I tried to organise a contact visit – my blood sister's just recently had a kid. I just want to hold my nephew – my first nephew, you know what I mean? … Can't do it, can't do it, you know what I mean. It's…

> I: Why did they say no? Did they give you a reason?

> P: No, not really. This is what I believe, right. I been coming to this place for years, right, mate. When I first come here, right, this place was – this place, right, had 50 per cent less rules than it does now. It's like…we're all relaxed, the whole unit's all cool, man, you know, we're doin' our own thing, right, and they bring a new rule in, right, and it turns the unit upside down. Couple of weeks later, acceptance, it's all calmed down. We'll accept it, it's normal, back to normal. Bang! A new rule comes in. I swear to God…

> I: Sure, I understand what you're saying.

---

13   This was a line spoken by actor Russell Crowe in the Michael Mann film *The Insider*.

14   Such was the situation at various times within Cavan Training Centre from around 1994 to late 2007 when, according to one staff member, the ban was lifted because the Centre wanted to be seen to comply with the UN Convention on the Rights of the Child.

P: My opinion – soon as they see friggin' it's all cool man, they bring in [a new rule]. This place here is more strict than friggin' Yatala, you know what I mean? It's more strict than the Remand Centre, you know. It's – it's ridiculous, man, and I believe that they just like the power, man. It's the power. They can make us do [what they want] – we're like little puppets to them, you know what I mean? (E, 37:10, I2)

This participant, and many others, narrated that the official reason for banning contact visits was to prevent the supply of drugs in secure care. The residents' point, however, was a simple one: if each is strip searched at the conclusion of non-contact visits (as was the practice), then why couldn't they permit contact visits under such circumstances? When asked to name two things they would change if 'manager for a day', the two most common responses were cigarettes and contact visits. What is most interesting is that many young men initially were unable to think of anything they would change – these are sometimes hard to put into words since the structure and routine of lock up quickly becomes the norm and accepted as such. However, when prompted regarding the issue of visitation, the anecdotes and quite passionate pleas regarding this issue 'naturally' flowed. We believe there is good reason to question the mixture of practical utility and symbolic message which a ban on hugging a loved one or partner or child plays in relation to 15 to 17-year-old young men in custody. It seems, at best, a highly problematic attempt to contain emotions (and the supply of drugs) when visits by loved ones (where they exist and can present at such appointments) offer one of the few, if not the only, means for durable social connections to be supported.

Detention from a caregiver perspective

The aim in this section is to offer a brief counterpoint to the narrated material evidenced above. We are in the relatively fortunate position of probably having spoken/interacted with the same or similar groups of young men (or their relatives) over a considerable period from very different vantage points – that is, as a researcher interested in the lived experience of crime, incarceration and release, and as a youth worker and programme manager in a secure care centre. The purpose of this section therefore is not to undermine the force or 'truth' of the issues raised thus far. Instead, the objective is to examine the concept of care from the perspective of someone charged with the duty of caring for young men in lock up.

Although there are a range of rewarding aspects associated with caring for young people in detention, work in such places is extremely demanding and results in a high degree of staff burn out. One of the more difficult aspects is the need for caregivers to remain 'emotionally neutral'. They must avoid becoming too closely enmeshed in the world of those in their care, and must similarly find ways in which to resist being 'rattled' by residents. It is a slippery slope for any worker who too readily shows that their 'buttons' have been (and thus might again be) pushed. Remaining emotionally distant is, of course, easier said than done. In spite of the desire to appear composed and in-control, such 'neutrality' is underpinned by the inescapable reality that young people in secure care possess extremely complex needs (all of which are somehow to be managed – and where possible, effectively addressed – under the constraints of confinement). Caregivers work on a daily basis with young people who are dealing with the effects of substance abuse and/or withdrawal, who have grown up in dysfunctional and abusive family environments, and who all too often have few positive connections to the wider community beyond custody. The spectrum of personal dispositions (or coping mechanisms) ranging from extreme introversion to high extroversion can also be added to the residential biographical mix. Myers (1994, p.104) puts the situation aptly when he remarks, 'Many of the young people [in detention] are severely damaged – they have been 'got at' by society, their families, and a myriad of other forces…'. The task of undoing (even a portion of) this damage is monumental in scope and, as mentioned above, made infinitely more difficult in the closed world of the juvenile detention centre.

Detention is deemed by policymakers and the public to be a necessary option within the juvenile justice system. However, for those who have spent a good portion of their daily (and/or nightly) working lives in such places, they are not generally seen as the most appropriate setting to address the rehabilitation requirements of young people. The co-location of socially marginalised and sometimes psychologically troubled individuals who are witness not only to violence amongst residents, but to the sanctioned physical techniques used by staff to 'calm' those at risk to themselves or others, can impact negatively upon residents and workers alike. This juxtaposition which pits the force used to bring order and security to particular situations against the message (emanating from offender programmes and secure care manifestos) that physical and/or verbal aggression are in fact to be ruled out as legitimate forms of conflict resolution, is one of the foremost dilemmas in the struggle to provide a safe, nurturing and 'message consistent' environment for young people in detention. It is highly doubtful, in other words, whether it is possible to provide effective care and rehabilitative responses within the inherently inflexible and order driven institutional setting of secure care. Residents' views on issues ranging from the lack of culturally aware programmes (where the mandate is to engage Indigenous children in culturally appropriate ways) to the effects of 'power tripping' staff (where staff are trained youth workers required to bring a therapeutic approach to working with young people) to non-contact visits (where the mandate is to keep families together) to prolonged and harsh intra-facility based consequences (solitary confinement) (where there is the requirement to do no more harm) speak directly to this notion.

Detention – for recipients of care and caregivers – sets up a series of intolerable yet seemingly inevitable events. This uncomfortable juxtaposition of incapacitation (degradation of self) and reformation (recovery of self in connection with care from others) is no better illustrated than in the use of 'the cabin' (periods in solitary). On the one hand, this can be interpreted – even against the requisite ministerial and managerial approvals – as a cruel and unusual type of punishment. On the other hand, caregivers are obligated to ensure that staff and residents are provided with a safe living and working environment. In these kinds of situations, and many others, it is hard to see that anyone could be better off for having endured such events. In short, there are a multitude of rules, regulations and standard procedures which fundamentally inhibit and discourage sensitive and sustained social, psychological, educative and emotional support due young people in detention. Many workers, to their great credit, struggle to understand how such environments could nurture socially significant changes within residents when the system appears to reward emotional distance, masculine bravado and hyper-dependence on rules and routines. How, in short, are independent responsible persons supposed to surface within environments which require strict obedience to rules and routines over and above 'free' or relatively autonomous action (see Halsey 2008b)?

Given the above, it is clear that the role of caregiver is multi-faceted if not somewhat 'manic'. Not only do staff provide an integral custodial function by providing a safe, secure and caring environment, but in addition – and this applies particularly to juvenile settings – the caregiver is expected to be a mentor, counsellor, friend, life-coach, key-worker and the like, all within the space of the same day (and sometimes with respect to the same young person). Accordingly, the demands placed on a caregiver working in juvenile detention are considerable and often play out in apparently contradictory and unfortunate ways. Mixed signals often arise where staff impose a lock down on residents who may have thought they were 'mates' with the worker(s) imposing the consequence. This, it can be noted, is where juvenile detention differs fundamentally from prison. In the latter, all staff tend unanimously to be described as 'dogs', whereas staff (youth workers) in secure care facilities are more likely to be viewed as having at least some redeeming qualities.

Just as there is a need to humanise those sentenced to detention, there is also a need to humanise those who work in such places. Workers, to put it bluntly, are not automatons. They have emotions. They can be compassionate. They often advocate for the young people in their care. In particular, they are highly cognisant of the fact that young people import into custody a host of dysfunctional factors (poor literacy and numeracy, familial abuse, drug and alcohol dependency, few or no living skills). But the 'sting in the tail' for the reputation which precedes many caregivers, is that these factors – when situated within the custodial environment itself – have to be carefully managed. Sometimes, this means carrying out duties which – in the majority of other contexts – would be called degrading, even violent. In a very real sense, and without denying for a moment that there are particular staff who subscribe to the 'tough love' approach (as if residents had not had enough of this brand of care at other moments in their lives), caregivers deal with the aftermath of the pre-custodial systemic disadvantage and neglect experienced by those in their care. In Myers' (1994) terms, it is because so many of those in detention have been 'got at' (by families, peers, teachers, even police), that they lack the ability to manage relationships or understand the meanings of appropriate conduct with regard to different settings. Caregivers may be the first and only persons to have taken a genuine interest in their lives and needs.[15] Ward and Stewart (2003, pp.127, 137) make the important distinction between 'criminogenic needs' (such as 'pro-offending attitudes and values...poor problem solving, substance abuse...and criminal associates') as against 'basic needs' ('relatedness', 'competency' and 'autonomy') which feed into and help nurture more general 'human needs' (such as 'love, friendship, creativity, justice, work, aesthetic pleasure [and] sexuality'). The main emphasis in secure care (and prison) is to deal, if at all possible, with criminogenic needs. As important as these are (and it is important to oversee the safe withdrawal from heroin, alcohol, petrol sniffing and the like), it could be argued that the 'larger' person is left out of the frame – that residents' needs are considered through the lens of pathology and social control rather than through the panorama of social capacities and potentials.

When all is said and done, perhaps the most important currencies in the world of a caregiver (indeed in the world of most persons) are trust and respect. Generally speaking, caregivers who relate to young people in a consistent, supportive, encouraging and sympathetic manner will by and large be in a better position to do things *with* (rather than against) the willing participation of residents. Caregivers, just like those they are charged with caring for, are a diverse group and bring a range of stories and baggage (emotional and other) to the job. Until society expects and asks for something more from its detention facilities than retribution and incapacitation, it would seem that caregivers will be compelled to privilege order, routine and control at the expense of the social and cultural needs of residents.

Concluding remarks

What might one take from the above discussion? At least three things come to mind. First, and statistically speaking, juvenile detention in Australia (with the notable exception of Victoria) is on the incline in terms of rates per

---

15   From the vantage point of the general community, it is easy to under-estimate the impact of chaotic and absent families in young people's biographies. Armitage clearly recalls sitting at the dinner table beside a 16-year-old young man in Cavan Training Centre in order to teach him how to correctly hold a knife and fork. The embarrassment felt by the resident at not being able to use cutlery was significant – but he had never been *taught* how to do this (just like the majority in detention had never been taught (nor expected) to stay at school, to treat people and property with respect, to know that it is okay to ask for advice when life gets too tough and so on).

100,000 relevant population. The situation with regard to Indigenous young men in particular is dire with nearly one in two persons aged 10 to 17 in detention identifying as Indigenous. This is a remarkable and utterly shameful situation given that such persons make up less than 5 per cent of the general population in this age cohort. There can be no starker example of the link between social disadvantage, desperation, crime and incarceration than the plight of Indigenous Australians. We add our voice to those calling for policies which conceive of Indigenous offending as a fundamentally *social* rather than criminal issue. A second point arising from our discussion concerns the distinct lack of opportunities or avenues for young people in detention to speak of their lives and to have their voices heard. There are, in short, precious few studies or government initiatives devoted to permitting secure care residents to relay their experiences, hopes and fears (complete with all the messiness that this entails) to audiences situated beyond the custodial or juvenile justice environments. Such stories are urgently needed in order to challenge the traditional discourses governing how young people in detention are popularly – even professionally – perceived.

Finally, our discussion tries to bring to the fore something of the dilemmas faced by caregivers. From a critical criminological perspective, it is all too easy to construe the problems of incarceration as the problems 'caused' and/or perpetuated by staff. The situation is far more complex than this. Detention centre staff, whilst obviously permitted to walk out of the complex at the end of each shift, nonetheless also 'do' a form of time for the duration of these shifts. *Their* agency – their capacity to experiment, to try new ways of working with young people in custody, to bend or break the rules on occasion for the greater 'social good', to take control over 'non-trivial' things – is severely limited. Accordingly, to change the experience of detention means to change it for staff and residents alike. We wonder, however naively, what might eventuate were caregivers *and* recipients of care given the mandate to speak openly, often and constructively *with each other* about the precursors to, and possibility of, a less damaging carceral experience.

Short of abolishing such institutions, dialogue between those who have the greatest knowledge of their problems (residents and workers) would seem as good a place as any to start the journey toward new kinds of custodial practices and spaces. This requires, at the very least, more than acting on the oft repeated refrain to 'put all complaints in writing' – to make things official.

Far from solving problems, bureaucratisation reinforces the routinised, hierarchical and in many ways faceless dimensions of custodial life. Workers and residents need to invent – and be permitted to engage in – a different kind of language (perhaps one based around restorativeness as opposed to punitiveness) capable of reorienting the starkly rigid conceptions of who workers ('power trippers') and residents ('lost causes', 'run amoks', the 'unteachable') are perceived to be. In short, those who live and work in custody need to take a leap of faith. One such leap could entail regular ongoing meetings where residents and staff discuss – under amnesty type conditions – things which could be improved or perhaps tried for the first time. The point would be to create a space (however limited) for discussion and debate rather than for commanding and controlling. This goes to the issue of building a different and better relationship between the caregiver and the recipient of care. Secure care facilities could enact educational/orientational sessions which require young people and youth workers to *jointly* participate in exercises and discussion concerning the challenges posed by one's status as resident or worker. Such sessions could be 'chaired' by ex-residents and more senior residential care workers and could reflect the cultural/ethnic diversity of those who live and work in such places. Much more needs to be done, in other words, to prepare those about to enter secure care as a vocation or as a result of a detention order.

Liebling and Arnold's (2005) work on the moral performance of prisons comes to mind here. It is not merely the material aspects of custodial life which effect what happens within such spaces. Rather, and perhaps more importantly, it is the *affective* dimensions which are more likely to dislodge the fairly static and dysfunctional custodial subjectivities tied to bravado, distrust, violence and an aversion to all things 'intellectual'. To our way of thinking, Liebling and Arnold (2005, pp.205–228) are right on track in suggesting that transforming custodial life means paying much closer attention to the way such notions as respect and humanity are embodied, performed and reformed between recipients of care and caregivers (prisoners and correctional officials). They ask two simple but fundamentally critical questions about the nature of penal environments: '[H]ow much trust, fairness, and co-operation is there in the prison? [And] [t]o what is this related?' (ibid., p.206). In the current context we can only venture a very cursory reply to the first of these questions: namely, there is very little trust, fairness and co-operation in custodial environments. At least, there are not the kinds of trust, fairness and co-operation needed to encourage moves away from cycles of crime, violence and incarceration. In response to the second question, the type and intensity of such things as trust, fairness and the like are directly related to the visions each worker and resident (but also each politician, judge, citizen and so forth) adhere to regarding who or what it is possible to become or do whilst serving time. This is why we believe the practice and reinvention of caregiving and detention is as much a social question as it is an institutional or administrative one.

References

Ashkar, P. and Kenny, D. (2008) 'Views from the inside: Young offenders' subjective experience of incarceration.' *International Journal of Offender Therapy and Comparative Criminology 52*, 5, 584–597.

Australian Institute of Health and Welfare (2008) *Juvenile Justice in Australia, 2006–07.* Canberra: Australian Institute of Health and Welfare.

Edgar, K., O'Donnell, I. and Martin, C. (2002) *Prison Violence: The Dynamics of Conflict, Fear and Power.* Cullompton: Willan Publishing.

Halsey, M. (2006) 'Negotiating conditional release: Juvenile narratives of repeat incarceration.' *Punishment and Society 8*, 2, 147–182.

Halsey, M. (2007a) 'On confinement: Client perspectives of secure care and imprisonment.' *Probation Journal 54*, 4, 339–368.

Halsey, M. (2007b) 'Assembling recidivism: The promise and contingencies of post-release life.' *Journal of Criminal Law and Criminology 97*, 4, 1209–1260.

Halsey, M. (2008a) 'Pathways into prison: Biographies, crimes, punishment.' *Current Issues in Criminal Justice 20*, 1, 95–110.

Halsey, M. (2008b) 'Risking Desistance: Respect and Responsibility in Custodial and Post-release Contexts.' In P. Carlen (ed) *Imaginary Penalities*. Cullompton: Willan Publishing.

Harvey, J. (2007) *Young Men in Prison*. Cullompton: Willan Publishing.

Irwin, J. (1970) *The Felon*. Englewood Cliffs, NJ: Prentice-Hall.

Johnston, E. (1991) *National Report, 5 Volumes, Royal Commission into Aboriginal Deaths in Custody.* Canberra: AGPS.

Liebling, A. (with Arnold, H.) (2005) *Prisons and Their Moral Performance*. Oxford: Oxford University Press.

Liebling, A. and Maruna, S. (eds) (2005) *The Effects of Imprisonment.* Cullompton: Willan Publishing.

Lyon, J., Dennison, C. and Wilson, A. (2000) *'Tell Them So They Listen': Messages from Young People in Custody.* Home Office Research Study 201. London: Home Office.

Maruna, S. and Immarigeon, R. (eds) (2004) *After Crime and Punishment.* Cullompton: Willan Publishing.

McNeill, F. (2006) 'A desistance paradigm for offender management.' *Criminology and Criminal Justice 6*, 1, 39–62.

Myers, L. (1994) 'Detention as a Last Resort: End of the Line or a New Beginning?' In L. Atkinson and S. Gerull (eds) *National Conference on Juvenile Detention: Proceedings of a Conference Held 10–13 August 1993.* AIC Conference Proceedings no. 25. Canberra: Australian Institute of Criminology.

Office of Crime Statistics and Research (2006) *Crime and Justice in SA, 2005, Juvenile Justice.* Adelaide: South Australian Department of Justice.

Payne, J. (2007) *Recidivism in Australia: Findings and Future Research.* Research and Public Policy Series No. 80. Canberra: Australian Institute of Criminology.

Sykes, G. (1999) [1958] *The Society of Captives.* Princeton, NJ: Princeton University Press.

Taylor, N. (2007) *Juveniles in Detention in Australia, 1981–2006.* Technical and Background Paper no. 26. Canberra: Australian Institute of Criminology.

Toch, H. (2002) *Living in Prison: The Ecology of Survival.* Washington, DC: American Psychological Association.

Van der Laan, A., Vervoorn, L., van der Schans, C. and Bogaerts, S. (2008) *Being Inside: An Explorative Study into Emotional Reactions of Juvenile Offenders to Custody.* Cullompton: Willan Publishing.

Ward, T. and Stewart, C. (2003) 'Criminogenic needs and human needs: A theoretical model.' *Psychology, Crime and Law 9*, 2, 125–143.

CHAPTER 10

Doing Youth Justice: Beyond Boundaries?

Anna Souhami

Introduction

In recent decades a consensus has emerged in youth justice systems about the benefits of working beyond professional boundaries. Across all UK jurisdictions practitioners and policymakers espouse the importance of 'joining up' practice, pooling resources and expertise and removing barriers to professional collaboration (e.g. Criminal Justice System Northern Ireland 2007; Dillane *et al.* 2001; Scottish Executive 2004, 2006a, 2006b). It appears that a multi-agency orthodoxy has developed in youth justice practice.

However, it is in the English and Welsh youth justice system where multi-agency practice is most fully developed. Under the Crime and Disorder Act 1998, the delivery, organisation and management of youth justice services became a multi-agency responsibility. The formation of Youth Offending Teams (YOTs) were the cornerstone of this approach. YOTs replaced the specialist teams of social workers in Local Authority Social Services 'youth justice' or 'juvenile justice' teams. They are 'stand alone' units which do not belong to any one department or agency but instead draw together practitioners from all the core agencies that work with young offenders – social work, probation, police, education and health authorities – with scope to involve staff from other agencies or organisations, such as the prison service, local authority youth services and voluntary organisations. These staff can be seconded to the YOT, or employed directly to the YOT by the local authority. They are managed directly by a YOT manager, who can be appointed from any of the core partner agencies, and managed locally by multi-agency 'steering groups' and chief executives' departments. They are accountable nationally to the Youth Justice Board (YJB), a non-departmental public body (NDPB) also established under the Crime and Disorder Act with responsibility for the central supervision of youth justice services. In addition, YOTs work in partnership with a range of services across the statutory, voluntary, faith and corporate sectors.

In this way, the entire operation of the youth justice system in England and Wales now operates beyond agency boundaries. It therefore brings into focus the problems and possibilities of multi-agency practice in youth justice.

This chapter explores the implications of experiences in the English and Welsh youth justice system for multi-agency practice in working with young offenders. What are its advantages? What challenges does it hold for practitioners? And what are its implications for the nature of work with young offenders? In exploring these questions the chapter draws on qualitative research with youth justice practitioners which explores both the development of multi-agency work on the cusp of the youth justice reforms and its impact on the shape of youth justice practice nearly ten years on.

Multi-agency practice and youth justice

The consensus about the benefits of multi-agency practice has developed alongside a series of shifts in thinking about youth crime and its management over the last 20 years. Youth justice practice has long been preoccupied by the tension inherent in the youth justice system, where the requirement to punish is coupled with a duty to protect young people's welfare. The conflicts between 'welfare' and 'justice' became manifested in two dominant approaches to dealing with young people in trouble in the UK, both of which incorporate incompatible assumptions and principles about work with young offenders (Muncie 2004). However, during the 1980s a further strategy emerged for working with young offenders which was not connected to traditional questions of care or control, but with managing the offending population as efficiently and effectively as possible (for example, see Feeley and Simon 1992; Pratt 1989). Instead of aiming to reform or rehabilitate young offenders, policies aimed to make youth crime tolerable in the most efficient, economic way.

In line with this approach, it was recognised that it is more effective – and cheaper – to tackle offending behaviour at an early stage (for example, Audit Commission 1996). Reflecting this, the Crime and Disorder Act 1998 established 'preventing offending by children and young persons' as the principal aim of the English and Welsh youth justice system, in which the aim was to halt offending by 'nipping it in the bud' (Home Office 1997).

At the same time, there was an increasing optimism about the ability of the youth justice system to affect change in young people. In contrast to the orthodoxy of previous decades that criminal justice interventions were unable to prevent re-offending and could in fact do more harm than good (e.g. Martinson 1974), the emerging 'what works' agenda suggested that, if informed by evaluative research and targeted appropriately, some forms of intervention could be successful in reducing offending behaviour for some young people (Muncie 2004). Youth justice services have therefore become refocused on identifying and directing services towards selected 'risk conditions' associated with offending such as poor parenting, chaotic family life, truancy and school exclusion, and associating with delinquent peers.

Finally, there has been a shift in the way that offending behaviour itself has come to be thought about. Crime became seen as a complex phenomenon with multiple causes and effects. In other words, young people who offend present multiple problems, which may be connected to a range of factors related to, for example, their family, schooling, health or social needs (e.g. Graham and Bowling 1995; Home Office 1997). By this understanding, offending behaviour cannot be effectively addressed by any single agency. Instead, an efficient, effective approach to youth justice requires input from a range of agencies to address the multi-faceted nature of youth crime.

In this way, an effective approach to youth offending has come to be seen to require efficiency, a proactive 'problem-solving' approach, and the involvement of a range of agencies. In this context, multi-agency work can be seen to have a number of significant benefits.

HOLISTIC

First, because they draw together representatives from all the relevant agencies, multi-agency teams can both identify the range of needs experienced by their service users and provide a holistic service to address them. Further, because they can pool information and expertise, they are well placed to identify those young people considered to be most at risk of offending across a range of different 'risk factors' and attempt to prevent them from doing so. In a policy climate which increasingly prioritises pre-emptive targeting and intervention with young people, this is considered to be a particularly important benefit of YOTs (Youth Justice Board 2004a).

EFFICIENT

Second, by consolidating the diverse expertise and resources of staff from different agencies into a single structure, multi-agency work can allow for a better co-ordinated and more efficient use of resources, whether funding, expertise, effort or information. In particular, it can remove obstructions to co-operation between agencies. As Burnett (2005) puts it, staff can effectively become 'brokers' for their home agency, allowing the team direct access into local services which may have previously been unresponsive. Multi-agency work thus allows practitioners to make faster and easier referrals and provides quicker and easier access to information held by different agencies.

ACTIVE

Third, because staff are able to work outside their traditional structures and practices, multi-agency practice allows for the development of new and innovative ways of working. In other words, multi-agency teams provide for an environment where creativity is encouraged (Burnett and Appleton 2004; Souhami 2007).

COHERENT

Finally, it is thought that multi-agency teams bring about a more coherent approach to youth justice work. By pulling together different agencies into a collective whole with common objectives, multi-agency work aims to resolve tensions in the aims and approach of different agencies and bring about a shared approach to youth offending, thereby reducing conflict and disruption. In other words, dissolving boundaries between agencies is an attempt to 'design out' conflict (Pitts 2000, p.9) in the youth justice system and allow for its smooth running.

Multi-agency practice has therefore come to be seen as having a number of important advantages in youth justice practice. However, it also raises some significant challenges for practitioners. Drawing on an ethnographic study of the formation of multi-agency practice in a developing Midlands YOT (Souhami 2007), the following pages consider some of the implications of developing practice beyond professional boundaries. In particular they explore how, rather than straightforwardly bringing about the emergence of an efficient, coherent approach to practice, multi-agency work instead brings into focus fundamental questions about the purpose and values of youth justice practice.

Working beyond boundaries

The immediate question for practitioners joining a multi-agency team is how to adapt their practice to a multi-agency context. Experiences in the Midlands YOT indicate that this is in fact a highly complex process.

Specialist skills

First, practitioners' specialist skills and expertise cannot always be easily transferred to a multi-agency environment. Even where the role of staff from partner agencies appears relatively straightforward, the new context may demand fundamental changes in the way practitioners approach their work. For example, health and education staff in the Midlands YOT understood that their role was to provide specialist input into social casework where young people had particular health or education needs. However, whilst both were highly experienced in their respective fields, neither had previously focused on offending behaviour or worked in a context in which their interventions were compulsory. Moving to a YOT therefore required critical shifts in the approach and scope of their work. As a health officer said, 'it's trying to get in my head it's a completely different way of working. In my previous line you accepted that clients offended but it really wasn't that much of an interest to us. If somebody didn't turn up that's OK, it was up to them, it was really very much their choice.' In addition, the technical vocabulary of youth justice can act as a further barrier to practice. For example, the health officer in the Midlands YOT described feeling bewildered and excluded by both the terminology used and the prolific use of abbreviations such as PACE, TWOC and PSR. As she explained, 'social work is a different language to me'.

Moreover, some staff may find it difficult to employ their core professional skills at all. For example, while it may seem relatively clear how the expertise of practitioners from health or education could contribute to case work, it is perhaps less obvious what input a police officer could provide. Indeed, in the Midlands YOT staff struggled to find a role for police staff. As one social worker put it, 'we all thought, police, oh God, what are we going to do with a policeman'.

Generic practice

But in addition, although multi-agency work aims to bring together a diverse range of specialist skills, resources and services, the development of work that is common to all practitioners is intrinsic to multi-agency practice. As staff are brought together to address a common problem with shared objectives, they are to some extent required to put aside their usual roles and become involved in new, shared ways of working and thinking. Indeed, in the case of YOTs the development of generic work is envisaged as a central strand of youth justice practice. Early guidance on establishing YOTs stated that practitioners' roles should be developed 'in the light of their personal skills and experience, not solely because of their professional background': while some degree of specialist input can be maintained, 'in principle' any team member can undertake any function including writing pre-sentence reports (PSRs) and supervising offenders (Home Office *et al.* 1998). In this way, professional boundaries become blurred.

For many specialist staff in the Midlands YOT, the chance to transcend their usual role was an important attraction of inter-agency work. As an education officer explained: 'I've learned loads and loads and loads. I was used to my old job, just thinking I was brilliant at it. It's good to take yourself out of that environment, it's better for me, definitely better for my development.' However, the development of generic practice raises some important questions for multi-agency staff.

FINDING A BALANCE

First, what is an appropriate balance between the generic and specialist elements of practitioners' roles? In other words, to what extent should they retain a distinct identity as specialist practitioners, and how far should they take on new, shared responsibilities defined by the partnership? This is a central question in multi-agency work (e.g. Burnett 2005; Burnett and Appleton 2004) and one which experiences in the Midlands YOT suggest is vital for multi-agency workers' job satisfaction and sense of inclusion. For example, education and health staff in the Midlands YOT felt they were spending more time in general casework than specialist interventions. As a result, they felt their professional expertise and experience had been made redundant and described feeling devalued, undermined and deskilled. Moreover, they felt they were not only losing their own professional identity but replacing it with that of another profession: they were 'becoming social workers'.

Yet while the balance between specialist input and new, shared tasks appears to be crucial for the cohesion of multi-agency teams and thus their effective functioning, it is also difficult to negotiate. In particular, it can be complicated by pressures inherent in multi-agency work. Because of the high workloads experienced within teams, staff can feel under pressure to take on generic or administrative duties rather than working within their areas of expertise (Youth Justice Board 2004b). This became a cause of considerable resentment in the Midlands YOT. As the education officer put it, 'it detracts from what I'm here for, doesn't it? If I'd wanted to be a social worker on the YOT, I would have trained as one, wouldn't I?'

QUALIFICATION

Second, how far are practitioners qualified to take on new, shared practice? Although staff may have extensive experience in their home agency, they may be new to the kind of work required in the multi-agency organisation. Indeed, where the recruitment of a diverse workforce is encouraged, such as in the case of YOTs, it is likely that some new staff will not have professional qualifications in work with children in trouble. For example, probation staff in the Midlands YOT had no previous experience of working with children at all and found that they were, as a probation officer put it, 'totally different clients', which required a completely different approach. If practitioners' roles are closely determined according to professional expertise, questions of qualification might not be as acute. But if there is some development of generic roles, how do agency-specific qualifications translate? For example, it might be quite appropriate for a health officer in a YOT to provide assessments or interventions for young people with mental health or substance misuse needs. But are they qualified to be a case worker, or to write PSRs?

This issue became of crucial importance in the Midlands YOT. Staff from partner agencies who were tasked with work of this kind said they felt inexperienced and unprepared to undertake to do the work now required of them. This made for an unhappy and anxious working life: practitioners described themselves as feeling 'totally out of my depth', 'like a piece of shit'. But moreover, as an education officer explained, their lack of confidence and training had serious implications: 'I've just done a PSR on my own... I don't think it's right that I should be doing it... I think it's a very grave thing, it's somebody's justice, it's somebody's liberty.'

APPROPRIATE PRACTICE

In addition, given the diverse professional backgrounds of multi-agency practitioners, is it *appropriate* for all staff to become involved in all duties? For example, social work staff were initially unsure about how to involve police officers in the generic work of the Midlands YOT. Whilst health and education staff had been encouraged to take on a caseload or write PSRs, many social workers felt it was inappropriate for a police officer to do so. This was not a question of qualification or individual expertise: indeed, none of the staff from partner agencies had experience of work of this kind. Instead, practitioners were concerned that there was something intrinsic in the outlook of police staff that made certain roles inappropriate. As one practitioner put it, 'When you look at things we're very much social workers, he's very much a police officer, and I don't know how that would affect writing a PSR.' However, this raises the question of what professional identity actually means. What does it mean to be 'very much a police officer', and why should that affect the way a practitioner completes a PSR?

In other words, the development of multi-agency roles puts at issue a number of questions about the nature of professional practice. Do the various agencies that work with young offenders differ in their ethos and values? And if so, are these differences apparent in the way individual staff work? In other words, how are the relationships between agencies manifested beyond boundaries? These questions become particularly apparent in relation to problems of conflict in multi-agency work.

Culture and conflict

Conflict is often argued to be an inherent feature of multi-agency work (for example, Crawford 1994, 1997; Crawford and Jones 1995; Gilling 1994; Pearson *et al.* 1992; Sampson *et al.* 1988). Because of their different traditions, cultures and working assumptions, staff are likely to have different conceptions of the problems at hand and thus a different understanding of the appropriate approach to them (Crawford and Jones 1995; Gilling 1994): in fact, it has been argued that 'it is naive to expect them to act otherwise' (Gilling 1994, p.254). Indeed, conflict can be seen to be built into the structure of YOTs which, after all, were formed in an attempt to consolidate and resolve such differences of approaches between youth justice agencies.

The implication is that conflicts in the cultures of different agencies may undermine working relationships and thus be a barrier to multi-agency practice. In particular, conflicts are often expected between practitioners from the police and social work, who 'represent, at least symbolically, important polar interests within the system of crime control and the criminal justice process' (Crawford 1997, p.97). Reflecting this, former youth justice social workers in the Midlands YOT thought that the two agencies were fundamentally incompatible. In contrast to the 'welfarist' approach of social work, the police had a punitive, inflexible 'cop culture' which was geared towards 'criminalising' or 'nicking' young people. As one social worker put it, 'the police have always seen social workers as in league with the service user. Social workers have always seen the police as bastards who are locking them up.' How, then, can functional relationships develop? However, the notion of clear conflicts between agencies in fact may mask a more complex picture, as outlined below.

INDIVIDUALS OR AGENCIES?

First, the question of inter-agency conflict calls into question the relationship between practitioners and their parent agencies. If different agencies have competing ideas about the aims and approach to work with offenders, will these be straightforwardly understood and played out among their representatives? In other words, will conflicts in working cultures necessarily be translated into conflicts between multi-agency staff?

In fact, the relationship of multi-agency practitioners to their parent agency is likely to be particularly complex. Because multi-agency work separates staff from their home agency, especially in organisations such as YOTs which operate outside traditional organisational structures, roles and practices (Crawford 1994, 1997), it is more likely to appeal to those who feel to some extent detached from their work and colleagues. This is particularly likely to be the case where partnership work is felt to conflict with important aspects of the organisational life of the parent agency. For example, Crawford and Jones (1995) found that in the climate of 'old fashioned machismo' (Reiner 2000, p.97) in the police service in which action, excitement and a punitive approach to offenders is prized, inter-agency work which does not have these characteristics is often regarded pejoratively as 'social work' rather than 'real police work' and therefore 'women's work'. This is perhaps particularly likely to be the case in the field of youth justice, where staff are required to take on work which, until recently, was 'owned' by social workers, was traditionally welfarist in approach and was differently gendered. It is therefore likely that some sense of disconnection is necessary for police staff to be able to take up a position on a YOT. In the Midlands YOT for example, both (male) police officers said that they felt uncomfortable and out of place in the police service and saw this as an integral part of their move to the YOT. As one of them explained, 'I have nothing in common with younger police officers. They're different animals... I don't get on well with police officers generally.'

In this way, a paradox of multi-agency work is that the representatives of parent agencies are likely to be unrepresentative of those who work in them. In practice, this can be a great advantage. The ability for practitioners in multi-agency teams to 'get on' with their colleagues is crucial for developing relationships, which in turn is essential for partnerships to function (Crawford and Jones 1995). As a YOT manager put it, 'partnerships are often about relationships with people. I don't think agencies have relationships, I think people have relationships'. Where there are thought to be conflicts between the work of the partnership and particular agencies, the ability of staff from these agencies to appear somehow atypical can greatly smooth inter-agency relations. However, as Crawford and Jones (1995) point out, the atypicality of many inter-agency staff also suggests that the relationship between practitioners and their colleagues in their parent agencies should not be taken for granted, which may have implications for the ability of staff to act as 'brokers' for their parent agency.

CONFLICTS OR CONFUSION?

But, moreover, the development of multi-agency practice puts at issue the very idea of a distinct occupational approach. It brings into focus not just the differences between the culture and approach of different agencies, but the similarities, complexity and confusion within and between them as well.

The need to develop new forms of multi-agency practice requires staff explicitly to engage with fundamental questions about the aims and purpose of youth justice interventions. What forms of work and administrative routines should the partnership develop, and what is the underlying ethos and purpose that should shape it? For example, the establishment of group work with young offenders was the first new, multi-agency programme developed in the Midlands YOT. The development of these groups required staff to think about a number of practical issues: should young people be breached for non-attendance, or should the groups be voluntary? Should staff provide transport to the sessions or should young people make their own way there? Yet underlying these issues were core questions about the values and purpose of youth justice practice. To what extent should young people be considered responsible for their offending? How far should practitioners help them? And was in fact the role of the team to help or to punish? Practitioners were now engaged in explicit debates about the purpose and values of youth justice work. As a result the inherent ambiguity and incoherence at the heart of youth justice practice became exposed. It became clear that there was no clear position within each agency about these issues. Instead, disagreement, diversity and confusion were widespread among practitioners from all agencies. As the education officer said, 'everybody within our group, and we're multi-agency group-workers, we all disagreed on what we should do...

There's a lot of different philosophies out there about what the team is, punitive approaches, and welfare approaches... I think it's individual.'

Moving forwards: challenges for practice

In this way, by relocating youth justice practice beyond agency boundaries, multi-agency work exposes the conflicts, tensions and uncertainties at the heart of youth justice practice. These dilemmas will of course always have been present beneath the work of the various youth justice agencies. However, by moving beyond the established practice of participating agencies they are brought to the surface.

This puts in question a central strand of the rationale for multi-agency work. As outlined above, the consolidation of work with young offenders into single structures was intended to resolve inter-agency tensions about the purpose of youth justice work being about a shared approach to practice. It appears, however, that multi-agency practice instead exposes the confusion at its core. This can be a deeply unsettling process. In the Midlands YOT it was experienced as the partnership collapsing: staff felt the team had 'disintegrated', 'fragmented', that they were 'in chaos'. But as some have suggested (e.g. Crawford 1994; Sampson *et al.* 1988) such tensions can instead be seen as desirable and productive. The acknowledgement of shared uncertainties can be an important basis on which to start building a common approach to addressing offending behaviour. The crucial challenge for multi-agency teams, therefore, is to tackle these issues in a constructive manner which allows the conflicts and uncertainties within and between agencies to be recognised and addressed (Crawford 1994).

Drawing on current research with senior youth justice practitioners, the final section of this chapter explores how these questions have played out in the English and Welsh youth justice system. To what extent have these tensions and uncertainties been resolved? And what is the shape of youth justice practice that has emerged?

Youth justice beyond boundaries

Nearly a decade after the 'radical overhaul' of the youth justice system, the formation of multi-agency practice in England and Wales has been considered a great success by central government, the YJB and, crucially, youth justice practitioners themselves (for example, Audit Commission 2004; Youth Justice Board 2005). Despite the difficulties and tensions it creates, practitioners suggest that it also brings considerable rewards. Staff most commonly described inter-agency work in YOTs as innovative, active and exciting and long-serving staff report a significant and positive cultural change in services in a relatively short time.

Most significantly, perhaps, YOT staff all reported a dramatic increase in the status of youth justice practice at a local level. Since their launch in 2000, YOTs have grown from relatively small units of around 10 or 20 staff to expansive, complex organisations, some with over 100 staff and an equal number of volunteers. This increase in size appears to have been accompanied by a burgeoning confidence. Youth justice services have transformed from being what one practitioner described as 'small [teams] that you didn't really care about', to a position where, as one YOT manager put it, 'we think we can do anything... OK, we know what we want, how are we going to get it.'

The removal of youth justice services from agency boundaries appears to be directly responsible for their growth in both size and status. Removing YOTs from the ownership of any one department or agency appears to have encouraged local authorities and statutory partners to accept corporate responsibility for youth justice services and participate in both the management of YOT performance and the provision of staffing, funding and services (Youth Justice Board 2004a). Or, as one YOT manager put it, multi-agency management boards are able to 'embarrass people to take part, and embarrassment's quite a strong lever'.

In addition, the scope for work in partnership across other sectors has significantly increased both the size and skills available to YOTs. This is particularly apparent in the alliances formed with the voluntary and community sector which in many areas is responsible for the entire operation of specific youth justice services, such as 'prevention' programmes with young people thought to be at 'high risk' of offending. Indeed, the YJB estimate that there are currently over 10,000 volunteers engaged in the youth justice system through services such as these and they are seeking to increase this number (Youth Justice Board 2007).

It appears therefore that relocating youth justice practice beyond boundaries has significantly changed the landscape of youth justice services in England and Wales. However, these developments appear to be bringing about some important shifts in the nature of youth justice practice.

Re-drawing boundaries

First, expansive partnership work appears to have blurred the boundaries between youth justice services and other agencies and sectors. In other words, through the increased flows of people, practice and ideas between the YOT and other agencies it becomes difficult to know where the YOT – and thus the youth justice system – begins and ends. The advantage of the ambiguity surrounding the status of services such as those run by the voluntary and community sector is that it enables youth justice programmes to reach young people who have not yet come into contact with mainstream youth justice services and thus divert them from offending (Youth Justice Board 2008b). Yet, at the same time, by blurring the boundaries of the youth justice system, partnership work risks widening and deepening the reach of youth justice services into young people's lives.

But, in addition, it appears that the relocation of youth justice services beyond agency boundaries may paradoxically have led to the development of a new, multi-agency profession. The expansion in their size, funds and status appears to have led working in a YOT to become seen by practitioners across a range of agencies as a long-term career choice rather than a short-term secondment. An increasing proportion of staff are now permanently employed as YOT workers or in 'technical' secondments whereby staff are unlikely to return to their home agency. Rather than operating beyond boundaries, it appears new boundaries are now becoming drawn around YOTs.

The development of an increasingly permanent workforce raises the possibility of the emergence of a new form of multi-agency profession, with its own knowledge base, training, values and skills (see, for example, Goldson, 2000). In fact, this appears to have been actively encouraged by the YJB through the development of a new core qualification in 'effective practice' with young people who offend, aimed at all multi-agency youth justice practitioners (Fulwood and Powell 2004).

However, these developments put in question fundamental aspects of the purpose of multi-agency work. First, an increasing proportion of permanent staff obstructs the refreshing of specialist skills and services that secondment provides, thereby losing an important strand of the rationale for multi-agency practice (Youth Justice Board 2008a). Second, whilst it appears to provide the basis of a shared, multi-agency form of professional practice, 'effective practice' may in fact perpetuate the tensions and uncertainties about the purpose and practice of work with young offenders. Despite its technical appearance, notions of effective practice of course contain important assumptions about the nature of youth justice practice and the values that underlie it (see e.g. Muncie 2004; Stephenson, Giller and Brown 2007). Most obviously perhaps, the notion that practice should be closely prescribed and assessed sharply conflicts with the individualised approach that had until very recently been a core and defining value of social work practice (e.g. Meyerson 1994; Rojek, Peacock and Collins 1998). It is possible therefore that the technical language of efficacy has obscured rather than resolved the tensions that were briefly brought to the surface by the development of multi-agency work.

Conclusions

While multi-agency practice may be particularly entrenched in England and Wales, other UK jurisdictions appear to be eager to embrace it as a central strand of youth justice strategy. The ability of multi-agency teams to identify a diverse range of needs and address them through a coherent, holistic service appears to resonate with a youth justice climate which both recognises the complex and multi-faceted nature of youth offending and demands proactive, efficient strategies to address it. But what lessons can be drawn from the English and Welsh experience for multi-agency youth justice practice in other systems?

First, staff who join multi-agency teams may need considerable support. They may find themselves in a context in which they are required to alter fundamentally their approaches to work or even abandon them altogether, negotiate the balance between specialist and generic input and manage the development of new practice for which they may feel unqualified and ill-equipped. A challenge for both the multi-agency organisation and its parent agency is to allow practitioners the freedom to experiment and innovate whilst providing adequate guidance to alleviate their sense of isolation and confusion.

Second, whilst the benefits of multi-agency work may largely be understood in terms of economic, administrative rationales, working beyond professional boundaries in fact confronts staff with fundamental ideological and conceptual questions about both the purpose and values of working with young offenders and the nature of professional identity. What does it mean to represent an agency on a team? Do practitioners bring with them a distinct ethos as well as distinct skills? What are the perceived differences in the way staff understand the aims and approach of work with young offenders? And how should conflicts and uncertainties be resolved? In other words, what does it mean to work in a multi-agency way? Whilst there are clearly no definitive answers to these complex questions, experiences in England and Wales suggest that recognising and explicitly engaging with them is essential in order to recognise the tensions and conflicts within and between agencies and provide a constructive basis on which to start building a shared approach to addressing offending behaviour.

Despite these challenges, the English and Welsh example indicates that working beyond professional boundaries is highly rewarding and exciting and appears to have brought about a dramatic growth in the size, status and confidence of youth justice services. However, the apparent success and sustainability of multi-agency work in England and Wales suggests further lessons for practice elsewhere. As outlined above, the benefits of working beyond occupational boundaries derive from the diversity of multi-agency teams. It is the mix of professional skills, approaches and backgrounds which is considered central both to the emergence of a coherent, holistic and creative approach to practice and to overcoming traditional barriers to inter-agency corporation. Yet as multi-agency work becomes more deeply embedded and more professionalised it appears to be eroding the diversity at its core. Further, where this process occurs without explicitly addressing the ideological tensions and uncertainties at the heart of youth justice practice, the shared practice into which practitioners become assimilated risks not only leaving these untouched but institutionalising the conflicts that it is intended to resolve. In this way, a central challenge for multi-agency practice in the youth justice system is ensuring the sustainability wrought by its success does not paradoxically undermine its fundamental rationale.

References

Audit Commission (1996) *Misspent Youth.* London: Audit Commission.

Audit Commission (2004) *Youth Justice 2004: A Review of the Reformed Youth Justice System.* London: Audit Commission.

Burnett, R. (2005) 'Youth Offending Teams.' In T. Bateman and J. Pitts (eds) *The RHP Companion to Youth Justice.* Lyme Regis: Russell House Publishing.

Burnett, R. and Appleton, C. (2004) 'Joined up services to tackle youth crime: a case-study in England'. *British Journal of Criminology 44*, 1, 34–55.

Crawford, A. (1994) 'The partnership approach: Corporatism at the local level?' *Social and Legal Studies 3*, 4, 497–519

Crawford, A. (1997) *The Local Governance of Crime: Appeals to Community and Partnerships.* Oxford: Clarendon Press

Crawford, A. and Jones, M. (1995) 'Interagency cooperation ans community-based crime prevention: Some reflections on the work of Pearson and colleagues.' *British Journal of Criminology 35*, 1, 17–33.

Criminal Justice System Northern Ireland (2007) 'A Charter for Youth Justice.' Available at www.youthjusticeagencyni.gov.uk/document_uploads/NIO_Charter_for_Youth_Justice.PDF, accessed 17 March 2009.

Dillane, J., Hill, M., Bannister, J. and Scott, S (2001) *Evaluation of the Dundee Families Project: Final Report.* Edinburgh: Scottish Executive.

Feeley, M. and Simon, J. (1992) 'The new penology.' *Criminology 30*, 4, 452–474.

Fulwood, C. and Powell, H. (2004) 'Towards Effective Practice in the Youth Justice System.' In R. Burnett and C. Roberts (eds) *What Works in Probation and Youth Justice: Developing Evidence-based Practice.* Cullompton: Willan.

Gilling, D.J. (1994) 'Multi-agency crime prevention: some barriers to collaboration.' *Howard Journal 33*, 3, 246–257

Goldson, B. (2000) '"Children in need" or "young offenders"? Hardening ideology, organizational change and new challenges for social work with children in trouble.' *Child and Family Social Work 5*, 255–265.

Graham, J. and Bowling, B. (1995) *Young People and Crime.* Home Office Research Study no. 145. London: Home Office.

Home Office (1997) *No More Excuses: A New Approach to Tackling Youth Crime in England and Wales.* London: HMSO.

Home Office, Department of Health, Welsh Office and Department for Education and Employment (1998) *Establishing Youth Offending Teams.* London: HMSO.

Martinson, R. (1974) 'What works? Questions and answers about prison reform.' *The Public Interest 35*, 22–54.

Meyerson, D.E. (1994) 'Interpretations of stress in institutions: The cultural production of ambiguity and burnout.' *Administrative Science Quarterly 39*, 628–653.

Muncie, J. (2004) *Youth and Crime*, 2nd edn. London: Sage.

Pearson, G., Blagg, H., Smith, D., Sampson, A. and Stubbs, P. (1992) 'Crime, Community and Conflict: The Multi-agency Approach.' In D. Downes (ed.) *Unravelling Criminal Justice*. London: Macmillan.

Pitts, J. (2000) 'The New Youth Justice and the Politics of Electoral Anxiety.' In B. Goldson (ed.) *The New Youth Justice*. Lyme Regis: Russell House Publishing.

Pratt, J. (1989) 'Corporatism: the third model of juvenile justice.' *British Journal of Criminology 29*, 3, 236–254.

Reiner, R. (2000) *The Politics of the Police*, 3rd edn. Oxford: Oxford University Press.

Rojek, C., Peacock, G. and Collins, S. (1988) *Social Work and Received Ideas*. London: Routledge.

Sampson, A., Stubbs, D., Smith, D., Pearson, G. and Blagg, H. (1988) 'Crime, localities and the multi-agency approach.' *British Journal of Criminology 28*, 4, 473–93

Scottish Executive (2004) *Getting it Right for Every Child: Report on the Responses to the Phase One Consultation on the Review of the Children's Hearings System*. Edinburgh: Scottish Executive.

Scottish Executive (2006a) *Getting It Right for Every Child: Implementation Plan*. Edinburgh: Scottish Executive.

Scottish Executive (2006b) *Report of the Youth Justice Improvement Group*. Edinburgh: Scottish Executive.

Souhami, A. (2007) *Transforming Youth Justice: Occupational Identity and Cultural Change*. Cullompton: Willan.

Stephenson, M., Giller, M. and Brown, S. (2007) *Effective Practice in Youth Justice*. Cullompton: Willan.

Youth Justice Board (2004a) *Sustaining the Success: Extending the Guidance Establishing Youth Offending Teams*. London: Youth Justice Board.

Youth Justice Board (2004b) *The Provision of Health, Education and Substance Misuse Workers in Youth Offending Teams and the Health/Education Needs of Young People Supervised by Youth Offending Teams*. London: Youth Justice Board.

Youth Justice Board (2005) 'YOTs improve practice and partnership work.' *YJB News*, December, 32.

Youth Justice Board (2007) *Volunteering in the Youth Justice System: Guidance for Youth Offending Teams and Secure Establishments*. London: Youth Justice Board.

Youth Justice Board (2008a) 'Strands and structures of the workforce.' www.yjb.gov.uk/en-gb/practitioners/WorkforceDevelopment/WorkforceStrategies/forYOTs/StrandsandStructureoftheWorkforce

Youth Justice Board (2008b) *Evaluation of the Youth Inclusion Programme: Phase 2*. London: Youth Justice Board.

CHAPTER 11

Conclusions

Fergus McNeill and Monica Barry

Introduction

As we said in introducing this collection, the contributors were given minimal guidance on the focus of the book overall or of each particular chapter (other than in very broad terms), although we did ask them to engage critically but constructively with contemporary research, policy and practice. This minimal guidance and coordination makes it all the more remarkable, therefore, that we find clearly recurring themes running through the chapters, despite their considerable variety and despite the diverse experiences and perspectives of the contributors. In introducing and revisiting these recurring themes it is perhaps worth noting that although most of our contributors currently occupy academic posts many of them have experience of professional roles in youth justice policy or practice.

Some readers may find that the overall tone of the book and of this conclusion seems too critical and that not enough has been made of the many constructive developments in youth justice across and beyond the UK jurisdictions in recent years. If that is the case we would offer just two comments in reply. First, we think that the contributors have tried to offer balanced accounts and have, albeit to varying degrees, given praise where the evidence suggested it was merited. That said, our second response must inevitably be that it is right and proper for researchers and scholars to act as 'critical friends' of the fields of policy and practice.[1] The value of academic research and scholarship must surely rest on its capacity to interrogate policy and practice in relation to its evidence base, to challenge misconceptions and false assumptions, to expose the adverse unintended consequences of policies and practices, and to generate new ways of looking at, thinking about and tackling seemingly perennial problems so as to stimulate constructive and progressive innovation. Naturally, this will sometimes mean that the friendship becomes strained when the criticism is at its most intense. But, equally, there are reciprocal obligations on academics too: if academics are quick to demand research-minded policy and practice, it must sometimes seem to policymakers and practitioners that they are slow to deliver policy and practice-minded research.

If this book errs too much on the side of critique, and we are not at all sure that it does, we nonetheless hope that it can resist a second charge, that is, that the book's critique fails to engage with the needs of policymakers and practitioners and, worse still, of young people. Some of the chapters offer more than others in making suggestions for a better way forward. In setting out below what seem to us to be the recurring critical themes of this volume, we aim at the same time to at least sketch out, admittedly in the broadest of terms, what kinds of policy and practice responses might be required.

Criminalisation and stigmatisation

Young people are being criminalised at an earlier age and for a wider range of behaviours than ever before (see Brown, Chapter 2, McVie, Chapter 3, Morgan, Chapter 4, Halsey and Armitage, Chapter 9, this volume). Their parents are also the target of criminalising practices, from which it can be implied not only that children and young people are brought up to be 'offenders', inadvertently or otherwise, but also that parents must be held responsible for the behaviour of their children. The narrowness of this responsibilising gaze renders invisible the state's responsibilities to the wider

---

1   If anyone requires persuading of this, they could do no better than to listen to Rod Morgan's lecture 'Critical Friends: The Honest Politicians Need For…' at the Scottish Centre for Crime and Justice Research. Available at: www.sccjr.ac.uk/av/2007–SCCJR-Annual-LectureRod-Morgan/1, accessed 18 March 2009.

needs of families affected by the social and cultural conditions within which offending emerges, often alongside and sometimes because of, other social problems.

Whatever the arguments about the influence of social problems in the aetiology of youthful offending, it is clear that the majority of young people embroiled in youth justice systems are disadvantaged in other respects too – for example, in terms of education, levels of poverty and marginalisation from mainstream opportunities. Those with the added label of 'ethnic minority' or 'mental health needs' are doubly disadvantaged through being disproportionately represented in youth justice systems.

Stigmatisation of young people is now enacted not just through familiar labelling processes and the attendant social reactions but, also, more subtly, in the form of risk assessment procedures which are increasingly used to predict the risks posed by children and young people with problematic behaviours and to ascertain the intensity of intervention which is required (see McVie, Chapter 3, Phoenix, Chapter 7, this volume). Such methods of risk identification and prediction are often inaccurate but are nonetheless used increasingly to justify and determine the extent of intrusion into the lives of young people. Critically, this means that stigma is connected not only to what has been done by young people – for which they are to be held personally responsible as if in a social vacuum – but also to dubious judgements about what they *may* do. This is a kind of prospective stigmatisation of perceived riskiness, a sort of pseudo-scientific identification of bad character, rather than a 'mere' question of bad conduct.

Other means of stigmatisation and criminalisation come in the form of so-called 'summary justice', which Morgan (Chapter 4, this volume) refers to as 'punishment without prosecution', where pre-prosecution decision making by the police and the Crown Prosecution Service can result in large numbers of young people being criminalised without due legal process, and being subject to a confusing array of measures, mainly financial, which are aimed not only at deterring young people from crime but, one might cynically suppose, also at boosting the public purse.

So what needs to be done about criminalisation and stigmatisation? First, we need to be much more judicious and reserved in our use of criminalisation as a means of tackling children's and young people's sometimes difficult behaviours and problems. The more behaviour that we criminalise and the more young people that we criminalise, the more obstacles we create to youthful desistance. Similarly, we need to be much more hesitant and much more measured about our deployment of risk discourses and practices, as indeed of any discourses and practices that create dangers of stigmatisation. If 'risk' constructs its bearers as threats or dangers, and 'need' constructs its bearers as deficient or passive, then at the very least we need to encourage counterbalancing discourses and practices focused on strengths, resources, potential and resilience. Stigmatising labels are by their nature exceptionally difficult to remove and deleterious in their short and long-term consequences; they often function as markers for exclusion, thus triggering precisely the social problems that led to the behaviours that precipitated their application. This suggests both a systems focus on persevering as long as possible with informal non-criminalising means of tackling young people's problems, and a practice focus on identifying and releasing the potential of young people.

Punishment and containment

Criminalisation usually comes hand in hand with punishment and as Morgan (Chapter 4, this volume) points out, roughly one half of all criminalised young people appear before the court. The other half are dealt with by summary justice measures as described above. The lack of accountability implicit in and net-widening effects of such out-of-court 'justice' merely serve to further discriminate against young people who are arguably the most vulnerable and least able to defend themselves.

For those brought before the court, where too many now arrive precisely for breaching out-of-court summary justice requirements, an increasing number are being detained in custody for longer periods and for less serious offences, despite an overall drop in youth crime in recent years. Too often, detention equates with mere containment, not only of the individual but of the wider problem of youth crime. It is a reactive rather than a proactive response to the problem of youth crime and limits the opportunity for restorative practices which, ironically, have recently been promoted in the youth justice field (Cavadino and Dignan 2006).

Although the question of punishing young people leads us to normative questions about the ethical principles that should govern youth justice –

questions that have not been a major focus of this collection – there is no doubt that our contributors have highlighted not only the increasingly punitive *effect* of many recent developments, but also the social context and extent of punitiveness towards youth (as well as its limits) and the extent to which young people *feel* punished, even where punishment is not the stated aim of the systems or practices concerned. Taken together, these insights raise very significant concerns for two important reasons. First of all, as we discuss further in the next section, punitiveness is particularly worrying when set alongside a decline in social and political acceptance of collective responsibility for youth crime and, at the same time, a concomitant increase in the willingness – perhaps even determination (against any and all evidence) – to see young people as solely and personally responsible for their actions. Second, and more worrying still, the rise of punitiveness (whether in the intent of sanctions, in public opinion or in young people's experience) is not accompanied, so it seems to us, by any reassertion of a rights-based approach to youth justice. Indeed, as we have said, due process rights are being eroded – so, to paraphrase a term from the philosophy of punishment, it is not so much a case of 'limiting retributivism' (Tonry and Rex 2002, p.3) (by means of due process guarantees of proportionate and parsimonious punishment) as 'limitless retributivism'.

Responding constructively to these sorts of developments is far from simple. Intimidating though it may seem, it is hard to dismiss the suggestion that what is required, at the least, is the sponsorship of a meaningful and informed public debate about how we understand youth crime, as well as thoroughgoing re-engagement with the principled basis of youth *justice*. Both discussions would require brave, bold and astute political leadership, as well as a commitment to engage from the relevant professions and the rest of civil society, and indeed some mechanism for engaging young people themselves.

Responsibilisation

Policymakers have latched onto the possibility that young people *choose* to commit crimes for purely personal reasons and the naive suggestion that (only) by cognitive behavioural training will young people learn that crime does not necessarily pay. Young people are seen as, in effect, wholly to blame for youth crime and they – and increasingly their families – are made responsible for their own behaviour and their own rehabilitation, or as Maruna and King (Chapter 6, this volume) describe it, their own 'redeem-ability'. The abolition some ten years ago of the doctrine of *doli incapax*, which had hitherto given the benefit of the doubt to 10–13-year-olds about their ability or otherwise to know right from wrong, was a stark message to children that they were now to be held responsible in law for their actions.

This focus on the individualisation of the problem and responsibilisation of the youthful actor has been equated by several contributors to this volume with earlier criminalisation, increased punishment, more intrusive interven-tions, a greater use of imprisonment for young people and a policy rationale which denies the need for structural change (see, for example, Brown, Chapter 2, Morgan, Chapter 4, Barry, Chapter 5, Maruna and King, Chapter 6, Phoenix, Chapter 7, McNeill, Chapter 8, this volume). Risk assessment in this process of responsibilisation targets only the 'criminogenic needs' or 'dynamic risk factors' (rather than the developmental needs) *of* young offenders, and neglects both the socio-structural contexts of these 'factors' and the risks posed *to* young offenders from the wider environment. As Phoenix (Chapter 7, this volume) points out, responsibilisation of young people is an excuse for the lack of responsibilisation of policymakers to address the wider needs of young people in trouble.

We have already alluded to the dangers of such approaches in terms of criminalisation and stigmatisation. But there is a more generalised threat here too – the threat of damaging the collective efficacy of communities and of society itself by colluding in the all too familiar process of setting 'us' (law-abiding adults) against 'them' ('feral youth'), a depressing process which is exemplified in many social fields beyond those concerned with youth crime and justice (see, for example, McCulloch and McNeill 2007). To the extent that the responsibilisation of the 'deviant' represents an exoneration of the (apparently) conformist, it is a dagger in the heart not only of collective social responsibility but also of social and community cohesion. Clearly this broader malaise speaks to some of the more fundamental economic, social and political challenges of our times. That said, it is impossible to resist the temptation, in thinking about the proper policy response here, to note the alacrity and seemingly limitless largesse with which government can rise to the challenge of rescuing the financial system from its current crisis – with

'our' money and apparently in all of 'our' collective interests. If the collectiv-
isation of risks can work for capital, perhaps it can be made to work for young
people too.

Policies and practices that may exacerbate youth crime

Yet the weight of evidence, in this collection at least, would suggest that such
a collectivist approach to youth justice seems an unlikely development.
Rather, it seems that too often policies are built on political expedience and
perceptions of the public mood, rather than on sound evidence. Given that the
adverse circumstances that often influence young people to commit crime are
so rarely the focus of the subsequent intervention (the so-called 'solution'), it
is hardly surprising that youth crime seems intractable. Young people
themselves suggest how they may be encouraged to stop offending but such
suggestions are rarely taken on board. Instead, interventions too often have
the opposite effect of encouraging a continuation of offending by young
people because such interventions – despite the elusive promise of partnership working that Souhami (Chapter 10, this volume) explores – fail to
deliver meaningful alternative lifestyle opportunities.

As we have already said, because young people are blamed for their own
predicament, punishment is seen as more appropriate than offering welfare-
oriented alternatives. But this can obviously prove counterproductive. Less
help and more punishment, in many young offenders' eyes, leads to more
offending and less concern for the consequences. Too often they have no
stake in the future to protect through conforming and see no feasible means
of acquiring one. Equally, managerialised systems and practices, even those
that draw welfare professionals into youth justice systems in an effort to
provide holistic responses (see Souhami, Chapter 10, this volume), nonetheless result in even welfare practitioners being confined to 'criminal' justice interventions at the expense of negotiating wider structural opportunities for
young people (see, for example, Phoenix, Chapter 7, this volume).

The desistance literature, reference to which has seasoned this collection
(see, for example, Barry, Chapter 5, McNeill, Chapter 8, this volume),
suggests that young offenders will respond positively to relationships with
professionals that are deemed legitimate, encouraging and fair. However,
approaches that are punitive, dogmatic, coercive or even just standardised and

lacking in human warmth and engagement may all too often exacerbate rather than alleviate youth crime.

Once again, the remedies to these problems are easier to identify than to deliver. Clearly the relationships between research and politics, policy and practice are pivotal, but as we have argued above, it is hard to nurture and sustain these critical friendships. If researchers want research-minded policies and practices, then they have to work harder at meaningfully engaging with these fields – even when that means risking what their more critical colleagues might consider cooptation or contamination. It is surely too easy to stand on the outside finding fault. But, equally, even if researchers *can* act as honest brokers of what is always contested evidence, politicians and policymakers need to be prepared to lead rather than follow public and media debates. In the arena of systems and practices, much more attention needs to be paid to young people's experiences of developing and desisting, and of their experiences of the practices that exist precisely to support these processes. As contributors to this volume have argued, this is as much to do with the moral quality of the interactions between young people and their workers as it is about the technical methods deployed. It follows that finding ways to develop legitimate, respectful, individualised and constructive modes of intervention, with the active engagement of young people in that process, must be a priority for politicians, policymakers and practitioners alike.

Concluding remarks

Though 'common sense' might see an obvious connection between the concepts of youth offending and youth justice, they turn out to be uneasy bedfellows. Certainly the inference that youth justice is the answer to the problem of youth crime is not borne out by the evidence, not least the important evidence coming from the voices of young offenders themselves. The two terms 'youth offending' and 'youth justice', which make up the title of this collection, and the policies, systems and practices discussed within this collection, are embroiled in a marriage of convenience and, as is so often the case with such marriages, it is the children who suffer most.

The contributions in this volume spell out the same message about youth justice time and again: namely that there is a seeming preoccupation with 'youth' at the expense of 'justice'. Too readily such systems exist or at least function so as to punish and to challenge individual young people rather than to question the extent to which the wider society is as much, if not more, to blame for the disadvantages young people face. When this crude reductionism is set aside, it becomes obvious why youth justice in and of itself can have only a limited effect on youth crime; too many of the real drivers of youth crime – those drivers that reside in the fabric of our late-modern societies and the inequalities that they perpetuate – are beyond its reach. But herein lies both the paradox and the ultimate solution; youth justice is the answer to youth crime – but only in the sense that were we ever to arrive at a society that did justice to and by its children and young people, that really acted as if *Every Child Matters*, that genuinely ordered its affairs so as to secure children and young people's health, safety, achievement, positive involvement and economic wellbeing, then we would find ourselves in a society much less troubled by youth crime.

References

Cavadino, M. and Dignan, J. (2006) *Penal Systems: A Comparative Approach.* London: Sage.

McCulloch, P. and McNeill, F. (2007) 'Consumer society, commodification and offender management.' *Criminology and Criminal Justice* 7, 3, 223–242.

Tonry, M. and Rex, S. (2002) 'Reconsidering Sentence and Punishment.' In S. Rex and M. Tonry (eds) *Reform and Punishment: The Future of Sentencing.* Cullompton: Willan Publishing.

The Contributors

Monica Barry is a Senior Research Fellow at the Glasgow School of Social Work and at the Scottish Centre for Crime and Justice Research, based at Strathclyde University. Her work includes evaluations of criminal justice policy and practice and her research interests centre on youth and criminal justice, desistance from crime, youth policy and the impact of youth transitions on offending behaviour. She is the author of *Youth Offending in Transition: The Search for Social Recognition* (2006), and editor of *Youth Policy and Social Inclusion: Critical Debates with Young People* (2005).

Fergus McNeill is Professor of Criminology and Social Work in the Glasgow School of Social Work and in the Scottish Centre for Crime and Justice Research at the University of Glasgow. His research interests explore the interfaces between criminology, criminal justice and social work, including sentencing, community penalties and youth justice. Latterly his work has focused on the policy and practice implications of research evidence about the process of desistance from offending. His book, *Reducing Reoffending: Social Work and Community Justice in Scotland* (co-authored with Bill Whyte), was published in 2007.

James Armitage is the Regional Coordinator of the Indigenous Law and Justice Branch of the Attorney-General's Department, Australian Government. Formerly, he was the Director of the South Australian Government's Crime Prevention Unit where he managed crime prevention initiatives throughout the State. James has developed and delivered a number of programmes for young offenders and staff, including the Challenging Offending Behaviour curriculum, Victim Awareness and various Pre-Release programmes. His work has appeared in a number of juvenile justice related reports and crime prevention publications.

Sheila Brown is a criminologist based at the University of Plymouth. She has extensive experience in researching childhood and youth and has led numerous projects on youth and crime, listening to youth, and young people as victims. Other research interests include questions of children's rights and a critical assessment of global issues facing criminologies of childhood and youth. She works across academic and policy sectors and in consultancy for partnerships and third sector organisations. She has written academic books and articles, journalistic pieces and policy reports on the sentencing of young people, media and youth crime and justice.

Mark Halsey is an Associate Professor of Criminal Justice in the Law School at Flinders University. Funded by the Australian Research Council (ARC), he has recently completed a five-year interview-based study of the custodial and post-custodial issues facing a cohort of young males aged 15 to 24. His current research is entitled 'Generativity in young male (ex)prisoners: Caring for self, other, and future within prison and beyond'. Based on interviews with (ex)prisoners, their nominated significant others, correctional officers and prison managers, the study explores the conditions for positive legacy making in the lives of (ex)prisoners aged 18 to 28.

Anna King is a post-doctoral Research Fellow at the Center for Mental Health Services and Criminal Justice Research at Rutgers University, USA, and a former Gates Scholar. She has taught courses in public attitudes towards crime, crime and the mass media, and research methods in social sciences. Her research interests include policy evaluation, programme evaluation, crime and the mass media and public attitudes towards offenders and re-entry policy. Anna was a Lecturer in criminology in the UK before returning to the USA in 2007.

Susan McVie is a Senior Research Fellow in the School of Law, University of Edinburgh. She is Co-Director of the Edinburgh Study of Youth Transitions and Crime, a longitudinal programme of research exploring offending amongst 4000 Scottish youths. A specialist in quantitative criminology, her research interests include patterns in youth offending and victimisation, individual criminal careers and life-course criminology, and transitions from juvenile to adult criminal justice systems. Recent publications include a book chapter on self-report offending surveys in the UK, and journal articles exploring the impact of policing and youth justice systems on individual offending behaviour.

Shadd Maruna is Professor of Human Development and Justice Studies at the School of Law, Queen's University Belfast. His research focuses on ex-prisoner reintegration and community attitudes regarding crime and justice issues. His book *Making Good: How Ex-Convicts Reform and Rebuild Their Lives* was named the Outstanding Contribution to Criminology by the American Society of Criminology in 2001. More recent books include *Rehabilitation: Beyond the Risk Paradigm* (with Tony Ward), *After Crime and Punishment* (with Russ Immarigeon) and *Fifty Key Thinkers in Criminology* (with Keith Hayward and Jayne Mooney).

Rod Morgan is Professor of Criminal Justice, University of Bristol and Visiting Professor at the Police Science Institute, Cardiff University and at the London School of Economics. He was Chairman of the Youth Justice Board for England and Wales from 2004 to 2007 and HM Chief Inspector of Probation for England and Wales from 2001 to 2004. During his academic career he has held almost every post within the criminal justice system it is possible to hold part time. He is a prolific author on criminal justice issues and is co-editor of the leading British criminology text, *The Oxford Handbook of Criminology* (2007).

Jo Phoenix is Reader in Criminology in the School of Applied Social Sciences, Durham University. Her research interests are youth justice and prostitution, the contradictory effects of contemporary attempts to govern groups defined as both 'needy' and 'risky' and how professionals come to make decisions about these groups. She is the author of *Making Sense of Prostitution* (2001), *Illegal and Illicit* (with Sarah Oerton, 2005) and *Sex for Sale: Regulating Prostitution in the UK* (forthcoming) as well as numerous articles on youth justice, prostitution policy reforms, and women and young people's involvement in the sex industry.

Anna Souhami is Lecturer in Criminology at the School of Law, Edinburgh University. Her main research interests lie in the sociology of criminal justice policy and practice, in particular in the area of youth justice. Her current research explores the emergent system for the governance of youth crime in England and Wales. Her previous research in youth justice examined the radical restructuring of youth justice services under the Crime and Disorder Act 1998 and its effects on youth justice professionals' sense of identity and culture. She is the author of *Transforming Youth Justice: Occupational Identity and Cultural Change* (2007).

Subject Index

Author Index